W9-AVC-449

Bloom's Literary Themes

Alienation
The American Dream
Civil Disobedience
Dark Humor
Death and Dying
Enslavement and Emancipation
Exploration and Colonization
The Grotesque
The Hero's Journey
Human Sexuality
The Labyrinth
Rebirth and Renewal
Sin and Redemption
The Sublime
The Taboo
The Trickster

Bloom's Literary Themes

CIVIL DISOBEDIENCE

Bloom's Literary Themes

CIVIL DISOBEDIENCE

Edited and with an introduction by
Harold Bloom
Sterling Professor of the Humanities
Yale University

Volume Editor
Blake Hobby

BLOOM'S
LITERARY CRITICISM
An imprint of Infobase Publishing

Bloom's Literary Themes: Civil Disobedience

Copyright ©2010 by Infobase Publishing
Introduction ©2010 by Harold Bloom

Bloom's Literary Criticism
An imprint of Infobase Publishing
132 West 31st Street
New York NY 10001

Library of Congress Cataloging-in-Publication Data
Bloom's literary themes. Civil disobedience / edited and with an introduction by
Harold Bloom ; volume editor, Blake Hobby.
p. cm.
Includes bibliographical references and index.
ISBN 978-1-60413-439-1 (hc : alk. paper)
1. Civil disobedience in literature.   I. Bloom, Harold.   II. Hobby, Blake.
III. Title: Civil disobedience.
PN56.C58B56 2010
809'.933581—dc22
                                        2009038087

Bloom's Literary Criticism books are available at special discounts when purchased in
bulk quantities for businesses, associations, institutions, or sales promotions. Please call
our Special Sales Department in New York at (212) 967-8800 or (800) 322-8755.

You can find Bloom's Literary Criticism on the World Wide Web at
http://www.chelseahouse.com

Text design by Kerry Casey
Cover design by Takeshi Takahashi
Composition by IBT Global, Inc.
Cover printed by Yurchak Printing, Landisville, Pa.
Book printed and bound by Yurchak Printing, Landisville, Pa.
Printed in the United States of America

This book is printed on acid-free paper.

Contents

Series Introduction by Harold Bloom: Themes and Metaphors

1. Topos and Trope

What we now call a theme or topic or subject initially was named a *topos*, ancient Greek for "place." Literary *topoi* are commonplaces, but also arguments or assertions. A topos can be regarded as literal when opposed to a trope or turning which is figurative and which can be a metaphor or some related departure from the literal: ironies, synecdoches (part for whole), metonymies (representations by contiguity) or hyperboles (overstatements). Themes and metaphors engender one another in all significant literary compositions.

As a theoretician of the relation between the matter and the rhetoric of high literature, I tend to define metaphor as a figure of desire rather than a figure of knowledge. We welcome literary metaphor because it enables fictions to persuade us of beautiful untrue things, as Oscar Wilde phrased it. Literary *topoi* can be regarded as places where we store information, in order to amplify the themes that interest us.

This series of volumes, *Bloom's Literary Themes*, offers students and general readers helpful essays on such perpetually crucial topics as the Hero's Journey, the Labyrinth, the Sublime, Death and Dying, the Taboo, the Trickster and many more. These subjects are chosen for their prevalence yet also for their centrality. They express the whole concern of human existence now in the twenty-first century of the Common Era. Some of the topics would have seemed odd at another time, another land: the American Dream, Enslavement and Emancipation, Civil Disobedience.

I suspect though that our current preoccupations would have existed always and everywhere, under other names. Tropes change across the centuries: The irony of one age is rarely the irony of another. But the themes of great literature, though immensely varied, undergo transmemberment and show up barely disguised in different contexts. The power of imaginative literature relies upon three constants: aesthetic splendor, cognitive power, wisdom. These are not bound by societal constraints or resentments, and ultimately are universals, and so not culture-bound. Shakespeare, except for the world's scriptures, is the one universal author, whether he is read and played in Bulgaria or Indonesia or wherever. His supremacy at creating human beings breaks through even the barrier of language and puts everyone on his stage. This means that the matter of his work has migrated everywhere, reinforcing the common places we all inhabit in his themes.

2. CONTEST AS BOTH THEME AND TROPE

Great writing or the Sublime rarely emanates directly from themes since all authors are mediated by forerunners and by contemporary rivals. Nietzsche enhanced our awareness of the agonistic foundations of ancient Greek literature and culture, from Hesiod's contest with Homer on to the Hellenistic critic Longinus in his treatise *On the Sublime*. Even Shakespeare had to begin by overcoming Christopher Marlowe, only a few months his senior. William Faulkner stemmed from the Polish-English novelist Joseph Conrad, and our best living author of prose fiction, Philip Roth, is inconceivable without his descent from the major Jewish literary phenomenon of the twentieth century, Franz Kafka of Prague, who wrote the most lucid German since Goethe.

The contest with past achievement is the hidden theme of all major canonical literature in Western tradition. Literary influence is both an overwhelming metaphor for literature itself, and a common topic for all criticism, whether or not the critic knows her immersion in the incessant flood.

Every theme in this series touches upon a contest with anteriority, whether with the presence of death, the hero's quest, the overcoming of taboos, or all of the other concerns, volume by volume. From Monteverdi through Bach to Stravinsky, or from the Italian Renaissance through the agon of Matisse and Picasso, the history of all the arts demonstrates the same patterns as literature's thematic struggle with itself. Our country's great original art, jazz, is illuminated by what the great creators called "cutting contests," from Louis Armstrong and Duke Ellington on to the emergence of Charlie Parker's Bop or revisionist jazz.

A literary theme, however authentic, would come to nothing without rhetorical eloquence or mastery of metaphor. But to experience the study of the common places of invention is an apt training in the apprehension of aesthetic value in poetry and in prose.

Volume Introduction by Harold Bloom

As a term, "civil disobedience" for most of us evokes the activists of the twentieth century who followed Thoreau: Mahatma Gandhi, Nelson Mandela, Martin Luther King, Jr., and our protestors down to the present moment. Yet its literary history is far richer than Henry David Thoreau, and goes back to Sophocles, Aristophanes, Machiavelli, Shakespeare, Milton, Melville, Hawthorne, Dostoyevsky, Kafka, and Ralph Waldo Ellison.

What possibly can unite figures so diverse as Antigone, Hamlet, Milton's Samson, Bartleby the Scrivener, Hester Prynne, Svidrigailov, Joseph K., and Ellison's Invisible Man? I hold aside, for now, the literary master of civil disobedience, my hero Sir John Falstaff. When rhetoric and dramatic representation replace civic action and suffering, civil disobedience can begin to mean everything and nothing. Antigone asserts a private ethic against the state, yet the ironist Hamlet disdains assertion and questions even his own questionings. Milton's Samson like blind Milton himself asserts the God within against all outward authority.

Melville's Bartleby would prefer not to, and declines explanation, while Hester Prynne stubbornly will outwait all of male society. The most fascinating of all is *Crime and Punishment*'s Svidrigailov, who ends himself with a pistol-shot to his forehead while cheerfully explaining to a policeman that he is "Going to America!"

What literature can teach us is that our sociopolitical ideas of civil disobedience are too limited in imagination. Svidrigailov the nihilist refused to teach us anything but the wise comedian Falstaff is our Montaigne-like Socrates, and he provides us with the ultimate demand that animates all civil disobedience, everywhere: "Give me life."

1984
(George Orwell)

"Of Man's Last Disobedience:
Zamiatin's *We* and Orwell's *1984*"

by Gorman Beauchamp, in
Comparative Literature Studies (1973)

Introduction

Gorman Beauchamp argues that both Eugene Zamiatin's *We* and George Orwell's *1984* are dystopian novels in which individuals perform acts of civil disobedience. According to Beauchamp, these individuals mirror Adam's disobedience in the Garden of Eden. Beauchamp describes how literary characters in these novels rebel against a tyrannical, God-like state and, in doing so, fall from grace in dystopias that are grotesque metaphorical Edens. Beauchamp articulates how this rebellion mirrors the world as described by Freud's *Civilization and Its Discontents*, in which modern human beings, constricted and suppressed by the social order, find their source of discontent in civilization's utopian dreams.

Beauchamp, Gorman. "Of Man's Last Disobedience: Zamiatin's *We* and Orwell's *1984*." *Comparative Literature Studies* 10.4 (Dec 1973) 285–301.

Utopia can be defined as civilization-only-more-so: that is, as a systematic intensification of the restraints upon which all society rests.[1] All civilization is predicated on order, regulation, some degree of regimentation—limitations that conflict with man's natural or instinctual drives and result in the phenomenon Freud called repression. Because repression is the inevitable cost exacted for civilization, man will, on an instinctual, subconscious level, always remain its enemy. Primitive man, Freud argues, was psychically "better off knowing no restraints on instinct. To counterbalance this, his prospects of enjoying . . . happiness for any length of time were very slender. Civilized man has exchanged a portion of his possibilities for happiness for a portion of security."[2]

In the tradition of rationally planned utopias, from Plato's *Republic* to B. F. Skinner's *Walden Two*, the ideal has been to enlarge that "portion of security" by increasing the degree of civilization—to reorder society into a more harmonious, efficient (but more regimented, repressed) whole, in which each "unit" plays only his socially determined role. Lewis Mumford has likened the utopian model to the military one: "total control from above, absolute obedience from below," whether the "above" be occupied by philosopher kings or behavioral engineers. The price of utopia, he says, is total submission to a central authority, forced labor, lifetime specialization, and inflexible regimentation.[3] A reader familiar with Freud's psychosocial theory, set out most fully in *Civilization and Its Discontents*, will recognize the utopian ideal as but a more systematic, rigorous application of civilization's existing prohibitions and restraints—will recognize, that is, that the dreamworld of chiliastic social planners can be realized only at further, and extreme, expense of individual, instinctual freedom.[4]

The claims of utopianism are essentially religious ones. In the vacuum created by the breakup of "the medieval synthesis," a *Weltanschauung* that subsumed all social activity in one embracing theocentric enterprise overseen by the Church, there grew up anew secularized religion that dominated men's lives: *étatisme*, or worship of the State. The State, as the Church's successor, became the object of what Paul Tillich has called "ultimate concern"—became, that is, the supreme value in men's lives to which all other values are subordinated. When a people makes the nation its ultimate concern, he wrote, "it demands that all other concerns, economic well-being, health and life, family, aesthetic and cognitive truth, justice and humanity, be sacrificed . . . Everything is centered in the only god, the nation."[5] Utopianism is the most extreme form of *étatisme*, claiming for the State a godlike efficacy. Like its predecessor in divinity, the State offers salvation, not in the next world, however, but in this; not through eschatology, but through utopianism.[6] The State can effect the millennium, but only, of course, if its creatures obey its dictates. The new god is not less jealous than the old, and, like the old, aspires to omniscience and omnipotence, for only with such divine powers can it know of and punish the deviations of the sinner who would resist its enforced salvation. Thus even the most benevolently intended utopias are, by the very nature of their claims, totalitarian, demanding the ultimate concern of their subjects and asserting ultimate control of their destinies.[7]

The dream of social redemption through the State, dawning with such bright hopes in the decade of the French Revolution and growing ever brighter through the nineteenth century, became for many in the twentieth century a nightmare. The reasons are historical: the rise of messianic totalitarian regimes, whose utopianistic schemas resulted not in man's salvation but his damnation. The more humane among utopian thinkers would claim Nazism and Stalinist Communism to be aberrations, bastards rather than true heirs of Plato and More and Wells; but Mumford has argued—correctly, I believe—that these regimes arose logically from the assumptions of venerable utopian ideals:

> Isolation, stratification, fixation, regimentation, standardization, militarism—one or more of these attributes enter into the conception of the utopian city, as expounded by the Greeks. And these same features, in open or disguised form, remain even in the supposedly more democratic utopias of the nineteenth century.... In the end, utopia merges into the dystopia of the twentieth century; and one suddenly realizes that the distance between the positive ideal and the negative one was never so great as the advocates or admirers of utopia had professed.[8]

Such a realization underlies the emergence of a distinctly twentieth-century literary subgenre, the dystopian novel, a *roman à thèse* whose purpose, clearly ideological, is to assert the ultimate value of man's instinctual freedom over the putatively melioristic repression of utopian civilization.[9]

In two dystopian novels in particular—Eugene Zamiatin's *We* and George Orwell's *1984*—the central conflict of the individual's rebellion against the State reenacts the Christian myth of man's first disobedience, Adam's against God. For in each novel there is a god figure, the embodiment of the State, who demands absolute adoration and obedience. And in each there is an Adam-like protagonist who, for love of an Eve, defies this god by asserting his instinctual freedom and thus "falls" from the utopianistic new Eden. This mythic conflict—Adam rebelling against the *étatist* god figure—is a fictional manifestation of the psychic conflict that Freud posited between the individual and society.

Freud shared, on the one hand, the belief of Dostoevsky's Grand Inquisitor that man needed, and wanted, a dominant figure to rule and protect him. The "coercive characteristic of group formation" Freud traced back to "the fact of their origin from the primal horde. The leader of the group is still the dread primal father; the group still wishes to be governed by unrestricted force; it has an extreme passion for authority, . . . a thirst for obedience."[10] This political führer is "loved" in the same ambivalent way the personal father is "loved"; and, as Philip Rieff points out, "Freud's belief that politics is founded on the group's erotic relation with authority is made concrete by his claim that authority is always *personified*." Love for this power-as-person, then, constitutes "the most fundamental source of authority."[11] In dystopian fiction, the embodiment of the state is always such a figure: Zamiatin's Well-Doer, Orwell's Big Brother, Huxley's World Controller, even Forster's Machine (in "The Machine Stops"), all of them incarnations of the Grand Inquisitor. And no clearer confirmation of the "displacement" of Eros which Freud saw underlying all authority can be found than in the erotic language Orwell's disobedient Adam uses to express his ultimate submission: "I love Big Brother." In the megacivilization of utopia, man's whole duty is to love the führer and serve him.

On the other hand, however, Freud himself had little faith in the efficacy of utopias. Dostoevsky's implacable dystopian, the Underground Man, accused utopians of wanting to convert society into a human anthill, but man's instincts—his desire to follow "his own foolish will"—would (he asserted) thwart all their efforts to regiment him. Freud, employing a similar insect metaphor, agreed: "It does not seem as though any influence could induce a man to change, his nature into a termite's. No doubt he will always defend his claim to individual liberty against the will of the group."[12] His "urge to freedom" is forever pitted against the coercive unity of society, so that the conflict between the individual, "I," and the group or State, "We," appears from a Freudian vantage point irreconcilable.

"I do not want to be 'I,'" cried Bakunin a century ago; "I want to be 'We.'" His sentiment informs utopianism, historical as well as fictional, so that in the dream-turned-nightmare world of Koestler's *Darkness at Noon*, the I has become suspect, a "grammatical fiction." "The Party did not recognize its existence. The definition of the individual was: a multitude of one million divided by one million."[13] Whatever encourages individualism, "I-ness," is the enemy, for it separates the one from the many, man from the godlike State. Prime among such estranging emotions is sexuality: in the new Edens, as in the old, the serpent that seduces man into disobedience is sexual, Adam's love for Eve. "Present-day civilization makes it plain," Freud points out in *Civilization and Its Discontents*, "that it does not like sexuality as a source of pleasure in its own right and is only prepared to tolerate it because there is so far no substitute for it as a means of propagating the human race."[14] (In *Brave New World*, of course, a substitute *has* been found: the bottled baby.) Elsewhere, Freud explains the reason for this animus:

> Sexual impulsions are unfavorable to the formation of groups. . . . The more important sexual love became for the ego, and the more it developed the characteristics of being in love, the more urgently it required to be limited to two people. . . . Two people coming together for the purpose of sexual satisfaction, in so far as they seek solitude, are making a demonstration against the herd instinct, the group feeling. . . .
>
> In the great artificial groups, the church and the army, there is no room for woman as the sexual object. The love relation between man and woman remains outside these organizations. . . . Even in a person who has in other respects become absorbed in a group, the directly sexual impulses preserve a little of his individual activity. If they become too strong, they disintegrate every group formation.[15]

This conflict, then, that Freud postulated between the individual and civilization adumbrates the central struggle in the dystopian novel:

"the dreadful father," a secularized god demanding total allegiance and obedience to the utopian decalogue, challenged by the individual's instinctual will to freedom. And particularly with respect to the sexual nature of that challenge, the conflict recapitulates the myth of Adam's rebellion against God. With this background, let us turn to an examination of the dystopian versions of paradise lost, *We* and *1984*.

"Put me in a System and you negate me," Kierkegaard declared; "I am not just a mathematical symbol—I *am*." This affirmation underlies Zamiatin's *We*, a satirical depiction of a futuristic United State whose members have become, almost literally, mathematical symbols: they have no names and are known only by their numbers, indeed are called Numbers. Sealed off from the natural world in a glass-walled city, they function as interchangeable parts of one vast machine, regulated by a Table of Hours: "Every morning, with six-wheeled precision, at the same hour, at the same minute, we wake up, millions of us at once. At the very same hour, millions like one, we begin our work, and millions like one, we finish it. United in a single body with a million hands, at the very same second, designated by the Tables, we carry the spoons to our mouths; at the very same second we all go out to walk, go to the auditorium, to the halls for Taylor exercises, and then to bed."[16] Zamiatin's imagination has projected the ideal of utopian organization to its logical extreme: "A magnificent celebration of the victory of *all* over *one*, of the *sum* over the *individual*" (p. 44).

In the United State, not surprisingly, freedom is equated with sin. Employing the Eden metaphor, one Number explains:

> That legend referred to us of today, did it not? Yes. Only think of it for a moment. There were two in paradise and the choice was offered to them: happiness without freedom or freedom without happiness. No other choice. . . . They, fools that they were, chose freedom. Naturally, for centuries afterward they longed for fetters, for the fetters of yore. . . . For centuries! And only we found the way to regain happiness. . . . The ancient god and we, side by side at the same table! We helped god defeat the devil definitely and finally. It was he, the devil, who led people to transgression, to taste pernicious freedom—he, the cunning serpent. And we came along, planted a boot on his head, and . . . squash! Down with him! Paradise again! We returned to the simple-mindedness of Adam and Eve. (p. 59)

The god who oversees this paradise regained is the Well-Doer, a remote, ironclad figure who emerges annually to be reelected on the Day of Unanimity: "This was always the most magnificent moment of our celebration: all would remain sitting motionless, joyfully bowing their heads under the salutary yoke of that Number of Numbers" (p. 134) as "He descend[ed] to us from the sky, He—the new Jehovah—in an aero, He, as wise and lovingly cruel as the Jehovah of the ancients" (p. 131).

Since all Eros in this utopian anthill is channeled into worship of the Well-Doer, there are no marriages nor families, and all children become property of the State; so that having precluded all emotional ties and "having identified itself with man's only permissible aspiration," as one writer notes, the State "emerges as the only possible object of man's affection, thus fulfilling his need for emotional relationships."[17] In a State striving for a monopoly on love, sex is suspect, tolerated as a necessary evil, but strictly controlled:

> Naturally, having conquered hunger ..., the United State directed its attack against the second ruler of the world, against love. At last this element was conquered, that is, organized and put into a mathematical formula.... You are carefully examined in the laboratory of the Sexual Department where they find the content of the sexual hormones in your blood, and they accordingly make out for you a Table of sexual days. Then you file an application to enjoy the services of Number so and so, or Number so and so. (p. 22)

On these occasions, one "received a certificate permitting the use of curtains. This right exists in our State only on sexual days. Normally we live surrounded by transparent walls ... beneath the eyes of everyone" (p. 19). Not content with such restrictions, the State is seeking ways to reduce the number of sexual days, for these moments of privacy are subversive of its group values, impediments to total We-ness.

In his prelapsarian state at the novel's outset, the protagonist, D-503, is perfectly content in this new, de-eroticized Eden: he has his work as a designer of spacecraft, a sweetly simple sex partner, and his love for the State, for the Well-Doer. He prizes his non-freedom: "It is pleasant to feel that somebody's penetrating eye is watching you from behind your shoulder, lovingly guarding you from the most minute mistake, from the most minute incorrect step" (p. 63). Like all good Numbers, D-503 knows that We is of God, I is of the devil, and the reports he hears of a secret organization that "aims at liberation from the beneficent yoke of the State" (p. 34) puzzle and upset him. But just as the United State has not succeeded in eradicating every vestige of desire for freedom for all its Numbers, neither has D-503 succeeded in eradicating all trace of his instinctual, irrational, "animal" nature. His hands are covered with hair, "a stupid atavism," and he hates having anyone look at them; yet this atavism portends deeper, unconscious desires—Freud's instinctual drives—that are soon stirred to life in him. He is tempted to taste the forbidden fruit of love, and he falls.

The Eve who seduces him to experience his own sexuality, and concomitantly his individuality, is a dark, enigmatic Number, I-330. D-503's first encounter with this mysterious woman "had a strange effect on me, like an irrational component of an equation which you cannot eliminate" (p. 10). He becomes fascinated, however, with his temptress, is lured by her to a secret rendezvous, offered a "forbidden fruit," which is liquor ("drink this charming poison with me"), and succumbs: "Suddenly her arms were around my neck . . . her lips grew into mine, even somewhere much deeper, much more terrible" (p. 53). The experience proves a shattering one:

> I became glass-like and saw within myself. There were two selves in me. One, the former D-503, Number D-503; and the other. . . . Before, that other used to show his hairy paws from time to time, but now that whole other self left his shell. The shell was breaking. . . . (p. 54)

The other (unconscious) self emerging from the shell its civilization had constructed around it begins now to dream, a state symptomatic among the Numbers of mental disorder. And, indeed, by the utopian standard of the United State, D-503 has become "sick."[18]

> I *felt* myself. To feel one's self, to be conscious of one's personality, is the lot of an eye inflamed by a cinder, or an infected finger, or a bad tooth. A healthy eye, or finger, or tooth is not felt; it is non-existent, as it were. Is it not clear, then, that consciousness of oneself is sickness? (p. 121)

The question is, of course, ironic, since D-503's "sickness" constitutes for Zamiatin the essence of being human, that which separates man from the robot. And sexuality he presents as the force that liberates consciousness, frees man from civilization's ultrarepression of his instincts, and gives rise to individuality, to imagination. "I know that I have imagination," the postlapsarian Adam realizes, "that is what my illness consists of. And more than that: I know that it is a wonderful illness—one does not want to be cured, simply does not want to!" (p. 78). Elsewhere Zamiatin wrote that "there are two priceless fountainheads in man: brains and sex. From the first proceeds all science, from the second all art. And to cut off all art from yourself or to force it into your brain would mean to cut off . . . well, yes."[19] In a society that *has* forced all art into the brain—whose poetry is all in praise of mathematics and whose "immortal tragedy" is entitled *He Who Comes Late to Work*!—the personal, passionate emotions are considered dangerously subversive: thus the attempt to emasculate the Numbers, to cut off . . . well, yes.

I-330's rebellion against utopia's repression is overtly political: she belongs to the secret underground movement (MEPHI, derived from Mephistopheles) dedicated to overthrowing the Well-Doer, to tearing down the Wall "so that the green wind may blow over the earth, from end to end" (p. 145). D-503's rebellion, however, is purely instinctual, that of a man blindly following his heart: "I want to be with I-330. I want her every minute, every second, to be with me, with no one else. All that I wrote about Unanimity is of no value. . . . For I know (be it sacrilege, yet it is the truth) that a Glorious Day is possible only with her and only when we are side by side" (p. 130). Passion has restored to D-503 his sexuality and, with it, consciousness, imagination, I-ness; thus disintegrating in him, in Freud's words, "the herd instinct, the group feeling." Willing now to do anything to keep her love, Adam follows his Eve into rebellion against God. He agrees to turn over to the MEPHI the spacecraft he has built, to be used to destroy the Wall and topple the Well-Doer.

But their plan fails, thwarted by the Gestapo-like Bureau of Guardians, and D-503 is forced to undergo the Great Operation, a fantasiectomy that serves to numericalize completely the wayward sinners against the State. The proclamation issued by the Well-Doer epitomizes Zamiatin's view of utopia:

> The latest discovery of our State science is that there is a center
> for fancy—a miserable little nervous knot in the lower region
> of the frontal lobe of the brain. A triple treatment of the knot
> with X-rays will cure you of fancy,
>
> *Forever!*
>
> You are perfect; you are mechanized; the road to one-
> hundred-per-cent happiness is open! Hasten then all of you,
> young and old, hasten to undergo the Great Operation! Long
> Live the Great Operation! Long live the United State! Long
> Live the Well-Doer. (p. 167)

His "fancy" removed, D-503 reverts to perfect Numberhood: docile,
content, unable to feel love for any but the Well-Doer; again a
smoothly functioning part of We. Sitting beside the Well-Doer, D-
503 now watches I-330 tortured to death and knows it to be right, "for
reason must prevail" (p. 218). Rebellion has been rendered impossible
in the utopian Eden; his has been man's last disobedience.

The influence of Zamiatin's work on *1984* is pronounced and
pervasive; indeed, one critic has called *We* Orwell's *Holinshed*.[20] Many
of the features of the United State reappear in Orwell's Oceania, not
least of which is the systematic repression of the sexual drives. Thus
the rebellion of the individual against the State, in *1984* as in *We*, is
presented as a sexual one, the struggle for instinctual freedom against
the enforced conformity of an omniscient, omnipotent *étatisme*.
Orwell's Winston Smith, like Zamiatin's D-503, is the last Adam,
reenacting the myth of the Fall, following his Eve into disobedience
against God.

The topography of Oceania is well enough known that I need
not dwell on it: the telescreens, Big Brother's electronic eyes that
are always "watching you"; the phenomena of *newspeak* and *double-
think* and *blackwhite*; the ubiquitous slogans proclaiming war to be
peace and freedom slavery. Nor need I stress the dystopian nature of
Orwell's vision of utopia at dead end, all its perverted values terroristi-
cally enforced by the Ministry of Love.[21] What should be pointed out,
however, is the remarkably precise way in which Orwell has embodied,
in the conditioned hysteria of love for Big Brother, Freud's theory
of eroticism displaced. In the daily Two-Minute Hate (the Oceanic
equivalent of prayer), the telescreens project the image of Goldstein, the satan of this State, against whom the increasingly frenzied

faithful hurl their hatred. Then (Winston recounts of one such Hate) "drawing a sigh of relief from everybody, the hostile figure melted into the face of Big Brother ... full of power and mysterious calm, and so vast that it filled the screen ... The little sandy-haired woman had flung herself over the chair in front of her. With a tremendous murmur that sounded like 'My savior!' she extended her arms to the screen."[22] Julia, Winston's Eve, explains "the inner meaning of the Party's sexual puritanism."

> It was not merely that the sex instinct created a world of its own which was outside the Party's control and which therefore had to be destroyed if possible. What was more important was that sexual privation induced hysteria, which was desirable because it could be transformed into war fever and hero worship. The way she put it was:
>
> "When you make love you're using up energy; and afterwards you feel happy and don't give a damn for anyone. They can't bear you to feel like that. They want you to be bursting with energy all the time. All this marching up and down and cheering and waving flags is simply sex gone sour. If you're happy inside yourself, why should you get excited about Big Brother?" (pp. 110–11)

In order to ensure that the Oceanians *do* get excited about Big Brother—displace, that is, eroticism from its natural object, another individual, to the State—the Party attempts in every way "to remove all pleasure from the sex act.... The only recognized purpose of marriage was to beget children for the service of the Party. Sexual intercourse was to be looked on as a slightly disgusting operation, like having an enema" (p. 57). Thus the Party instigated organizations like the Junior Anti-Sex League, a sort of celibate Scouts, whose chastity, like that of medieval monks and nuns, demonstrated their superior love for and loyalty to their god. For the Party's ultimate aim, as the Inquisitorial figure O'Brien explains to Winston, is the total abolition of the sex instinct: "We shall abolish the orgasm. Our neurologists are at work upon it now ... There will be no love, except love for Big Brother" (p. 220). Even more clearly than in Zamiatin's United State, the rulers of Oceania have grasped the threat to utopianism posed by man's sexuality and are moving drastically to destroy or displace it.

As Adam in this perverted paradise, where the only love allowed is the love for Big Brother, Winston differs from D-503 and their biblical archetype in one important respect: even before he is tempted into erotic rebellion, he already hates the führer. In his furtively kept journal, he has written, over and over again, the phrase "DOWN WITH BIG BROTHER." Guilty though he is of *thoughtcrime* (Oceanians, like Christians, are culpable not only for what they do but also for what they think), Winston falls into overt rebellion only when he falls in love. In this respect, the biblical myth and the novel's mythos are the same: it is an Eve who lures Adam to sin against God.

This sin—Julia and Winston's—consists essentially of an emotion. They have illicit rendezvous, they attempt to join the Brotherhood (the probably nonexistent underground resistance movement led by the probably nonexistent Goldstein), but their real lese majesty is simply being in love, giving free rein to their instinctual eroticism. Julia, Winston realizes, is thoroughly apolitical, "a rebel only from the waist down"; she falls asleep while he reads her Goldstein's banned expose of Ingsoc, the philosophy of Oceanic *étatisme*. But because the whole duty of citizens is to love Big Brother, their love for one another is perforce politically subversive. "Their embrace had been a battle, their climax a victory. It was a blow struck against the Party. It was a political act" (p. 105). Thus when they are arrested by the Thought Police, it is not their lives but their love that must be extinguished.

Julia and Winston had all along known that they were doomed, would sooner or later be caught, yet they had held onto the belief that "they can't get inside you" and therefore that their love was inviolable, something beyond the power of even the State to destroy. O'Brien sets about to demonstrate to Winston that it is not. In the long, excruciating torture sessions that make up the last third of the book, O'Brien systematically undercuts and refutes every belief Winston held, beats and brainwashes away every trace of human dignity, until he is left with only one vestige of his humanity, his love for Julia.

> "Can you think of a single degradation that has not happened
> to you?"
>
> Winston had stopped weeping, though the tears were still
> in his eyes. He looked up at O'Brien.
>
> "I have not betrayed Julia," he said.

O'Brien looked down at him thoughtfully. "No," he said, "no; that is perfectly true. You have not betrayed Julia." ... Never did O'Brien fail to understand what was said to him. Anyone else on earth would have answered promptly that he *had* betrayed Julia. For what was there that they had not screwed out of him under torture? He had told them everything he knew about her, her habits, her character, her past life; he had confessed in the most trivial detail everything that had happened at their meetings, all that he had said to her and she to him ... everything. And yet, in the sense in which he intended the word, he had not betrayed her. He had not stopped loving her; his feelings toward her had remained the same. O'Brien had seen what he meant without the need of explanation. (p. 225)

Winston hopes to be shot quickly, so that he will die still hating Big Brother, still loving Julia. But O'Brien understands this, too. It is not Winston's life he wants, but his soul, what is "inside him." Winston thus must be made to betray Julia, for only then can he be made to love Big Brother—must be emptied of one love to be filled with another. So he is taken to Room 101.

"The thing in Room 101," O'Brien explains, "is the worst thing in the world," each man's innermost fear. "In your case the worst thing in the world happens to be rats" (p. 233). The threat of having his face devoured by the squealing rats sends Winston into sheer panic, a panic that, as O'Brien had said, was beyond courage or cowardice, beyond all rational choice.

He suddenly understood that in the whole world there was just *one* person to whom he could transfer his punishment—*one* body that could be thrust between himself and the rats. And he was shouting frantically, over and over:

"Do it to Julia! Do it to Julia! Not to me! Julia!" (p. 236)

As George Woodcock noted, each dystopian writer stresses "the particular aspects of the trends toward Utopia which seem to him most dangerous." For Zamiatin these were technological, for Orwell they were bureaucratic, "the fear of man's being turned into a mind-less robot by predominantly political means."[23] Thus while D-503,

technologically lobotomized, sits in contented approval as I-330 is put
to death, Winston, psychologically terrorized by a brutally perfected
totalitarianism, is reduced to an even more appalling fate: screaming
for Julia's death to save his own life. They *have* gotten inside him and
destroyed his love.

The State's total victory is made evident when, "rehabilitated" and
released from prison, Winston encounters Julia again and feels toward
her—as she toward him—only guilt-induced antipathy. This loss of
love leaves Winston emptied of personality, malleable, defenseless
against the State whose purpose, O'Brien had explained, was to tear
the human mind to pieces and put it together in a shape of the State's
own choosing. With Winston their success is complete:

> He gazed up at the enormous face. Forty years it had taken
> him to learn what kind of smile was hidden beneath the dark
> mustache. O cruel, needless misunderstanding! O stubborn,
> self-willed exile from the loving breast! Two gin-scented
> tears trickled down the side of his nose. But it was all right,
> everything was all right, the struggle was finished. He had won
> the victory over himself. He loved Big Brother (p. 245).

During one of the torture sessions O'Brien had announced, "if
you are a man, Winston, you are the last man. Your kind is extinct;
we are the inheritors" (p. 222). Winston's, like D-503's, is man's last
disobedience; there will be no more Adams and no more Eves in
utopia.

Those more humanistically than theologically inclined have
tended—perversely, no doubt—to see in Adam's Fall something
heroic. Despite scriptural intent, they admire in his refusal to forsake
Eve, in his following her into disobedience against God, that spark
of Promethean grandeur, that unyielding pride of the rebel. From
a Freudian perspective, as we have seen, Adam's Fall embodies the
eternal struggle of the instinctual against civilization (the "security" of
paradise), of the individual against the father-god; in more explicitly
political terms, the myth serves as symbol of the erotic rebel who puts
love, and thus self, above the State. In this sense Aeneas, who deserts
Dido at the gods' command to remember his duty to Rome, stands as
Adam's antithesis, as the perfect *étatist* hero.

Given the archetypal nature of the myth of the Fall, it is hardly surprising that dystopian novelists should adapt it in terms of the new *étatist* theology, for it contains the essential elements of the conflict between the individual and utopia. Because the dystopian novel is necessarily futuristic (not so much prediction as warning), its redaction of the myth is Janus-like, facing backward and forward: the cast of characters is that of Genesis, the drama follows its accustomed course, yet the outcome is fundamentally different, a denouement possible only in the twentieth century. For only in the twentieth century has the possibility arisen that men could be made *incapable* of falling from some programmed paradise. Through conditioning or drugs, through physiological alteration or subliminal suggestion or technological coercion or sophisticated terrorism, or some combination of all of these, Adam's erotic rebellion could be rendered impossible. Man would be obedient to the State because he could not be otherwise.[24]

The history of our century lends credence to such fears. We have witnessed the rise of messianic regimes that pretend, in Hannah Arendt's words, "to have found a way to establish the rule of justice on earth," that essential promise of utopianism. The very phrasing of Miss Arendt's description of totalitarianism's goal—to impose on men "a band of iron which holds them so tightly together that it is as though their plurality had disappeared into One Man of gigantic proportions"—parallels that of the dystopian writers.[25] History reflects fiction, and vice versa. The critics who censure the dystopians for despairing of the resiliency of the human spirit, its innate will to freedom, have shown less understanding of the potentialities of totalitarian control than have those they criticize. As Miss Arendt has perceived, totalitarianism is an unprecedented phenomenon in human history, more frightening just because more *total* than any previous form of tyranny. Orwell understood the historically unique threat it posed:

> The terrifying thing about modern dictatorships is that they are something entirely unprecedented. Their end cannot be foreseen. In the past every tyranny was sooner or later overthrown, or at least resisted, because of "human nature," which as a matter of course desired liberty. But we cannot be at all certain that "human nature" is constant. It may be just as

possible to produce a breed of men who do not wish for liberty as to produce a breed of hornless cows. The Inquisition failed, but then the Inquisition had not the resources of the modern state. The radio, press-censorship, standardized education and the secret police have altered everything. Mass-suggestion is a science of the last twenty years, and we do not know how successful it will be.[26]

The control techniques enumerated in this passage written in 1939 already seem to us primitive as oxcarts: the technology for tyranny is infinitely more sophisticated today. And tomorrow . . . ?

The dystopian novel, to warn against such a totalitarian tomorrow, posits the existence of utopia: a world where Eros is reserved for the State alone, where Adam will have no Eve, where Eden will be inescapable, where the Fall will be as unimaginable as freedom. Utopia's dawning will signal an end to man's disobedience, and paradise, alas, will be regained.

Notes

1. By "utopia" I should be understood to mean not every sort of escapist eudaemonia where a miraculously rewrought mankind lolls about in effortless contentment but only those imagined societies that offer a *systematic program* for reshaping man's nature and restructuring his social relationships. In other words, for an image of man remade to be legitimately utopian, an at least theoretically viable methodology for effecting this remaking must be explicit, whether a political methodology (as in Plato) or a psychological methodology (as in Skinner).

2. Sigmund Freud, *Civilization and Its Discontents*, in *The Standard Edition of the Complete Psychological Works of Sigmund Freud*, trans. James Strachey, XXI (London, 1961), 115. This work is the locus classicus of Freud's views on the individual's conflict with civilization, but also see *The Future of an Illusion*, also in the *Standard Edition*, XXI, 5–20, and the studies of two neo-Freudian social thinkers: Norman O. Brown, *Life against Death: The Psychoanalytic Meaning of History* (Middletown, Conn., 1959), and Herbert Marcuse, *Eros and*

Civilization: A Philosophical Inquiry into Freud (New York, 1962).

3. Lewis Mumford, "Utopia, the City and the Machine," *Daedalus*, 94 (1965), 258.

4. The best known of contemporary utopians, B. F. Skinner, would, of course, dismiss the idea that man has an innate nature. His mouthpiece in *Walden Two* (New York, 1962), says, for instance: "What do you say to the design of personalities? Would that interest you? The control of temperament? Give me the specifications, and I'll give you the man!" (p. 292). The assumption here—one common, implicitly or explicitly, to all utopians—is that the human personality is limitlessly plastic, to be molded to whatever shape society desires. Freud's emphasis on an innate, biological donnée, however, as Lionel Trilling has pointed out, "proposes to us that culture is not all-powerful. It suggests that there is a residue of human quality beyond the reach of culture to control"; *Beyond Culture* (New York, 1968), p. 113. For Skinner's own estimation of his differences with Freud, see his essay "Critique of Psychoanalytic Concepts and Theories," in *Science and Theory in Psychoanalysis*, ed. Irwin G. Sarason (Princeton, N.J., 1965), pp. 137–49.

5. Paul Tillich, *Dynamics of Faith* (New York, 1958), pp. 1–2. See also J. L. Talmon, *The Origins of Totalitarian Democracy* (New York, 1960), pp. 21–24 et passim.

6. See Martin Buber, *Paths in Utopia*, trans. R. F. C. Hull (Boston, 1958), pp. 7–9; and Judith Shklar, "Political Theory in Utopia," *Daedalus*, 94 (1965), 370.

7. No utopian society was more benevolently intended than that of Sir Thomas More, nor more rigorously democratic, yet even there the State directs all major and most minor aspects of its citizens' lives. For example: "Now you can see how nowhere is there any license to waste time, nowhere any pretext to evade work—no wine shop, no alehouse, no brothel anywhere, no opportunity for corruption, no lurking hole, no secret meeting place. On the contrary, *being under the eyes of all*, people are bound either to be performing the usual labor or to be enjoying their leisure in a fashion not without decency"; *Utopia*, trans. Edward Surtz, S. J. (New Haven, Conn., 1964), pp. 82–83

(my italics). "Under the eyes of all" foreshadows the Guardians and glass houses of *We* and the telescreens and "Big Brother is watching you" slogan of *1984*.

8. Mumford, "Utopia, the City and the Machine," p. 277.

9. On the factors giving rise to dystopianism, see George Woodcock, "Utopias in Negative," *Sewanee Review*, 64 (1956), 81–97; and Irving Howe, "The Fiction of Anti-Utopia," *The Decline of the New* (New York, 1970), pp. 66–71.

10. Sigmund Freud, *Group Psychology and the Analysis of the Ego*, also in the *Standard Edition, XVIII* (1955), 127.

11. Philip Rieff, *Freud: The Mind of the Moralist* (Garden City, N.Y., 1961), p. 257.

12. Freud, *Civilization and Its Discontents*, p. 96. See also Paul Roazen, *Freud: Political and Social Thought* (New York, 1970), p. 159; "Freud thought deep within man there was an unbreakable nucleus, a central portion of the self ineluctably in opposition to society. Freud once wrote that 'for most people there is a limit beyond which their constitution cannot comply with the demands of civilization.' In that sense, 'every individual is virtually an enemy of civilization.'"

13. Arthur Koestler, *Darkness at Noon*, trans. Daphne Hardy (New York, 1970), p. 208. This point is made *ad nauseam* in Ayn Rand's execrably written but mercifully brief dystopian fiction, *Anthem*.

14. Freud, *Civilization and Its Discontents*, p. 105.

15. Freud, *Group Psychology and the Analysis of the Ego*, pp. 140–41 (see note 10 above). For Plato's parallel view on this matter, see A. E. Taylor, *Plato: The Man and His Works* (New York, 1956), p. 278.

16. Eugene Zamiatin, *We*, trans. Gregory Zilboorg (New York, 1959), p. 13. Page references are hereafter cited in the text.

17. Christopher Collins, "Zamiatin, Wells, and the Utopian Literary Tradition," *Slavonic and East European Review*, 44 (1966), 358.

18. The sentiment, language, and metaphor here and elsewhere clearly echo Dostoevsky's Underground Man. See Robert L. Jackson, *Dostoevsky's Underground Man in Russian Literature* (The Hague, 1958), pp. 150–57.

19. Eugene Zamiatin, quoted by Alex M. Shane, *The Life and Works of Evgenij Zamiatin* (Berkeley and Los Angeles, 1968), p. 142.

20. Christopher Hollis, A *Study of George Orwell* (London, 1956), p. 199. For the most instructive discussions of Orwell's debt to Zamiatin, and their differences, see Woodcock, "Utopias in Negative" (note 9 above); Isaac Deutscher, "*1984*—The Mysticism of Cruelty," *Heretics and Renegades* (London, 1955), pp. 35–50; and Jürgen Rühle, *Literature and Revolution*, trans. Jean Steinberg (New York, 1969), pp. 38–40. Orwell himself wrote an appreciative review of *We* in his column in the *Tribune* (London), 4 January 1946.

21. George Kateb in *Utopia and its Enemies* (New York, 1963), pp. 235–36, argues that Oceania ought not to be considered even a negative utopia, for O'Brien "describes the political system of *1984* as ' . . . the exact opposite of the hedonistic utopias that old reformers imagined.'" Kateb has a point, but it is rather strained and overly formalistic. Orwell's vision of the future is clearly intended to show utopian messianism gone sour, reflecting the historical reality of our century. Consider the reflection of Koestler's Rubashov: "Nobody foresaw the new mass movements, the great political landslides, nor the twisted roads, the bewildering stages which the Revolutionary State was to go through; at that time one believed that the gates of Utopia stood open, and that mankind stood on its threshold" (p. 106). For an excellent account of the dashing of these bright hopes, see Sir Isaiah Berlin's essay, "Political Ideas in the Twentieth Century," *Four Essays on Liberty* (New York, 1969), pp. 1–40.

22. George Orwell, *1984* (New York, New American Library, n.d.), p. 17. Page references are hereafter cited in the text.

23. Woodcock, "Utopias in Negative," pp. 91–92.

24. The evidence for this contention may never be deemed conclusive by skeptics, yet that a wide variety of control techniques is being perfected is indisputable: there are, for example, José Delgado's experiments with cerebral electrodes, Georges Unger's isolation and chemical duplication of a "memory molecule," the behavior-modifying drugs already administered to "problem" children (to 5 to 10 percent of Washington's school population, for instance), and so on. See also Aldous Huxley, *Brave New World Revisited* (New York, 1965); Seymour Farber and Roger Wilson, eds., *Control of the*

Mind (New York, 1961); and Perry London, *Behavior Control* (New York, 1971).

25. Hannah Arendt, *The Origins of Totalitarianism* (Cleveland and New York, 1958), pp. 465–66.

26. George Orwell, *The Collected Essays, Journalism, and Letters of George Orwell*, vol. 1, *An Age Like This* (New York, 1968), pp. 380–81.

THE ADVENTURES OF HUCKLEBERRY FINN
(MARK TWAIN)

"Civil Disobedience and the Ending of Mark Twain's *The Adventures of Huckleberry Finn*"
by Robert C. Evans, Auburn
University at Montgomery

In the simplest sense, any act of civil disobedience is rooted in a prior act of obedience to individual conscience. Persons who choose to disobey the laws of their lands or the moral teachings of their culture do so because they feel an obligation to higher kinds of law or to superior sorts of ethics, whether those are rooted in religious belief, natural "instincts," or some profound sense of sympathy or empathy for others. Conscience, then, is key: The person who practices civil disobedience obeys his own conscience, instead of society's conscience. And—just as significantly—he does so not primarily on his own behalf but on behalf of his unselfish allegiance to others or to some lofty moral principle. His chief commitment is not to himself, but to someone or something more important, such as God, other persons, or an ethical ideal.

Viewed in these terms, Mark Twain's novel *The Adventures of Huckleberry Finn* presents a number of characters who are capable of genuine civil disobedience and a number who are not. Huck and Jim, obviously, do possess this capacity; Huck's father, the Duke and the Dauphin, and (more ambiguously) Tom Sawyer do not. The famous scene in which, after much agonizing, Huck decides not to obey the conventional morality of his culture—which would dictate that he report the location of Jim, the runaway slave, to Miss Watson, Jim's owner—but instead decides to obey his own humane impulses (269–71), is a prime example of Huck's capacity for ideal civil disobedience. The Duke and Dauphin, on the other hand, never act from anything other than selfish motives. They break many laws and violate many standards of civil behavior, but they never do so on behalf of any principle higher than personal self-interest. Tom Sawyer is a more complicated case. In the final chapters of the book, he does go to elaborate lengths to free Jim by disobeying the adults who have imprisoned Jim, and he does persuade Huck to cooperate in his schemes. In the end, Jim is finally freed, but the effect of Tom's highly complicated "evasion" scheme often leaves many readers highly dissatisfied. Huck, the book, and Twain may seem (in the eyes of many readers) to lose moral stature in the final chapters.

The Adventures of Huckleberry Finn is a book that poses real moral dilemmas not only for its titular hero, but also (especially in its final chapters) for its readers. Viewing the novel as an extended meditation on the themes of conscience and civil disobedience can help us grasp more fully the subtlety of Twain's phrasing and characterizations, as well as better understand the novel's ending and more deeply appreciate the ways the novel is designed to trace the moral development of young Huck and also encourage and test the moral development of the reader. The concluding chapters are deliberately disturbing and unsettling; they are designed, in part, to test how carefully we have read the novel and how well we have understood and absorbed the "lessons" implied throughout. The conclusion of the novel is written in a way that frustrates any simple, straightforward, or conventionally satisfying response. Instead, the audience is tested, not only ethically but in terms of its ability to read closely, thoughtfully, and insightfully. By the time we reach the final chapters of *Huckleberry Finn*, we should be reading with a kind of alertness and sensitivity that can make the conclusion seem deliberately provocative rather than disappointingly lax. In the ethical problems posed by the final chapters, Twain leaves us with no simple or easy affirmations. Instead, he puts us to the test.

I.

One episode early in the book that is especially relevant to the themes of personal conscience and civil disobedience is the scene in Chapter 6 in which Pap Finn, Huck's drunken and ne'er-do-well father, protests vociferously against the "govment" (33). One might assume that any attack on governmental authority is a text-book example of at least potential civil disobedience, but Twain makes it clear that Pap is motivated not by any claims of selfless conscience but by pure and naked self-interest. Pap is angry that Huck—who has been adopted by the Widow Douglas and whose money is under the protection of Judge Thatcher—has slipped out of his fathers total control. Pap excoriates the "govment" because he thinks it has robbed him of a piece of valuable personal property ("a mans own son"), and indeed he speaks of Huck almost as if Huck were a slave: "Yes, just as that man has got that son raised at last, and ready to go to work and begin to do suthin for *him* and give him a rest, the law up and goes for him. And they call *that* govment!" (33). Pap Finn may be protesting against the law, but he does so only because the law has failed to benefit his very narrow self-interests; it has (he thinks) denied him his "property" and trampled on his "rights" (33). Paps treatment of Huck as a kind of slave is made even more obvious when Pap next objects to the governments excessively lenient treatment of a "free nigger" (34). Twain describes how Pap beats Huck and keeps him locked up (29), much as Jim is beaten and imprisoned later in the book. Moreover, Pap condemns Huck for being well dressed and "educated" (24) in much the same way that he later condemns an educated and well-dressed "free nigger" (33–34). Pap, then, despite his protests against the "govment," is hardly an exemplar of civil disobedience. He is not motivated by conscience, by concern for others, or by obedience to some higher principle. He is utterly selfish, and his attack on the "free nigger" is one of the many moments in this novel in which Twain obviously mocks racism and satirizes racial prejudice. Pap expresses contempt for education, but one of his own chief functions in the novel is to help educate readers about the idiocy and viciousness of racial prejudice and about the injustice and irrationality of slavery. By presenting such a blatantly unattractive advocate of racism and slavery, Twain condemns both.

In contrast to Pap, Huck's biological father, is Jim, who eventually becomes Huck's surrogate father. Jim has a highly developed conscience and is very capable of genuine civil disobedience. Jim proves his willingness to break the law, of course, when he runs away after overhearing that Miss Watson may be intending to sell him (53). Huck, having himself just escaped from a kind of slavery, now adheres to his own private vow and to his own sense of personal honesty by repeatedly promising not to reveal Jim's secret (53–54). Both the boy and the man, then, are already engaged in acts of civil disobedience, and Huck is already acting on behalf of another and at the behest of his own conscience. Although Jim may seem at first to be acting here mainly to protect himself, eventually it becomes clear that one of his chief motives is to win the freedom of his wife and children. In Chapter 16, he explains to Huck that the first thing he intends to do when he gets to a free state is to work to earn enough money to "buy his wife; and then they would both work to buy the two children; and if [the children's] master wouldn't sell them, they'd get an abolitionist to go and steal them" (124). Jim is perfectly willing to disobey the law if doing so is the only way he can help others; his personal flight toward freedom is fundamentally a way of making sure that he can eventually free his family. Huck is shocked by such talk; it troubles his conscience, but by this point the irony of Huck's references to his conscience is clear. We realize that by violating the laws and teachings of his society, Huck is actually doing the right thing. We understand that by transgressing against the kind of "conscience" society has tried to instill in him, he is actually obeying a higher kind of conscience. When Huck eventually decides that he would rather "go to hell" than turn Jim in (271), the irony of his words is obvious. By choosing civil disobedience, Huck obeys a higher, truer kind of conscience and is adhering to a higher, truer kind of law. Here and repeatedly throughout the book (see, for example, *HF* 104–05, 201–02, and 289–90), both Huck and Jim are depicted as characters who are capable of learning from their own mistakes, empathizing with others, and acting on the behalf of others. Both the boy and the man are capable not only of understanding but of practicing ideal civil disobedience.

II.

It is the sudden reappearance of Tom Sawyer, in the novel's final chapters, that has disappointed numerous readers of Twain's novel. The enormously complicated "evasion" scheme cooked up by Tom to free Jim from captivity (which is accepted by Huck and, perforce, by Jim as well) has struck many readers not only as overlong (and thus as tedious and tiresome) but also as morally disappointing and aesthetically ineffective (see, for example, Leonard et al.). Many readers wish that Huck had taken a more active hand in freeing Jim more quickly and with far less rigmarole; many readers feel that Tom, Huck, and even Twain are guilty of demeaning Jim by treating him as an amusing plaything rather than as the dignified human being the rest of the novel often shows him to be. The final chapters have become a major source of critical controversy, and few are the critics who feel entirely happy with Twain's artistry or moral judgment in this section of the novel.

However, the final chapters of *Huck Finn* can also be read as *deliberately* unsettling, disturbing, and provocative. By the time one reaches Chapter 33, which describes Tom's arrival at the Phelps farm (where Jim is being held captive), a thoughtful reader is in a position (thanks to everything that has preceded that chapter) to appreciate the text's rich resonances and multiple ironies. Twain doesn't need to spell out the ironies and moral "lessons" these chapters present; an alert reader will be able to infer them for himself.

When Tom first meets Huck (who Tom, along with practically everyone else who knows Huck, thinks is dead), Tom immediately suspects that he is dealing with a ghost—which is precisely the same as Jim's reaction when he first encounters Huck on Jackson's Island in Chapter 8 (51). Our sense of any fundamental human similarity between Jim and Tom is soon subverted, however, when Tom begins concocting his elaborate, self-centered, and therefore bogus plan for civil disobedience—a plan that is a shallow parody of the genuinely selfless acts of actual or planned civil disobedience by Huck and Jim that have gone before.

Indeed, Tom's plea to the supposedly ghostly Huck ("Don't you play nothing on me, because I wouldn't on you" (283)) seems especially ironic, because it is only a few lines later that Tom deliberately does "play" something on Huck by failing to reveal the crucial fact that the imprisoned Jim was freed months ago in the will of the now-dead Miss Watson. Instead of simply and plainly telling Huck that Jim is already legally free, Tom stops himself and goes "to studying" (284), much as Huck himself had "studied a minute" earlier in the book (270), right before he decided that he would rather go to hell than betray Jim. The ironic parallel between these two scenes (one boy chooses to act on Jim's behalf; the other chooses to treat Jim as a plaything) is enhanced all the more when Tom next volunteers to help Huck steal Jim. This offer would seem to be an admirable act of civil disobedience (an act motivated by conscience and selfless empathy) if it did not turn out to be grounded merely in a desire for selfish adventure. Astute readers can appreciate the full irony of his offer and can particularly appreciate the irony of his insistence, in responding to Huck, that "I ain't joking, either" (284) when it is later revealed that Tom, of course, *is* joking. The joke is not only on Huck and (more cruelly) on Jim but also on Twain's readers. What seems a plan for selfless civil disobedience is eventually revealed to be a scheme of self-indulgent entertainment.

There are many ironies in Huck's reactions when Tom explains his elaborate scheme to "free" the already-free Jim. Huck expresses amazement that "Tom Sawyer was in earnest" (292); ironically, it later becomes clear that Tom both is and is not "in earnest": he *is* in earnest in the sense that he does indeed intend to proceed with his complicated plan, but he is also *not* in earnest, because he knows that the plan is not really necessary; in fact, he plans to trick both Huck and Jim. Likewise, when Huck remarks that Tom is "knowing, and not ignorant," his words have an ironic double (or triple) edge that Huck himself probably does not intend. Tom is indeed "knowing" (in the sense that he knows that Jim is already free); he is also "knowing" in the sense that he has in fact been raised to know right from wrong (but chooses to violate those moral standards here); but he is also "ignorant" in the way he ignores Jim's best interests in pursuit of his own desire for adventure.

In fact, alert readers of the novel should, by this time, already be feeling some misgivings about the complexities of Tom's plan. That plan, as Huck has already conceded, stands a good chance of getting them all "killed" (Jim included). Thus, when Huck next says that Tom was raised to be "not mean, but kind," readers might begin to suspect the irony (probably unintended by Huck) of Huck's words. By this point we should already be suspecting that Tom's plan will not prove especially "kind" to Jim (although its true meanness will not become apparent until later). Similar irony appears in Huck's claim that Tom, "without any more pride, or rightness, or feeling" is choosing "to stoop to this business [of freeing Jim], and make himself a shame, and his family a shame, before everybody" (292). The ironies here are thick and rich, for Tom is motivated by "pride" of precisely the wrong sort, and he is also in fact ignoring both "rightness" and "feeling," and his later conduct will indeed prove shameful in many respects. Huck says that

Tom's conduct is "outrageous" (293) and readers will have to agree, but not in the sense Huck intends. Similarly, when Huck next says that he wanted to act as Tom's "true friend" and urge him to "save himself," readers cannot help but note, after reading the novel's conclusion, how false a friend Tom himself turns out to be (both to Huck and to Jim), and how implicitly selfish his conduct. As Tom himself asks Huck, with probably unintended irony, "Don't you reckon I know what I'm about? Don't I generly know what I'm about?" (293). Tom does know what he's about (i.e., lying both to Huck and to Jim), and it is precisely that fact that makes his conduct so troubling.

As these examples illustrate, readers alert to the moral complexities of the final chapters will perceive many more resonances in Twain's language than are immediately obvious. One effect of the complexity of Tom's plans is to enhance our sense of the complexity of Twain's artistic design. The novel is more, not less, aesthetically sophisticated thanks to Tom's evasion; certainly it provokes (and even demands) a more active kind of reading than a simpler and less morally disturbing ending would have elicited. Some of the complexities that Twain achieves can be glimpsed in Chapter 42, which focuses on the nearly tragic aftermath of the evasion's collapse. By this point, Tom has been shot, and Jim, because of his unwillingness to desert Tom in his time of need, has been recaptured and brutalized. By this point, too, the ironies built into the text have become so blatant, so blindingly obvious, that they must have been intentional. In fact, the existence of such transparent ironies strongly suggests that the whole design of the entire "evasion" section is deliberately ironical. Chapter 42 seems intended to provoke such clear outrage in any morally sensitive reader that it is difficult to believe that this was not Twain's precise purpose in composing the whole last portion of the book.

Thus, when Twain (via Huck) reports that some of the white captors "wanted to hang Jim . . . [for] making such a raft of trouble, and keeping a whole family scared most to death for days and nights" (352), the outrage that this statement provokes in any morally sensitive reader is both undeniable and double-edged: Not only do the captors seem cruel, but the phrasing implicitly reminds us that it was Tom, not Jim, who was responsible for scaring the Phelps family, and indeed for all the other pain caused by the scheme. Any reader who may, before this point, have simply been enjoying Tom's cleverness and ingenuity now is suddenly brought up short by the possibility that

Jim may die due to Tom's schemes gone bad. Most readers, however, will have become morally uncomfortable with Tom's cleverness long before now, and that is precisely the effect Twain intended. What began as a lark for Tom now is darkly dangerous, and Twain's irony is patently obvious. Similarly ironic is the ensuing report that some of the whites "said, don't do it [i.e., hang Jim], it wouldn't answer at all"—advice that at first seems rooted in basic decency and empathy until the sentence concludes as follows: "he ain't our nigger, and his owner would turn up and make us pay for him, sure" (352). Once again the irony is stunning, and the clearly implied indictment of the whites' racism and materialism impossible to overlook.

The sophistication of the syntax in the sentence just quoted—a sentence in which Twain first seems to suggest that the whites are decently motivated and then undercuts any optimistic assumptions about their character—is soon mimicked in another sentence. Huck reports that the disappointed whites "cussed Jim considerable, though"—an outcome that seems mild in contrast to the abandoned plan of hanging; but then the sentence continues as follows: "and [they] gave him a cuff or two, side of the head, once in a while" (352). The cruelty of these farmers, who probably consider themselves "good" men and "good" Christians in normal life, is clearly ironic. So, too, are the conduct and statements of the kindly doctor who initially treats Tom's wound. At first he commends Jim for his faithfulness to Tom, commenting, "I liked the nigger for that," but then he continues: "I tell you, gentlemen, a nigger like that is worth a thousand dollars—and kind treatment, too" (353). This sentence is skillfully constructed: it seems to begin with genuinely kind (if patronizing) sentiments, then it switches to naked materialism, and then it switches back to apparent kindness. The sentence is typical of the complex aesthetic and moral effects Twain achieves in the final chapters of *Huckleberry Finn*, especially in Chapter 42. There are many more examples of this, but by now the basic point is clear: The "evasion" chapters in general, and Chapter 42 in particular, seem to have been designed by Twain to provoke an ever-increasing sense of moral outrage and revulsion in his readers concerning the treatment of Jim. Readers who have paid attention to earlier depictions of moral behavior (by such characters as Huck and Jim) and immoral behavior (by such characters as Pap Finn and the Duke and Dauphin) will now be in a good position to notice the subtle ironies embedded in the "evasion" chapters almost from the start. Readers who are reading the book for a second time will be especially well positioned to notice and appreciate those subtle ironies. And, by the time we reach the second half of Chapter 42, the ironies have become so numerous and so insistent that they are almost impossible to ignore.

Huckleberry Finn is a novel in which the potential for true acts of conscience—and thus for true civil disobedience—is presented both straightforwardly and in parody. Huck and Jim (in particular) are revealed, in the first two-thirds of the book, as characters who are capable of truly conscientious behavior and therefore of genuine civil disobedience. In contrast, Pap Finn and Tom Sawyer are presented as characters who are more than willing to break rules and disobey laws, but only for corrupt or self-serving purposes. Part of what makes *Huckleberry Finn* such a morally complex book is its depiction of the ways in which Huck, by acquiescing so fully in Tom's schemes in the final chapters, loses some of the respect he has previously won from readers impressed by his acts of genuine civil disobedience. It is Huck himself, of course, who, as the narrator of the novel, depicts himself as partly the unwitting dupe of Tom's schemes, but partly also as Tom's willing accomplice. And it is also Huck, as narrator, who constructs the book in such a way that finally makes Jim, and Jim alone, seem the true embodiment of genuine conscience in a novel in which conscience is such a major and explicit theme.

WORKS CITED AND CONSULTED

Leonard, James S., Thomas A. Tenney, and Thadious M. Davis, eds. *Satire or Evasion? Black Perspectives on* Huckleberry Finn. Durham, NC: Duke University Press, 1992.

Twain, Mark. *The Adventures of Huckleberry Finn*. Edited by Victor Fischer and Lin Salamo. Berkeley: University of California Press, 2001.

ANTIGONE
(SOPHOCLES)

"Antigone's Unwritten Laws"
by Victor Ehrenberg,
in *Sophocles and Pericles* (1954)

INTRODUCTION

In this chapter from his book-length study of Sophoclean drama and the development of secular law in ancient Greece, Victor Ehrenberg asserts that *Antigone* is one of the earliest texts to deal with the conflict between rationally derived human law and the divinely given "unwritten" law. The discrepancy between human law and the "unwritten" dictates of conscience is, as Thoreau makes quite clear in his landmark essay, at the heart of any act of civil disobedience. Though careful not to reduce Sophocles' characters and their conflicts to a personified clash of ideas, Ehrenberg writes that the conflict between Antigone and Creon is a conflict between "two fundamental concepts of the order of the world": Antigone piously honors the "unwritten law" of the gods by burying her brother; Creon, by preventing the performance of burial rites and punishing Antigone for carrying them out, insists on the primacy of human authority and law over irrationality, cultural tradition, and the edicts of the gods. Thus Antigone, in accord with her

---

Ehrenberg, Victor. *Sophocles and Pericles*. Oxford: Oxford Blackwell, 1954. 28–37, 54–61.

moral conscience, disobeys the civil authority of Creon, who,
in turn, disobeys the authority of the gods.

Death and the dead impose on living men and women the most sacred
duties, and these duties are in the very centre of the eternal and divine
laws. It is in no way accidental that the sacred rites due to the dead play
a prominent part in several of Sophocles' plays. When the Atridae give
orders that Ajax's body shall remain unburied they outrage the 'laws of
the gods'.[1] Zeus, 'unforgetting Erinys and fulfilling Dike', would have
punished them, had not Odysseus prevented the crime (1390ff). Similarly, whatever interpretation is given to the struggle between Antigone
and Creon, her reference to the 'unwritten laws' is the point on which
it is focused. This is the earliest extant, and at the same time the most
famous, example of the unwritten laws, which above all include the
sacred rituals and obligations owed to the dead by their kith and kin.
They were the laws 'which Hades desires' (519), and Antigone, in her
conflict with the law and the ruler of the State, appeals to them.[2] To
bury the dead is not a demand of human ethics, nor even a general rule
of human society. It is necessary in order to avoid religious pollution.
No one can be more eager to avoid pollution—of the State as well as of
himself—than Creon when Antigone's death is concerned (775f, 889).
He thinks differently in the case of Polyneices because he who led an
army against Thebes is a traitor to his country.

According to Athenian law, no man convicted of treason was
allowed to be buried in Attic soil.[3] Although the law had hardly
been applied for some time, the audience would probably feel that
the Atridae in *Ajax* and Creon in *Antigone* in acting as they did had
some justification. Ajax who had desired to kill the Greek leaders, and
Polyneices who had attacked his native city, were traitors and therefore might have to suffer the evil due to them.[4] On the other hand,
in *Ajax* there can really be no question that right is not on the side of
the Atridae. Although that does not mean that Creon must be equally
wrong, it leaves no doubt about the moral issue. The religious duty to
bury a body, a duty particularly of the kinsfolk, was quite definite, and
Creon's announcement made it even impossible to bury Polyneices
outside Theban territory. In war, a defeated invader would usually take
his dead with him; when this could not be done it was appropriate for

the victors to bury them, as the Athenians did after Marathon. We realize that the purely legal conflict might appear somewhat confused. There were, in a sense, good reasons on both sides, and at least partially it will have been this very fact that caused Sophocles to choose this example to express his firm conviction, and to bring it home to his audience, that divine law was predominant over all political law.

It seems certain that the question of how to dispose of the dead was of particular interest to the Greeks of the fifth century. Otherwise, it would be hard to explain why Herodotus (III 38) selected this special subject when he wanted to show the power of the *nomoi*, and how every people took their own laws as alone valid and 'beautiful'. Thus, the power of the laws was absolute (πάντων βασιλεύς); but each set of laws, applicable to one people only, became relative. What to Sophocles was a matter of sacred tradition, was equally powerful and yet only a varying custom and mere convention to his friend Herodotus. Their, and their contemporaries', thoughts were much concerned with the conception of *nomos* in its different meanings. Sophocles, with his complete and fundamental devotion to religious traditions and standards, must have felt sore about any 'scientific' or relativist conception of *nomos*; to him the sanctity of the dead was at the very core of the matter. No doubt, the subject was most suitable to achieve dramatic tension and effects; it was also a matter of wide interest and discussion. Above all, however, to choose this theme meant to put the issue on the most fundamental basis. It was appropriate that the sacred rituals of burial were the battlefield on which religion as a whole was to be defended.

The unwritten laws which command the burial of the dead express ancient sacred duties of kinship and of piety. Burial, under normal conditions, was primarily a family matter. Antigone buried her brother; Ajax will be buried by Tecmessa and Teucrus. But this duty of the next of kin is not the motive that induces Odysseus to speak in favour of the burial; the point is, in fact, not mentioned at all. That ought to be sufficient to prevent us from believing that the impulse which caused Antigone to act as she did was 'sisterly love' or family duty. From all we can see in Sophocles' plays it is clear that the unwritten laws were not confined to family traditions or to the question of burial. They were the rules of the divine order of the world. For that very reason, however, they were particularly manifest in all matters of sacred traditions, and it would be almost natural if our evidence concentrated on the smaller communities in which such sacred traditions were most intensely alive: the family, the *phratry*, the *deme*. The *deme* was, in fact, responsible for the performance of a burial when the family neglected their duty.[5] If that is typical of Athens, it is not of Antigone. She performs the burial, or rather that symbolic and ceremonial act which is taken for it, because the gods demand it, and not so much because she loves her brother. The demands of kinship are not an expression of family love, but of religious tradition. Antigone's personal feeling of what is her sisterly duty is overshadowed by the general principle for which she stands.[6] Principle, of course, is a cold and abstract word. What it really means is expressed in every word of her replies to Creon, most superbly in the famous line which should not be degraded by applying it merely to her and Creon's feelings towards the dead brothers, that untranslatable line of confident and passionate womanhood (523): "I am made not to join in hatred but to join in love."[7]

This is also the voice of obedience to the eternal divine laws. If we understand 'love' without all the later undertones of erotics or charity—neither *eros* nor *agapê*—if we take it, as it is called here, as *philia*, then we are approaching one of the forces active in the concept of Antigone's unwritten laws. In φιλία, as opposed to 'hatred' or 'enmity' (it is the same word in Greek), nearer to friendship than to love, we recognize the bond between human beings which was one of the foundations of Greek society, and which for Creon means something almost political. 'The unwritten and unfailing laws of the gods,' proclaimed by Zeus and 'Dike, dwelling with the nether gods', are opposed as eternal and divine to Creon's proclamations (κηρύγματα) which are mere decrees by a human ruler. Those laws of Antigone 'live for ever, were not born to-day or yesterday, and nobody knows whence they sprang' (456f). These famous words, full of emotion and belief, clearly indicate something that is essential, fundamental and universal. 'I was not like, by fear of any man's pride, to pay penalty before the gods for breaking these laws' (458f). On these laws Antigone's world is founded. She mentions Zeus and Dike, and the latter is described as one of the deities of the realm of the dead. With the two gods she describes the whole extent of the world to which she belongs and the laws of which she obeys, the world reaching from Olympus to Hades.[8] There is no place in the Universe where the unwritten laws are not valid.[9]

Universal and fundamental as the unwritten laws is therefore also the nature of Antigone's conflict with Creon. It has found many and very varied interpretations. In contrast to most attempts at explanation by earlier generations we nowadays realize that *Antigone* is one of the tragedies most difficult to understand. None of the many single and simple formulas supposed to cover the issue has been generally accepted.[10] When recently the full importance and the tragedy of Creon was realized, it was at once over-emphasized, and the deeper sense of the whole play again, as we believe, misunderstood.[11] We are aware that also in the following discussion important aspects of the play will be neglected, but at the same time some of the explanations previously proposed will be covered. We believe that the conflict between Antigone and Creon is more than simply a fight between two powerful human beings. Alive and great and independent as Sophocles' characters are, they always stand for more than themselves. 'They cannot be understood by psychology only, for Sophocles is not interested in psychology for its own sake.'[12] It seems just as fundamental a mistake to explain the *Antigone* merely as a conflict of two characters as to see in the play nothing but a contest of ideas. Family and State, mysticism and rationalism, private conscience and public law—as far as there is some truth in these or in other contrasting concepts, it is all included in the conflict between two fundamental concepts of the order of the world.

These concepts are clearly not only individual ideas, originating in the minds and souls of the two opponents. We realize that Antigone's and Creon's lives, minds, characters are separated by an unbridgeable chasm, and labels such as 'conflict of duties' or 'contest of will' remain inadequate. Personal emotions or experiences are all subject to the struggle of the two concepts of the meaning of life. Antigone believes in a divine order of the world; Creon relies on human laws and standards, whether of individual man or the State.[13]

This is indeed the framework of most of Sophocles' plots.[14] The struggle between the leading characters can end in nothing but disaster, not because of the stubbornness and single-mindedness of their natures, but because there is no chance of reconciling the world of men with that of the gods, the world of Creon with that of Antigone. This exclusive contrast has been explained by the mysterious affinities of either sex—woman, family, religion on the one side; man, State, power on the other. There may be a deep truth in this background picture, but it is not Sophocles' truth. Nor is Antigone a Joan of Arc, a martyr who hears divine voices. It will suffice to repeat that Creon stands for the world of man-made politics, and Antigone for that of divine guidance and order. It was the essential error in Hegel's penetrating interpretation of *Antigone* that he believed in a higher unity of the two worlds instead of their complete incompatibility. Hegel's mistake was to take Sophocles for a Hegelian.[15] Antigone has to perish so that Creon's world will meet with destruction. It is by the ultimate greatness and value of man that the divine order prevails, the order which is Antigone's and, we may say, Sophocles' order.

Unwritten Laws

We have anticipated what is still to be shown: that Sophocles, through the mouth of Antigone, who nevertheless retains her great and unique character,[16] expressed his own views on life and world. The corroborative evidence from other plays is irrefutable. The 'greatest laws' which Electra observes in her unwavering hatred of her father's murderers, 'winning the highest reward through reverence for Zeus' (*El.* 1093f), although they can even justify matricide, are the same as 'the old laws by right of which ancient Dike sits enthroned with Zeus', the laws which Oedipus invokes to support his merciless curse of Polyneices (*OC.* 1381f) who had hoped to win his father's forgiveness and support by invoking 'Aidôs sitting with Zeus as partner of his throne' (1267).[17] Punishment awaits those who break the sacred laws of reverence and justice. Zeus values piety towards the gods above everything; 'it does not die with men, it never perishes whether men live or die' (*Ph.* 1441ff).

If we ask what are the eternal laws, the poet gives us at least one circumstantial, though not precise, answer: the famous choral song in *Oedipus Tyrannus* (865ff). Here 'the laws set up on high' are called the laws of 'reverent purity in every word and deed', words which fix the place of the laws in the sphere of religion and ritual. 'They were born in Heaven, Olympus alone is their father; they were not brought forth by the mortal nature of man, nor shall forgetfulness ever put them to sleep. A god is great in them, and he does not grow old.' The prayer of the chorus is for a life lived in accordance with these laws. Described as they are with beautiful and passionate emphasis, they are laws of divine origin, Olympian laws, comprehensive and universal.

The stanzas following depict the sinner against these laws, the man full of *hybris* which 'begets the tyrant'. The chorus prays that the Polis may keep its old traditions. The god must remain the State's *prostates*, its guardian and leader. For if this is not so, if impiety takes hold of the city, then, the chorus sings, 'what need I dance?' (896). Then its service in honour of the gods has become senseless. In obvious retort to Iocaste's sceptical utterances on the value of Apollo's oracles, the chorus appeals to Zeus to show his power and the truth of the oracles: 'No longer Apollo is honoured, worship is dead.'[18]

The song does not repeat the striking mention of the unwritten laws, but their spirit could hardly be made more manifest. Not only does the poet stress, once more and with words of the most emphatic conviction, that the world in general as well as the Polis are ruled by eternal and divine laws, and that the political ruler who does not submit to them will become unjust and a tyrant. We can also discover, under the beautiful veil of poetry, the features of a code of belief and behaviour which is opposed to all only man-made beliefs and rules. The eternal laws are the rules of a world, of a *kosmos*, of divine ordering and man's pious devotion, not of human morality and political common sense. When the Sophists discovered 'natural law', they denied the traditional (and Sophocles') divine order. For Sophocles there was only Oneness, unity: nature was divine, *physis* was *nomos*.

In opposing the unwritten laws to Creon's decree Sophocles made what could perhaps be called a logical mistake. Not the slightest hint is given, and it is in itself entirely unlikely, that Creon's law was written law.[19] It was a κήρυγμα, a *pronunciamento* or proclamation. Taken quite literally, there was no conflict between written and unwritten laws. Sophocles uses the expression *agrapta nomima* in a way suggesting that it was not a newly invented phrase. It is certain that in fifth-century Greece most laws were regarded as valid just because they were written.[20] Creon's decree is fundamentally of the same kind, and Sophocles' mistake (if we may call it so) is easily explained. He did not invent either the phrase or the matter, but he used the concept in his own way and to his own purposes; in fact, it was probably he who gave it its most forceful expression. Heraclitus was perhaps the first to speak of one divine law from which all human laws derive. He coined a striking phrase for the idea which, however vaguely, was generally held, that all law was of divine origin. During the sixth and the fifth centuries, with the growing separation of legislation and jurisdiction from religion—that is to say, above all, with the growth of democracy and democratic law-making—the Greeks came to realize the difference between divine and human law, and became aware of some of its implications.[21] *Nomos*, 'Law' as a general rule, as a moral obligation and command, as a power above human standards, was seen as something distinct from the *nomoi*, the particular laws of a State. Witness, for instance, Pindar's enigmatic fragment of the '*Nomos*, king of all' (frg. 169 = 152 Bowra), or Empedocles' *to men panton nomimon* (frg. 135), 'the law of all things that is extended without break through the wide-ruling heaven and the boundless light', a law that echoes the commandment 'Thou shalt not kill'. We can trace various forms of the idea of a universal law or of a plural of universal laws, though there was no generally accepted, or at least predominant, doctrine.[22]

The phrase Unwritten Laws, though it too may have various meanings, reflects a popular version of the same idea. We must be careful not to assume that Plato's statement about the popular use of the phrase (*ta kaloumena upo ton pollon agrapha nomima*) (*Laws* 793 A) was true for a period a century earlier, although he speaks like Sophocles of νόμιμα and not, as was more common, of νόμοι. On the other hand, there is no evidence to show that the phrase was invented by one of the outstanding thinkers, say Protagoras.[23] A popular origin seems far more likely. To Sophocles the unwritten laws are sacred and eternal laws through which the divine powers rule the world. They are not confined to any particular community, and are distinct from all merely human law. An integral and, in fact, dominating part of the poet's thought and belief, they were bound to meet with consent as well as opposition. The choral song of *Oedipus Tyrannus*, with its emphatic rebuke to those who did not believe in the divine origin of the laws and their holy nature, cannot be understood unless Sophocles wrote it while fully aware of such opposing views. It is, unless we are grossly in error, the poet's reply to an opponent, or at least to contrary convictions. It cannot have been a negligible opposition to which Sophocles replied in such a striking fashion. He says so himself: it is human greatness in particular that is in danger of breaking or neglecting the laws of the divine order. What, in the beginning, we said of unwritten laws in general is indeed true of those of Antigone or of the 'laws set up on high': they are a claim and a challenge.[24]

SOPHOCLEAN RULERS

The maxims which King Creon proclaims in his first speech as well as further on are the words of a man who takes the principles of ruling seriously. He will follow good counsels and therefore grant free speech (178), he puts State and country above everything (182ff), and when he announces his fateful decree he claims to be governed by purely patriotic and moral motives (207f). To him it is therefore criminal and wanton to transgress the laws set up by the rulers of the State, even though these laws may be petty and unjust (481, 663ff). He struggles for πειθαρχία, obedience to the ruler, against anarchy (672, 676). The point in all this is not so much whether he is sincere and remains faithful to his principles (though this too is important), but the fact that Creon's maxims, if taken at their face value, are morally sound but reveal the complete lack of any divine sanction. He lives in a world in which the gods have no say, a world of purely human and political standards.

We have emphasized before that the deepest roots of the conflict between Antigone and Creon are to be found in the complete incompatibility of their spiritual worlds. Creon is neither simply 'the typical tyrant' nor just the representative of the State. In either view there is, of course, some truth, and that is why the one or other has often been claimed as the one and only fact which explains Creon. Tyrant and State-bound though he is, the basis of his 'political' position is that he lives in a world alien and opposed to that of Antigone. To him religious duties are secondary to the supreme sovereignty of the State (e.g. 745, 775ff) and to the standards of human and political ethics (207ff, 514ff, 730ff). He wants to prevent the pollution of the city (776), because the unharmed greatness of the State is his chief aim, but his claim that men cannot pollute the gods (1044) is a household thought, well known from Euripides, of those who are fighting the old religion; they put the divine powers, if they still acknowledge them, so high above the human level that the link between men and gods breaks and the gods are powerless and meaningless.

Creon denies the very foundations of religion when he refuses to admit the right of honouring those in Hades (780). The order of the world includes necessarily the dead, but only in so far as the living, and in particular the rulers among men, consent. The gods of the State, as Creon understands them, follow the principles of patriotism and government. The hostile brother has become a hostile political exile, and the enemy of the State is also the enemy of the gods (199ff, 280ff); this State-absolutism culminates in the blasphemy that even the possible pollution of heaven shall not deter Creon from doing what he considers right (1040). Thus, the ruler's lack of piety, a theme first put forth in a saying of Agamemnon in *Ajax* (1350, see p. 53), is illustrated in various aspects. Creon acts as he does, not so much because of a personal whim or his individual character, but as a result of what is typical of an autocratic and a-religious ruler. We shall have to come back to this theme more than once. The tyrant is by necessity impious, just as Otanes (in Her. III 80, 3) claims that a man is corrupted by the advantages of his position as a tyrant.[25] The time of Sophocles and Herodotus had become aware of the demoralizing influence of absolute power, and that was something different from the democratic hatred of tyranny. The world in which Creon lives is narrow and blind, though his belief in it may be sincere. The poet leaves no doubt that this world is bound to be destroyed by the divine order.[26]

It is for this reason that time and again the fight between order and order which the woman and the man are fighting as fierce soldiers is measured by the criterion of their sense and wisdom. 'Think,' 'understand' (φρόνησον) is Ismene's first word when she tries to dissuade Antigone from her purpose which is 'senseless'. With the same word Teiresias tries to lead Creon back to the right way (1023). Antigone ironically affirms that she will suffer for her ill counsel (δυσβουλία, 95), and the chorus calls her attitude thoughtlessness (383), rashness (853) and 'folly of speech and madness of heart' (603). It is of folly and madness that Antigone and Creon accuse one another (469f, 492). Their opposites, good counsel and sane thought, are the first qualities necessary for the true ruler, and the decisive scenes before the disaster are dominated by the fact that Creon is lacking just in these qualities which he strongly claims to possess.[27] Creon 'learns' at last (cf. 992, 1023), but he learns too late (1270ff, 1348ff), and his understanding only follows his fear (1095ff). Antigone's pious crime (74) is contrasted with Creon's 'impiety' (1348). When the chorus meditates that 'to be reverent is piety,' but power ought to be respected (827f), this is an opportunist's compromise against which the last words of Antigone before she goes to die (943) and the last words of the whole play (1348ff) stand out: 'Wisdom is the supreme part of happiness. Irreverence towards the gods must never occur. Great words of haughty men are punished with great blows, and thus teach wisdom to old age.' These passages are forceful enough to leave no doubt about the true meaning of the issue. Piety and wisdom are one, for true wisdom realizes the divine order of the world.

There is no question of being more or less prudent and wise. All attempts to make Antigone's lack of wisdom, her rashness and stubbornness, the real cause of her tragedy, are utterly mistaken. Her 'lack of wisdom' is, in fact, true wisdom, although her singlemindedness is accessory to her personal disaster. What Sophocles fights is wisdom as purely human reason and intellect. There is, on the one side, a young girl, heart and soul at one with the divine order of the world, bound to her kith and kin by strong emotion as well as sacred tradition, and with the heroic devotion that only a woman is able to display. There is, on the other side, an old man, proud of his brain as well as his power, relying on nobody and nothing but himself as the ruler and representative of the State, blind and blasphemous, but convinced of the truth and value of his political law (though, as eventually shown, not in the same degree) as Antigone is of her unwritten laws. Behind and beyond the two characters the fundamental contrast can always be seen.

One or two examples will make it clear that some of the obvious 'truths' about this tragedy are only part of the truth. There can be no doubt, for instance, that the contrast between family and State is of importance. In the notorious and much disputed lines (905ff) in which Sophocles reflects one of Herodotus' stories, Antigone makes a strange, though no less significant, attempt at justifying her action by emphasizing that she had to break the law of the State because she was faithful to the law of 'love' between brother and sister, the sacred obligations of close kinship, of that tie of blood which, if lost, can never be restored.[28] The very fact, however, that in these lines of poor poetry but strong reasoning, Antigone, up to a point, acknowledges the duty of obedience to the State makes it quite clear that it is not the State as such that is opposed to the demands of the family, but that State only which neglects the higher laws of piety.

Another example is even closer to our particular questions. Creon certainly is a tyrant. His doctrinairism, his extreme trust in his own infallibility, his sudden fits of rage, his blind actions, his readiness in suspecting treason—all these may be called qualities, at least some undoubtedly typical qualities, of a tyrant. The whole atmosphere

of court and city is such that we are all the time aware of a 'tyrannical' or, to say the least, of a forceful and violent ruler. The effects
of his personality on the citizens of the chorus are manifest, and the
slightly comical figure of the guard shows the impact of the tyrant on
an ordinary human being who, above all, wants to save his own skin.
There is probably none of the famous tyrants of history to whom we
could compare Creon, but a tyrant he is. We can perhaps say that the
picture which the fifth century had in general of a tyrant was largely
that of a man who set his own power and ambition over and against
any other claim, in particular the claim of justice, and served his own
aims and desires irrespectively of any moral standards. As soon as this
picture rose above the level of merely popular opinions, it provided
material to be shaped by the more extreme theories of the Sophists.
Sophocles drew up a character, not a mere résumé of certain doctrines.
His deep psychological insight is, for instance, displayed in the way
Creon expresses his hatred of the idea of being overcome by a woman;
it is the outburst of a man who wants to compensate for some inward
weakness by special manliness and cruelty (484f, 525, 579, 756). But
that man would still be a tyrant. Creon, however, is at the same time
something else.

If his decree were only the result of tyrannical arbitrariness, it
would not mean very much, and *Antigone* would not be the great
tragedy it is. Melodramatic tyrants like Lycus in Euripides' *Heracles*
are impossible in a Sophoclean play. Creon is, in fact, the legitimate
king, and this very fact is the basis of both his position in the State
and his own proud consciousness of this position. He has a firm and
genuine, if narrow, belief in the supreme importance of the State. As
the State has become absolute, it is only natural that the head of the
State is absolute as well. *L'État c'est moi* is the inevitable expression of
totalitarian absolutism. In identifying himself with the State (738),
Creon displays a genuine will to strengthen it (191); equally genuine
is the ethical force which compels him—without any prospect of
personal or general advantage—to distinguish between the dead man
who fought for his city, and the other who fought against it (207ff).
It is his honest conviction that only wanton insolence will break the
existing laws of the State (481). The same man who holds the citizens
in such fear that they dare not speak their own mind (504ff, 690ff)
proclaims that he regards it as a sign of a bad ruler not to listen to
anybody's free speech and good counsel (178ff). He has conceived a

programme of government full of excellent principles, but his deeds differ from his words. Nevertheless he is no hypocrite.

If it were so obvious as some scholars believe that he is 'maske-rading' or, in fact, lying, he and, indeed, his conflict with Antigone would be without true interest, an elementary tale in black and white which would never be tragic in the way Sophocles contemplated tragedy. Nor is it sufficient to say that Sophocles deals with Creon in a kind of obvious irony which would cause every spectator immediately to realize that he describes the typical doctrinaire and his foolish belief in his own unlimited competence. There is irony indeed, but it is the irony of that higher wisdom which looks at human efforts *sub specie aeternitatis*, and thus regards them as inevitably futile and tragic.

The connection between Creon's maxims and his decree is loose enough even in his own words. He does not defend his action by proclaiming his principles, but he recites Polonius-like the principles in which he believes,[29] and merely adds that he had given his decree 'in accord with them' (192). There is room enough to doubt whether it was in any way in the interest of the State to leave Polyneices unburied; but that is off the point. Creon with all his principles *is* the State, and to him no doubt and no problem can arise. When, as Virginia Woolf once pointed out, the spectator at the end of the play feels even sympathy with Creon, this is so, not because of any trick of the poet's, but because the man, however mistaken in his outlook and outrageous in his methods, is a victim of his principles as well as his misdeeds and has become human under the final blows of fate.

Creon has his standards, but none outside the State, and as he identifies himself with the State, none outside his own mind and reason. When the chorus replies to his announcement (211), the men dare not oppose him, but they realize the crucial point. 'This is thy pleasure, for thou hast power to use any law, both for the dead and for those alive.' They know in their hearts that this is all wrong; but they submit. The will of the ruler has become the law of the State, and it is encroaching upon a field outside politics. The 'tyrant' Creon, who demands obedience even in unjust matters (666f), is more than merely an autocrat. In his conviction, the State is omnipotent and absolute, overriding even the demands of tradition and religion. It is 'totali-tarian'. Creon does not deny the gods. Even in expressing his own will as the will of the State he believes that he follows the will of the gods. Totalitarian politics are by their very nature antagonistic to the claims of religion and the demands of private conscience. Sophocles, though without the experiences of the twentieth century A.D., realized this.[30] He was no politician. His tragedies are political only in the sense that they are 'Polis-minded' or 'Polis-bound', keeping apart from everyday politics. Sophocles fulfilled public duties, but his outlook was unpolitical because it was more than political. Yet, as he saw life as a whole he fully recognized the part played in life by politics.

We can underline this description of the poet's insight by a characteristic and important inference from *Antigone* which has not yet been mentioned. Two strong attempts are made to dissuade Creon from his decision to kill Antigone, the first by Haemon, the second by Teiresias. Haemon's plea is addressed to the king rather than the father, and eventually he uses the typical political arguments of the Polis against tyranny. Creon feels safe on that ground; it is that of his own world of politics, and the thought that the citizens might object to his action does not arouse any fear in him; this, after all, is a question of power. His absolutism finally turns against his proclaimed principles, and at the same time makes him incapable of understanding his son's deep sincerity. Teiresias, on the other hand, threatens him with disaster because the pollution spreads and the gods of the nether world are offended. At that moment, Antigone and Haemon are already dead, and disaster is bound to come to Creon himself. The gods are not going to act; for that, it is too late just as it is too late for Creon to repent. But Teiresias' intervention is nevertheless necessary because it has to bring about Creon's change of mind.[31] Teiresias is the natural adviser of the king, the man who is able to convey to him the divine knowledge which he has learnt by his prophetic insight. The part played in public life by soothsayers and interpreters of oracles is reflected in this figure, but he is at the same time the voice which announces the impending disaster, the voice of the divine order which the king has violated. As later in *OT.*, 'the blind prophet is the one who sees, and the clear-eyed sceptics are those who are blind'.[32] Creon gives in completely and almost without hesitation. He feels the menace of a world he had despised, in which he is not at home. There is a weakness in the boastful tyrant to which this sudden change is due, and this weakness is disclosed at the moment when Creon realizes that his narrow world has been overcome. From the psychological as well as the theatrical point of view the rapid change in Creon's mind may be unsatisfactory; but it reveals the more clearly the poet's intention to emphasize the fundamental issue and to show the weakness of Creon's world. A few words of the holy prophet who speaks the divine truth achieve what no political reasoning or human pleading could do, and the whole artificial building of human pride and human reason falls shattered to the ground.

NOTES

1. *Aj.* 1129ff, 1343
2. I believe that the uniform reading of the mss. is right, and not the correction by more recent scholars.
3. *Thuc.* I 126, 12. 138, 6. *Plut. Sol.* 12, 4, and especially Xen. *hell.* I 7, 22. Cf. W. Vischer, *Kleine Schriften* II, 632ff.
4. *Ant.* 10
5. *Dem.* XLIII 57f. I owe this quotation to Bowra, [*Sophoclean Tragedy* (1944)] 92. But according to him (98ff) the unwritten laws, at least 'in ordinary life and among more ordinary people', were concerned mainly with the ties of family. Apart from the vagueness of what he calls 'ordinary', I do not think his view is supported, as he claims, by the discussion of Socrates and Hippias in Xen. *mem.* IV 4, 19f, about incest between parents and children. This (hardly 'ordinary') example is used to show the relevance of only one of the three commandments [...]
6. Bowra, 96, writes: 'She does the last services to Polyneices because she loves him and because the gods demand it'. I think the order of these two motives ought to be reversed. Cf. also Mary R. Glover, *CR.* 42 (1928), 97ff.
7. Cf. A. Lesky, *Hermes* 80 (1952), 95ff. But the curious analogy *Aj.* 1376ff should not be quite forgotten.
8. Cf. Reinhardt [*Sophokles* (1947)], 86. The argument is confirmed by the fact that it is Dike, usually πάρεδρος Διός (cf. my *Rechtsidee im frühen Griechentum.* 67ff), who has become the representative of the nether world.
9. It would be in accordance with this essential fact if the lines 853ff are to be understood as Lesky understands them (l.c. 91ff) that Antigone, 'overcoming the menace of human power, has boldly advanced to the throne of Dike'. But I am not sure whether his interpretation is right. [...]

10. Cf., e.g., Jebb: 'The simplicity of the plot due to the clearness with which two principles are opposed to each other . . . the duty of obeying the State's laws . . . and . . . the duty of listening to the private conscience'. An awe-inspiring survey of all, or at least most of, the interpretations of the play is given by Mrs. M. K. Flickinger in her otherwise quite unimportant thesis, "The 'AMAPTIA of Sophocles' Antigone' (*Iowa Studies in Class. Phil.* II, 1935). Cf. also L. Bieler, *Antigones Schuld* (1937).

11. That is what in my view happened to the subtle interpretation by H. D. F. Kitto, *Greek Tragedy* (1950), 123ff. Whitman, on the other hand, rather disappointingly, sees 'nothing tragic or even morally interesting about Creon' ([*Sophocles* (1951)] p. 90).

12. Quoted from my *Aspects of the Ancient World.* [Oxford: Basil Blackwell, 1946] 149.

13. The same essential contrast can be found, e.g., between Sophocles' and Euripides' Heracles tragedies; cf. my *Aspects*, 164.

14. Cf. Bowra, 366: 'The conflict in Sophoclean tragedy is mainly between divine and human purposes'; cf. also p. 380.

15. Bowra, 65f, partly following A. C. Bradley, tries to show that Hegel did not 'maintain that Creon and Antigone were equally right in the eyes of their creator', but used *Antigone* as an illustration only of his general view of human existence. I cannot accept this distinction. When Hegel chose *Antigone* to confirm his philosophy, the play was for him a reality. The poet, in Hegel's view, expressed in his way the idea of a higher morality which the philosopher put into his general formula: 'Es ist nur die Einseitigkeit, gegen die die Gerechtigkeit auftritt'. Does Sir Maurice believe that Hegel attributed to Sophocles' own verdict onesidedness rather than justice? Cf. also the discussion of Bradley's views by Waldock, [*Sophocles the Dramatist* (1951)] 28ff.

16. Reinhardt, 84.

17. If the text in *Ant.* 797 is sound, Eros is called by the chorus 'sitting in power beside the great laws'. These must be the unwritten laws; but with quite a different meaning the chorus in 802 exclaims: 'I myself too am moved beyond the laws,' by pity—as Haemon was by love.

18. It is necessary to mention here Whitman's view which, if accepted, would invalidate much of our argument. He sees in the words of the chorus only 'a popular reflection', showing

'the somewhat confused morality of the bourgeoisie' (135). I cannot accept an interpretation in which the great song with its praise of the eternal laws, anticipated and echoed as it is by many other passages and in particular by Antigone's passionate pleading, is regarded as an expression of ordinary popular beliefs at variance with Sophocles' own beliefs, while, for instance, the almost incidental words of Hyllus against the gods in a moment of deepest suffering (*Trach.* 1266), words of which Whitman says himself that 'the outcry against the insufficiency of the gods arises most directly from the sense of the insufficiency of men', are taken as a reflection of Sophocles' own fundamental views about the gods. Moreover, if it is true, as we believe, that the song in *O.T.* is aware of opposing views, Whitman's interpretation would mean that Sophocles' chorus reacted most strongly against the poet's deepest convictions! We do not deny that the chorus here reflects public opinion; but who are we to maintain that Sophocles was fundamentally at variance with it? Whitman makes the mistake of assuming that the chorus never expresses the true views of the poet because it sometimes (e.g. *Phil.* 833ff, 850ff) does not.

19. In another passage we learn that Creon who had fought for the public law 'set forth' (481) has eventually to submit to what is called 'the established laws' (1113). The distinctions are far from being clear; cf. also *Ai.* 1246f.

20. The Wade-Gery objection (*CQ.* 38, 1944, 7, n. 5) misses my point.

21. The history of the meaning and importance of θεσμός and νόμος during the sixth century reflects these facts. Cf. my *Rechtsidee im frühen Griechentum*, ch. 3. We are, of course, not speaking of a distinction between sacred and profane law; as far as that distinction existed it remained within the limits of human, that is to say, State, law.

22. Hirzel ([Hirzel, R. 'Agraphos Nomos', *Abhandl. Sächs. Ges. d. Wiss., Phil.-hist.* Kl., XX, 1900]) provides rich material and illuminating interpretations, though he frequently neglects the historical and chronological connections.

23. Cf. I. Düring, *Eranos* 44 (1946), 99.

24. They thus become a vehicle of expression for that general attitude which, e.g., Turolla [in *Saggio sulla poesia di Sofocle*

(1934)] characterizes when, contrasting the poet in his middle age, the author of *Ajax*, *Antigone*, *OT.* and *Trachiniae*, with the later Sophocles, he calls the former '*l'apologeta*'.

25. This is stressed and expounded by G. Vlastos in a forthcoming paper on 'Isonomia', of which, by kindness of the author, I have seen a draft. [See now *AJP.* 1953.]

26. Cf. Reinhardt, 88, and elsewhere. I cannot accept the view expressed by W. Schadewaldt, *Aias und Antigone* (1929), 82ff, that Antigone's death is, at least partly, the punishment for the wrong she is supposed to have done to the Polis. What to some extent justifies Creon, does not necessarily condemn Antigone to a similar extent, and Polis and Polis may mean very different things. It seems that Hegel's monumental, if erroneous, interpretation will reappear, as it does in Schadewaldt's view, as long as the discussion goes on. In general cf. also M. Tierney, *Studies* 1943, 327.

27. See lines 1015, 1050f, 1090, 1242, 1261, 1269, 1339—176ff, 207; cf. the chorus 682.

28. Cf. Webster [*Introduction to Sophocles* (1935)], 99. Reinhardt, 92f. Bowra, 93ff.

29. The lines are repeated with equal sincerity and complete lack of irony by Demosthenes (19, 247), just as a modern headmaster might (and once did) repeat to his pupils Polonius' advice to Laërtes.

30. Of course, he did not condemn the Polis as such, though he objected to a totalitarian policy. Whitman's statement (233) that Creon 'embodies the moral atrophy of civic institutions', as contrasted with Antigone presenting 'the ideal of individual moral perception', uses modern and misleading notions, while at the same time putting nineteenth-century views into twentieth-century language.

31. Cf. Whitman, 96: 'we did not need the gods to tell us Antigone was right, though doubtless Creon did'.

32. H. D. F. Kitto, *Greek Tragedy* (1939), 137. The sentence is left out in the second edition.

THE PLAYS OF ARISTOPHANES

"Aristophanes and His Contemporaries"
by Alfred and Maurice Croiset, in *Abridged History of Greek Literature* (1904)

INTRODUCTION

In their summary of Aristophanes' life and accomplishments, Alfred and Maurice Croiset give us a valuable picture of the dramatist, his satirical comedies, and their relation to the political life of Athens. The Croisets, after discussing his extant plays, describe Aristophanes as a civil disobedient, a playwright who could not let the rhetorical manipulation of Athenians by demagogues pass without speaking against them. While the Croisets note the occasional injustice of Aristophanes' fictional portraits of these demagogues, his form of civil disobedience, both satirical and dramatic, "brought to light the secret viciousness of their policy, or better, that of all policy which cannot live without public approval, thinks itself justified in flattering public opinion, and in deceiving it for the sake of retaining power."

Croiset, Alfred and Croiset, Maurice. "Aristophanes and His Contemporaries." *Abridged History of Greek Literature*. New York: MacMillan, 1904. 248–55.

1. Life of Aristophanes, and his Works. The Extant Plays.[1]—

The work of Aristophanes is fairly well known, but not his personality, except for the declarations that he gave the public in his *parabases*. The only events of his life, however, seem to have been the production of his dramas. Hence it is impossible to separate the biography of the poet from the account of his works.

He was born about 450 B.C., and his parents were free-born Athenians, possessors of a small estate at Aegina, which they managed as *cleruchs*. Aristophanes was a talented youth. While still very young he brought out, in 427, his first play, now lost, the *Banqueters of Heracles* (*Daitaleis*), which won the second prize. Already a moralist and a sharp critic of the new tendencies, he followed the fashion of the day in making his plays educational. The next year, in 426, in another play now lost, the Babylonians, with true juvenile audacity, he attacked the demagogues, and particularly Cleon. This brought on him an exciting lawsuit, from which he appears to have come off victorious. He was, however, neither intimidated nor discouraged. In 425 he presented the *Acharnians*, the oldest of his extant comedies, which, though in competition with Cratinus and Eupolis, raised him to the first rank. In it he represents a sturdy peasant, Dicaeopolis, whom the war has forced to leave his estate and take refuge in the city. The good fellow wants peace at any price, and as he is the only one who wants it, he concludes a treaty on his own behalf. The charcoal-burners of Acharnae, who form the chorus, hasten to attack the traitor; but he succeeds in convincing them that he is right. Then, in a series of joyous scenes, we see him reaping the benefits of peace, buying, selling, and making merry, whereas the others suffer from hunger and the miseries of war. The play is excellent from end to end because of the gayety of its invention, its movement, its surprises, the renewal of its interest, and the poetic hardihood manifest at every instant.

Aristophanes brought out these first plays with the collaboration of a certain Callistratus, who undertook to make ready for the representation and direct it. There is reason to believe, however, that Aristophanes did not conceal his own authorship. It seems reasonable to interpret thus a rather obscure fact, which he himself attests; namely that, to the end of his life, he was accustomed frequently to employ either this same Callistratus or another man—a certain Philonides.

But in 424 he himself took charge of the representation of the *Knights*, the most violent attack he had made against the demagogue Cleon. Cleon had just won an unexpected victory at Sphacteria. Notwithstanding this, the young poet did not hesitate to turn to ridicule the favor Cleon was enjoying with the people. The Athenians laughed not only at their favorite, but also at themselves; and the play was a success. Under the name of Demos, he personified the people, in whose hands all power was vested; credulous old Demos was being duped by those who flattered him. He disgraced his faithful servants, in whom we recognize Nicias and Demosthenes, and substituted for them a cozening Paphlagonian, who while preying upon him pretends to be devoted to him. The rascal, of course, is Cleon. The disgraced servants attempt to raise a rival to the old man's favorite in the person of the sausage-seller Agoracritus. Impudent, ignorant, brawling, he finally supplants Cleon by the use of the same means that Cleon used. Demos, restored to reason, regains his youth with his senses. The strife of Agoracritus against Cleon forms the subject of the drama. It has not the gayety nor the rustic grace of the *Acharnians*, yet atones for this with a satiric and comic force not found so fully in any other play. The Athenian judges assigned it the first prize.

The next year, 423, Aristophanes, again taking up the theme treated in his *Babylonians*, satirized, in the *Clouds*, the sophists and the new education. Strepsiades, a humble peasant, laborious and thrifty, has a prodigal son who cannot pay his debts. The father is eager to learn rhetoric, which he regards as the art of eluding his creditors by deceiving the judges. This art is typified in Socrates, who is transformed for the occasion into a charlatan. But Strepsiades is too thickheaded to understand the lesson that he receives; and so he sends his son to study in his place. The son, Phidippides, when educated, mocks at and beats his father—such are the fruits of this much-lauded education. Strepsiades, converted and furious, sets fire to Socrates's school. The Clouds, who give their name to the play and form its chorus, represent the mazes before which philosophers bow in worship. The play obtained only the third prize. The author, more surprised than discouraged, rewrote it, but does not seem to have presented it again. The second edition is what we possess. The role of Strepsiades is excellent, giving the chief value to the drama. That of Socrates is only a gross slander; and though amusing, its injustice is offensive. It shows at least how far contemporary opinion was deceived by appearances in appreciating the great man. If the comedy did not contribute directly to his condemnation twenty-five years after, it would be rash to assert that it did not make ready for it indirectly by the false, odious image it created and kept alive in the public mind.

The *Wasps*, played in 422, seems to have had a less general aim. Aristophanes in this play derides the mania for lawsuits that had taken possession of the Athenians; but behind the somewhat thin veil, he sees and discloses the policy of the demagogues, who turn the leisure time of the people and the worst elements in its disposition to their own account. It is really still Cleon who is being censured. An old man named Philocleon is madly fond of lawsuits; around him buzzes the chorus of Wasps, representing the old *heliasts* whose sting is always threatening and who promote and profit by his folly. His son Bdelycleon undertakes to correct him. This difficult undertaking constitutes the real action of the play. Philocleon and his associates are finally converted. After that, the old man, free from the trouble of sitting in court, leads a joyous life. The play is vividly developed, full of spirit and of amusing incidents. It suggested to Racine some of the most successful portions of his *Plaideurs*.

The *Peace*, brought out in 421, was later rewritten. We have only the first edition. The subject is the same as that of the *Acharnians*, but the form is much inferior. The vine-dresser Trygaeus, weary of the war, mounts to Olympus on the back of a horned beetle and brings back Peace, whom he induces to dwell in his home, notwithstanding the opposition of certain lunatics. The action is uninteresting, and grows cold beneath the allegory. But the play is full of choice passages, all animate with the poetic charm of the country. Between 424 and 421 appeared also two lost plays, the *Laborers* and the *Merchant Vessels*, in which the poet pleaded for the cessation of hostilities.

From 421 to 414 there is a lacuna in the chronological series of his works; but we have no reason to believe that he maintained silence during this period. The years must have been occupied with plays that have not been transmitted to us. The series begins again in 414 with the *Amphiaraus*, of which, however, nothing is extant; and the *Birds*, which has been preserved. In this second group of plays the satire is generally less harsh and, above all, less personal.

The *Birds* is a charming fantasy mingled with satire, but without any marked general purpose. Two Athenians, Pithetaerus and Euelpidus, weary of living in a city where the courts are in session from morning to night, go away to find the birds, make an agreement with them, and induce them to build a new city between heaven and earth, called Nephelococcygia. The intriguers down below would fain win admission, but are driven away with clubs. The gods try unsuccessfully to govern the city; negotiations are entered into, and finally Pithetaerus assigns himself the kingdom, despite the claims of Zeus. All this is daring invention, as poetic as it is capricious and ingenious. The moral purpose, if there is one, consists chiefly in unmasking certain impostors and charlatans; but the poet seems to aim rather at amusing than at instructing his public.

Two years later, in 411, the *Lysistrata* was brought out, and also the *Thesmophoriazusae* (Θεσμοφοριάζουσαι). In the former, the poet once more pleaded against the war. This time the women demanded peace, or rather forced it by abandoning their husbands. The conspiracy is led by Lysistrata, who gives her name to the comedy. No other of the poet's plays is so bold in plot or incident, yet in no other is the action better managed. The aim of the *Thesmophoriazusae* is to turn Euripides into ridicule. By his attacks against women, the tragic poet is supposed to have offended them greatly. To spy out and amuse himself with their discussions, his father-in-law, Mnesilochus, disguised as a woman, slips in among the women of Athens, who are celebrating the festival of Demeter. There he meets with countless dangers, from which his son-in-law, the adroit Euripides, extricates him with great difficulty. The drama is spirited, but Aristophanes has neglected to give a summary of his griefs against Euripides. It is a game in satire rather than a satire proper—a series of skirmishes rather than a regular attack.

This second series was closed by the *Frogs*, one of the most important of Aristophanes's plays. It won the first prize at the Lenaean festival of 405. Here there is represented a formal judicial trial of Euripides and his art. He had just died, a year after Sophocles; the tragic poet Agatho was in Macedon; and Bacchus, patron of the theatre, is represented as anxious about the fate of tragedy. But he has no poet. Impelled by his fears, he decides to go and seek one among the dead. Whom shall he bring? He hesitates between Aeschylus and Euripides. A competition takes place; the two rivals mutually attack each other; thus all their art is criticised from the moral as well as the poetic point of view. Euripides is shown to be a sophist who has corrupted tragedy, degraded ideals, troubled men's spirits, and compromised good morality. Bacchus chooses Aeschylus and brings him back in triumph to the earth.

The years following were somewhat unfavorable to comedy. The close of the Peloponnesian War had left Athens under a burden. When the democracy was reestablished, the city took breath, but public spirit had not the same vigor as before. Comedy underwent a transformation. Though in his youth the poet was the incarnation of exuberant fancy and venturesomeness, he was obliged in his old age to conform to the new regime. This he did with a remarkable accommodation of spirit; yet he produced no masterpieces comparable to those of his earlier years.

In 392, he presented the *Ecclesiazusae*, an attack against contemporary theories. In this play the women of Athens, led by Praxagora, are represented as having got control of the assembly and having passed a vote establishing the principles of absolute communism. They abolished all rights of property and of the family. The theme of the play is the consequences that ensue. These are vividly portrayed. One no longer finds harsh satire directed against the powers of the day. The poet attacks a scholastic system, a chimera. Does he have specially in view a certain school, for example that of Plato, as has been supposed? He has not told us and we do not know. There is the same tendency in the *Plutus*, of which the first edition was brought out in 408, and the second, rewritten, in 388. The extant version is the second edition. A sturdy fellow, Chremylus, having found the god of riches, a blind god as everybody knows, takes him to the temple of Asclepias, gets him healed, and maintains him in his own home. In consequence a whole group of honest people, his neighbors and himself, become rich and devote themselves to banqueting. Under this guise is given a view of the ever recurring social question; and the intervention of Poverty, in a celebrated scene in which she extols her merits, gives the play a moral tone, that is unfortunately diminished and obscured by the final scene.

This was probably the last comedy that Aristophanes presented in his own name. He is said to have composed also the *Cocalus* and the *Eolosicon*, plays that have been lost. At the time they were represented as the works of his son Ararus, for whom he wished thus to win public favor. The former was, even at this early date, a comedy of intrigue; the latter, a parody.

Aristophanes died soon after this event. His anonymous biographer tells us that Plato composed for him this epitaph, "The Graces, seeking a temple which should not perish, chose the soul of Aristophanes." Besides the eleven plays that we possess and those that we have mentioned, he composed a number of others, of which we have only titles and fragments. The total appears to have been at least forty.

2. His General Tendencies. His Views: Political, Social, and Literary. His Religion.—

The first question that arises when one tries to appreciate this series of remarkable works is, How far can they be taken seriously? When taken together they suggest the idea of a system of political, social, and literary views from which might be deduced a doctrine. One is tempted to regard Aristophanes as a thinker well able to judge of affairs in his time, whose opinion merits much consideration. Is this really the case? Behind these brilliant invectives are we to look for a clearly defined policy, an established creed, and a criticism resting upon known principles?

If so, then surely Aristophanes would need to be regarded as a devotee of tradition, the resolute enemy of innovation. One would be obliged to suppose that from his youth, before he was twenty, he showed a constant inclination toward the past as against the future; and that, devoted to the ancient ideals which were being abandoned more and more, he did not cease to defend them and attack all that tended to corrupt them. And though in itself this would not appear improbable, yet it seems that one should then be able to deduce from his criticism a number of affirmations that would constitute his doctrine. But as soon as one seeks these, it is seen to be impossible to formulate them. Aristophanes censures democracy; is he, then, a partisan of aristocratic institutions, and would he institute a current of opinion tending to reestablish them? There is nothing in his plays that permits us to suppose this. What he censures is certain men and certain abuses; he lashes and turns to ridicule Cleon, Lamachus, Hyperbolus, Cleophon, and even makes sport of Pericles after his death. He shows how the people are deceived and sometimes wheedled by them. Does he, therefore, think that the state would be better governed by other masters? Really, we do not know. He denounces the impiety of the sophists, the dangerous subtleties of their instruction, the perilous seductions of that rhetoric which obliterates the sense of justice. Would he have wished men to abstain from learning the art of language and to return outright to the old education? [O]r did he mean simply to point out some deplorable excesses while advocating necessary changes? He has not said. The resolute adversary of Euripides, did he sustain the same relation to all contemporary poetry? It would appear not; for he at least admired the style of the poet whom he derided. As for religion, if he pretended to defend it against the theorists who advocated atheism, this was certainly not because he had a scrupulous respect for the gods. It is well known with what informality he treated them in more than one passage. All this, it must be confessed, does not give us the idea that he was a theologian, nor even a believer. We see, indeed, what he attacked; but when we endeavor to say precisely what he defended, we are at a loss.

May it not be that really he never comprehended himself, and possibly never felt the need of doing so? Let us consider how he was reared. From youth his instincts, which were only the consciousness of his rare powers, carried him toward comedy. His education was obtained while listening to the plays of Cratinus and his contemporaries, meditating upon them, and trying to imitate them. As soon as he began to think for himself, his thought was in a way moulded upon theirs. In trying to imitate their art, he adopted also their spirit, which was inseparable from it—a spirit of satire, opposition, and mockery at extravagance. The processes of the profession were therefore early adapted to the spontaneous trend of his genius, which was then just what it was later; and therefore he never became anxious to search for the true and the ideal. To seize upon the ridiculous and display it before all eyes, that was his calling. All his insight, natural good sense, and wit were used to disclose this, as was his poetic fancy and talent in exaggerating and adapting it for the stage. Characters thus formed do not have doctrines; for they are strangers to disinterested research. They have tendencies, whose principal element is the instinct of what their art demands and of what is most fitted to bring out the brilliance of their powers.

Must we say then, on the other hand, that the comedies of Aristophanes lack seriousness? We cannot go so far. When he attacks contemporary statesmen, it is true we cannot accept his testimony, because it is that of a pamphleteer and professional satirist. We have no reason for thinking him juster in this than he was when he portrayed Euripides. But he is just to as great an extent, and this makes his account worth attention. For, in criticising Euripides, if he sees only his defects and exaggerates them beyond all reason, he does evince, by the essential justice of his remarks, undoubted clearsightedness. And this is true of all his censures. That he calumniated Pericles, Cleon, and many others, we do not doubt. But in attributing to them intentions that they did not have and acts that they did not perform, he more than once perceived and brought to light the secret viciousness of their policy, or better, that of all policy which cannot live without public approval, thinks itself justified in flattering public opinion, and in deceiving it for the sake of retaining power. It would be much more unjust on the whole to degrade him to the rank of a simple jester than to raise him to that of a philosopher or political economist. Very keen good sense constituted the moral worth of his dramas; and even if it did not keep him from prejudice and injustice, it caused him to bring constantly to light truths whose particular application may have been doubtful, but whose eventual correctness is beyond dispute.

[. . .]

NOTES

1. Editions: Bekker, 5 vols., with Latin notes and translation, London, 1829; G. Dindorf, *Aristophanis Comaediae*, with fragments, excursus, notes, and scholia, 4 vols., Oxford, 1835–1839; Bergk, *Aristophanis Comaediae*, 2 vols., Leipsic, Teubner, 1852 and 1872; Meineke, Leipsic, 1860; Blaydes, *Aristophanis Comaediae*, with notes and the scholia, 12 vols, Halle, 1880–1899; von Velsen u. Zacher, *Aristophanis Comaediae*, Leipsic, 1869–1897. Dindorf's text, with a Latin translation, is found in the Didot Collection, *Aristophanis Comaediae*, Paris, 1839, in a volume containing also the fragments; the scholia form a separate volume. Th. Kock, *Ausgewählte Komödien des Aristophanes*, with introduction and notes, Berlin, 1876.

   Biographies and Ancient Testimony: The anonymous *Lives* collected at the beginning of the Didot edition of the *Scholia Graeca in Aristophanem*.

   Translations: French prose, by Poyard, Paris, 1898; and by Brotier, 2 vols., Paris, 1898. English translation of six plays, by B. B. Rogers, London, 1852–1902. The *Works of Aristophanes*, by J.H. Frere, 2nd ed., New York, 1874.

Consult: [. . . The] article *Aristophanes* in Pauly-Wissowa, *Realencyclopädie*; Deschanel, *Études sur Aristophane*, Paris, 1867; Th. Kock, *Aristophanes als Dichter und Politiker*, in *Rheinisches Museum*, 39, 1884, p. 119 ff.; Müller-Strübing, *Aristophanes und die historische Kritik*, Leipsic, 1873.

"Bartleby, the Scrivener"
(Herman Melville)

"A Second Look at 'Bartleby'"
by Egbert S. Oliver, in *College English* (1945)

Introduction

In "A Second Look at 'Bartleby,'" Egbert Oliver argues that Melville constructed his short story's protagonist as a caricature of Henry David Thoreau, whose desire to remain "aloof" from society is "carried to its logical and absurd conclusion." Egbert tries to demonstrate that certain passages from Thoreau's essay "On Civil Disobedience" correspond to the situation of Bartleby and his eventual disappearance into The Tombs. For Egbert, Bartleby's mantra, "I prefer not to," is a distillation of Thoreau's call to civil disobedience and radical individualism, one that, during the course of the narrative, is revealed to be both untenable and absurd.

Herman Melville's "Bartleby" has received little attention from the Melville critics or commentators, even though it stands as one of the two examples of his writing for 1853, the year following the writing and publication of *Pierre*, and at the beginning of his period of lesser

---

Oliver, Egbert S. "A Second Look at 'Bartleby.'" *College English* 6.8 (May 1945): 431–439.

prose writing before his long silence. Its position relative to his other work, if no other reason suffices, should assure it some attention, and it has not been entirely overlooked. In fact, a greater unanimity regarding it prevails among those Melville commentators who have mentioned it than on any of his major works. Two conclusions have several times been drawn regarding it, substantially in the same way: (1) that it is a good story and (2) that it is a picture of Melville's mind, both at the time the story was published and indicating what his attitude was to become.

John Freeman, the English biographer of Melville, asserted that, while the other stories in *The Piazza Tales* are comparatively insignificant, two of them, "Bartleby" and "Benito Cereno," are superb. "Bartleby," he wrote, "is an exercise in unrelieved pathos, the pathos of an exile in city life, faint counterpart of Melville's own isolation and gathering silence." Raymond Weaver, to whom admirers of Melville will be forever indebted for his competent critical and biographical work, reserves his highest praise of *The Piazza Tales* for "Benito Cereno" and "The Encantadas." But he does recognize the importance and value of this volume of stories in gaining a view of Melville as an artist: "They are of prime importance, not only for their inherent qualities as works of art, but because of the very peculiar position they hold in Melville's development both as an artist and as a man." Weaver included "Bartleby" in the volume *Shorter Novels of Herman Melville*, which he edited with a very fine Introduction. "And for twenty years," Weaver wrote, in the course of a biographical comment, "morning and evening, between 26th Street and the foot of Gansevoort Street, East River, an inconspicuous and elderly private citizen—a man whose history had been partly told and partly foreshadowed in *Bartleby the Scrivener*—walked with his own private thoughts."

Lewis Mumford, in his biography, saw in even more detail the mirrored view of Melville's mind in Bartleby's withdrawal from life. Mumford wrote:

> Bartleby is a good story in itself: it also affords us a glimpse of Melville's own drift of mind in this miserable year: the point of the story plainly indicates Melville's present dilemma. People would admit him to their circle and give him bread and employment only if he would abandon his inner purpose: to this his answer was—I would prefer not to.

This latter clause is Bartleby's answer, frequently repeated. Mumford supposes that Melville's persistence in minding his own spiritual affairs alienated those who could help him, made them impatient,

> for in the end, they foresaw they would be obliged to throw him off, and he would find himself in prison, not in the visible prison for restraining criminals, but in the pervasive prison of dull routine and meaningless activity. When that happened there would be no use assuring him that he lived in a kindly world of blue sky and green grass. "I know where I am!" Whether or not Melville consciously projected his own intuition of his fate, there is no doubt in my mind [this is Mumford's statement] that, as early as 1853, he was already formulating his answer. To those kind, pragmatic friends and relatives who suggested that he go into business and make a good living, or at least write the sort of books that the public would read—it amounts to pretty much the same thing—he kept on giving one stereotyped and monotonous answer: I would prefer not to. The dead-wall reverie would end in a resolution as blank and forbidding as the wall that faced him: a bleak face, a tight wounded mouth, the little blue eyes more dim, remote, and obstinate than ever: I would prefer not to!

"Bartleby" is the story of a man who gradually withdrew within himself, cutting off, one by one, the bonds of human fellowship and association until he stood alone, completely—blank and silent. His attitude toward life was a gradually progressive nonviolent noncooperation—even while he attached himself as a parasite to his employer and benevolent guardian. (This, the reader must be assured, is an inadequate and unfriendly summing-up of "Bartleby," which will be modified before this essay is finished.) I should like to suggest that the germ of the character Bartleby came not from Melville's searchings of his own relationship to society or from any bitterness in his hardening heart but from an external contemporary source, namely, Thoreau's withdrawal from society.

Melville, so far as I know, does not mention Thoreau directly by name in any of his writing, whether his literary work, letters, or various journal jottings. He mentions Emerson several times; he reviewed Cooper for the magazines; he has some comment to make on Dana,

Irving, and many minor writers. He, of course, has much comment on Hawthorne, with whom he was closely associated for a year and a half, and the various writers of the Duyckinck circle. However, his omission of Thoreau's name—while he was naming other writers—did not mean that he was ignoring Thoreau.

In 1850 Melville borrowed Thoreau's *Merrimack* from Evert Duyckinck's private library. He had ample opportunity to know much about Thoreau. His interest in Emerson in 1849 might have prompted him to ask Duyckinck for Thoreau's *Week on the Concord and Merrimack Rivers*. His friendship with the Hawthornes in the Berkshires in 1850 and 1851 certainly gave him occasion to hear of the various Concord characters. Hawthorne was for a time strongly attracted toward Thoreau. He greatly admired his workmanship and his skill in handling a small boat. Thoreau was, as Hawthorne tells us in his *Notebooks*, an occasional guest of the Hawthornes and a companion of Nathaniel in field and stream. Mrs. Hawthorne and her sister, Elizabeth Palmer Peabody, showed great interest in the American writers, especially in the Concord writers.

Hawthorne lived in Concord during the time of Thoreau's residence in the cabin by Walden Pond, his so-called hermitage, and Thoreau's experiment in withdrawing from society was probably discussed between the Melvilles and Hawthornes on occasion or on many occasions during their period of close relationship. However, even supposing that no one who knew Thoreau ever expressed an opinion of him to Melville—a most unlikely supposition—still Melville had ample opportunity to get the basis for his "Bartleby" from the so-called hermit of Walden Pond. He had available to him a published source which he used both in general outline and in some detail.

In 1849 Sophia Peabody Hawthorne's sister, a prominent member of the Transcendentalist group, Elizabeth Palmer Peabody, edited a book called *Aesthetic Papers*. This volume, which Melville undoubtedly had a chance to see in the Hawthorne home[1] if he did not himself have a copy of it, contained one of Hawthorne's longer historical tales, "Main-Street," Emerson's essay, "War," and an essay by Thoreau, "Resistance to Civil Government." This essay, now generally known as "On the Duty of Civil Disobedience," is known to all readers of Thoreau and is considered to have influenced Gandhi's activities in South Africa and India. It also served as a basis for Bartleby, who long preceded Gandhi in passive nonco-operation.

Thoreau argues that the American government—the government of slavery, engaged in the Mexican War unjustly—was such that a man "cannot without disgrace be associated with it. I cannot for an instant recognize that political organization as *my* government which is the *slave's* government also." Why do not people who want the Union dissolved, he asks, "dissolve it themselves—the union between themselves and the State?" "The proper place to-day, the only place which Massachusetts has provided for her freer and less desponding spirits, is in her prisons, to be put out and locked out of the State by her own act, as they have already put themselves out by their principles."

In this essay Thoreau tells the story of his own withdrawal from organized society and of his imprisonment for nonco-operation. "Pay, or be locked up in the jail," the state said. "I declined to pay." This is like Bartleby's often reiterated "I would prefer not to." Thoreau did not wish to pay a tax to aid in supporting the church. At the request of the selectmen, he gave them a formal statement:

> "Know all men by these presents, that I, Henry Thoreau, do not wish to be regarded as a member of any incorporated society which I have not joined." This I gave to the town clerk; and he has it. The State, having thus learned that I did not wish to be regarded as a member of that church, has never made a like demand on me since. . . . If I had known how to name them, I should then have signed off in detail from all the societies which I never signed on to; but I did not know where to find a complete list.

Thoreau then tells of his night in jail for not paying his poll tax. Here are some passages which suggested much to Melville. Thoreau says with a defiance which Melville must have admired: "I was not born to be forced. I will breathe after my own fashion." Bartleby's associates, his neighbors, his jailors even, did not know what to make of him, and Thoreau had found the same reaction of bewilderment. "They plainly did not know how to treat me. . . . for they thought that my chief desire was to stand the other side of that stone wall."

The kernel of Thoreau's thought is this: "It is for no particular item in the tax-bill that I refuse to pay it. I simply wish to refuse allegiance to the State, to withdraw and stand aloof from it effectually." This is the kind of challenge which intrigued Melville and set his mind to

working out implications. Here is a man who lives in society, certainly
to a real extent dependent upon it, yet withdrawing, aloof. Bartleby,
when asked to join in co-operative tasks, replies, "I would prefer not
to." He gives no reasons. He simply wishes to refuse. Thoreau's advice
is explicit. He is encouraging a withdrawal from life, even an attaching
of one's self to others, as he had built his cabin on Emerson's land.
"You must hire or squat somewhere, and raise but a small crop, and
eat that soon. You must live within yourself, and depend upon yourself,
always tucked up and ready for a start, and not have many affairs."
This is just the kind of practice which makes of Bartleby's life a cipher,
a zero: Squat somewhere, and live within yourself. "I can afford to
refuse allegiance to Massachusetts," Thoreau boasts, "and her right
to my property and life." Melville quietly writes a satire to show that
one cannot afford such a boast: to squat somewhere and live within
yourself is to refrain from living.

Bartleby in many ways, both outwardly and inwardly, parallels
Thoreau. Bartleby was a scrivener, that is, a writer, a copyist. When
once asked what he was doing, Thoreau replied, "Keeping a journal."
He, too, was a scrivener, a writer. In fact, Melville was undoubtedly
aware that Thoreau was generally accused of being a "copyist" himself,
a copyer of Emerson, as Lowell pictures him in *A Fable for Critics*.
Melville may or may not ever have seen Thoreau, but his first brief
glance at Bartleby and the comment it called forth might have been
made by many observers on seeing Thoreau. Bartleby, "a motionless
young man," stood at the door. "I can see that figure now—pallidly
neat, pitiably respectable, incurably forlorn!"

Bartleby is installed as scrivener in the law office in a manner such as
to leave him within call, yet out of sight of his employer. "And thus, in a
manner, privacy and society were conjoined." Even as Thoreau was, while
close to Concord, yet isolated from it, out of sight behind the screen of
green trees, so also Bartleby was installed in a hermitage behind a high
green folding screen near his employer's desk. The new scrivener at first
worked industriously: "As if long famishing for something to copy, he
seemed to gorge himself on my documents. There was no pause for
digestion. He ran a day and night line, copying by sun-light and by
candle-light." Melville may well have remembered the myriad classical
allusions, references, quotations in the *Week*. Probably he was aware of
Thoreau's lack of humor and local reputation for aloofness when he said
of Bartleby: "But he wrote on silently, palely, mechanically."

When Bartleby's copy is to be verified with the original, a type of work involving the joint labors of two or more men, Bartleby declines to help. "I would prefer not to," is his response. He is steadfast in his refusal. To the question "*Why* do you refuse?" he but answers, "I would prefer not to."

The three office clerks represent the variety of public opinion toward such a withdrawal from co-operative work. The employer appeals to them to support him in urging the adamant Bartleby to join in the work.

"Am I right?" he asks.

"With submission, sir," said Turkey, in his blandest tone, "I think you are."

"I think I should kick him out of the office," is Nippers' view.

"I think, sir, he's a little *luny*," replied Ginger Nut with a grin.

But Bartleby has his way. He does not choose to help verify copy. Others must do his work, the work which normally would be expected of him. Thoreau lived on Emerson's land by Walden Pond. He borrowed Alcott's ax. Someone else paid his tax to keep him out of prison. "In fact," Thoreau wrote in his essay, "I quietly declare war with the State, after my fashion, though I will still make what use and get what advantage of her I can, as is usual in such cases."

Melville was so fond of good food, good drink, and good fellow-ship that the vagaries in Thoreau's diet offered themselves as subject for jest. Bartleby remained in his "hermitage," his little corner of the office, even at mealtime. He was in the office first in the morning and last at night. In fact, he—like the camel which thrust its nose in the tent—took up quarters in the office. If he were to make his withdrawal effective, it must depend on someone else. He did not go out for food. Food must be brought to him. Ginger Nut, the office boy, is regularly sent out to return with a bag of ginger nuts, a dry, hard cookie.

> He lives, then, on ginger-nuts, thought I; never eats a dinner, properly speaking; he must be a vegetarian, then; but no; he never eats even vegetables, he eats nothing but ginger-nuts. My mind then ran on in reveries concerning the probable effects upon the human constitution of living entirely on ginger-nuts.

Bartleby's firm position, that of refusing to assist in verifying copy, is accepted by his employer with a tolerant ease. The eccentric scrivener was perfectly harmless in his passivity. Moreover, "it is plain he intends no insolence; his aspect sufficiently evinces that his eccentricities are involuntary." But the strange willfulness of Bartleby expresses itself in additional ways. At first he will not verify copy—"I would prefer not to," is his way of putting it. Then he also would prefer not to go to the post office to look for mail. He refuses to do an errand even within the office. In fact, he declines to hold his finger on a string to aid in tying a knot.

> Shall I acknowledge it? The conclusion of this whole business was, that it soon became a fixed fact of my chambers, that a pale young scrivener, by the name of Bartleby, had a desk there; that he copied for me . . . ; but he was permanently exempt from examining the work done by him . . . ; moreover, said Bartleby was never, on any account, to be dispatched on the most trivial errand of any sort; and that even if entreated to take upon him such a matter, it was generally understood that he would "prefer not to"—in other words, that he would refuse point-blank.

He is progressively living within himself!

This is Melville's picture of the Thoreau he abstracted from "Resistance to Civil Government," probably embellished and enlarged by Melville's conversations with Nathaniel and Mrs. Hawthorne. Bartleby is a *reductio ad absurdum* of the convictions Thoreau expressed: "I declined to pay." ". . . . I can afford to refuse allegiance. . . ." "I, Henry Thoreau, do not wish to be regarded as a member of any incorporated society which I have not joined." "I was not born to be forced. I will breathe after my own fashion." "It is for no particular item in the tax-bill that I refuse to pay it. I simply wish to refuse allegiance to the State, to withdraw and stand aloof from it effectually." Bartleby, too, simply wished to refuse. He stood aloof. He never gave reasons. He never argued. He embodied passive nonco-operation. He was a squatter, and he lived within himself.

Bartleby takes up quarters in the office—even his employer does not know when—spending his days and nights there, eating and sleeping there, attending to his personal toilet and laundry there. He takes over the offices, requesting the employer to come in only during working hours. But the employer-narrator of the story is not outraged by such usurpation. He is rather overwhelmed by the thought of Bartleby's loneliness, the solitude of his life.

Such an aspect of Thoreau's professed withdrawal from society and life alone in a cabin would have strongly impressed the companionable, sociable Melville. For he himself, too, was feeling the loneliness of the life at Arrowhead, away from the many friends he had enjoyed in New York. In 1850 and again in 1851 his New York friends had visited him. The Hawthornes had lived but a few miles away over the hills, and he had been meeting new friends. But in 1852 the Hawthornes were gone from the Berkshires; the Duyckincks and their circle of friends did not come again; Melville was feeling the loneliness of his new life. He had been feted in London, dined and entertained in New York, a popular author; but now even his neighbors were a little suspicious of him, and he was cut off from fellowship, by distance, by poverty, and by the feeling that his literary work was no longer given approval. It may well be that Melville's own sense of isolation entered into the employer's feeling toward Bartleby:

> For the first time in my life a feeling of overpowering stinging melancholy seized me. Before, I had never experienced aught but a not unpleasing sadness. The bond of a common humanity now drew me irresistibly to gloom. A fraternal melancholy! For both I and Bartleby were sons of Adam. . . . What I saw that morning persuaded me that the scrivener was the victim of innate and incurable disorder. I might give alms to his body; but his body did not pain him; it was his soul that suffered, and his soul I could not reach.

With all kindness the employer attempts to establish a fellow-communion with Bartleby. But Bartleby prefers not to talk, to answer questions, to say anything of himself or his circumstances. He even decides to do no more writing: "I have given up copying," he says. Now, doing no work, he was completely a squatter in the office. More than that, cut off from everyone, he was but a squatter in the universe, absolutely alone, "a bit of wreck in the mid-Atlantic."

Still he refuses to leave the office. Melville sees and enjoys the wry humor in such a situation. Bartleby is withdrawn from all social contacts, he is living within himself, but his very presence demonstrates the absurdity of his situation. Bartleby's employer contemplates the possibilities of an assumption on his own part. If Bartleby assumes that he has no relationships with or obligations to society, why not have society in turn assume that this assuming ex-scrivener did not exist? He thinks:

> I might enter my office in a great hurry, and pretending not to see Bartleby at all, walk straight against him as if he were air. Such a proceeding would in a singular degree have the appearance of a home-thrust. It was hardly possible that Bartleby could withstand such an application of the doctrine of assumptions.

But he decides against such direct action, instead accosting Bartleby with some impatience.

> "What earthly right have you to stay here? Do you pay any rent? Do you pay any taxes? Or is this property yours?"
> He answered nothing.
> "Are you ready to go on and write now? . . . In a word, will you do anything at all, to give a colouring to your refusal to depart the premises?"
> He silently retired into his hermitage.

Thoreau, in speaking of his experience in Concord jail in "Resistance to Civil Government," mentions how his fellow-prisoner occupied one window while he looked out the other and concludes, "I saw that if one stayed there long, his principal business would be to look out the window." Bartleby does find in his self-imprisonment that he leaves himself nothing to do but look out the window, in his case, a window opening on a blank wall. "I noticed," the employer observes, "that Bartleby did nothing but stand at his window in his dead-wall revery." Again: "Bartleby remained standing at his window in one of his profoundest dead-wall reveries."

Bartleby is established as a fixture in the office, as a piece of furniture, harmless, useless, silent. There the story reaches its extreme application, but for one turning. The employer was reconciled to Bartleby; the office workers were reconciled to him; he was accepted as a squatter and so might have continued. But the outside world, clients and visiting lawyers, did not understand Bartleby or the strange relationship—or lack of relationship—existing between him and the other people whose destiny it was to occupy the same bit of the world he inhabited. Other people, outsiders, made remarks. They thought the situation queer. The employer was becoming the subject of gossip.

"I resolved to gather all my faculties together, and forever rid me of this intolerable incubus." Go he must. But he would not go! "Since he will not quit me, I must quit him." However, even this stratagem is not enough to save him from the man of no obligation, the man who had withdrawn from everything. Bartleby remains in the emptied quarters. "You are responsible for the man you left there," the next tenant says accusingly to Bartleby's benefactor.

Bartleby—this man who would not feel the importance of human ties, who had cut himself off from all social contacts (so he foolishly imagined)—soon had the entire building, even the street, in a state of indignant excitement. Locked out of the offices, he persisted "in haunting the building generally, sitting upon the banisters of the stairs by day, and sleeping in the entry by night. Everybody is concerned; clients are leaving the offices; some fears are entertained of a mob; something you must do, and that without delay." This urgent challenge is hurled at the former employer, who had hoped to rid himself of Bartleby. But organized society could not dispense with Bartleby as easily as Bartleby could dispense with society.

The logical absurdity of Bartleby's position is emphasized in one brief conversation—brief, yet so much the longest of Bartleby's remarks as to appear loquacious.

> "What are you doing here, Bartleby?" said I.
> "Sitting upon the banister," he mildly replied. . . .
> "Would you like to re-engage in copying for someone?"
> "No; I would prefer not to make any change."
> "Would you like a clerkship in a dry-goods store?"
> "There is too much confinement about that. . . . But I am not particular."
> "Too much confinement," I cried. "Why, you keep yourself confined all the time!"
> "I would prefer not to take a clerkship," he rejoined, as if to settle that little item at once.

Bartender? No. Collecting bills for a merchant? No. Travel to Europe as a companion? No, but I am not particular! "I like to be stationary."

Bartleby gets that privilege in jail. Even as Henry Thoreau went quietly to the Concord jail with Constable Sam Staples, so, too, did Bartleby.

> As I afterward learned, the poor scrivener, when told that he must be conducted to the Tombs, offered not the slightest obstacle, but, in his pale, unmoving way, silently acquiesced.
>
> Some of the compassionate and curious bystanders joined the party; and headed by one of the constables arm in arm with Bartleby, the silent procession filed its way through all the noise, and heat, and joy of the roaring thoroughfares at noon.

Melville's plan of telling the story of Bartleby does not permit him to contemplate the thoughts of that prison inmate, as Thoreau could reveal his own thoughts in like circumstance. But Bartleby is found by his benefactor "standing all alone in the quietest of the yards, his face toward a high wall," much as Thoreau "stood considering the walls of solid stone." Thoreau wrote: "They plainly did not know how to treat me, but behaved like persons who are underbred. In every threat and in every compliment there was a blunder; for they thought that my chief desire was to stand the other side of that stone wall." Bartleby might well have said—or thought—the same. Melville in narrative form presents the ill-timed compliment and the underbred commentator, the loquacious grubman.

Bartleby avoids every attempt to establish relationships with him. He moves away even from food and takes up a position "fronting the dead wall." This is the ultimate in his withdrawal: he ceases to eat and is soon at peace, asleep "with kings and counsellors."

Such is the end to the kind of individualism Thoreau portrayed in "Resistance to Civil Government"—the end carried to its logical and absurd conclusion. "I declined to pay," said Thoreau, "I was not born to be forced. I will breathe after my own fashion." "Depend upon yourself." When Thoreau declined to pay, someone else paid for him, as he acknowledges in the essay. Melville was attracted by paradox. He often wished to imagine an example worked out to its logical conclusion. He certainly admired some of the heroic stubbornness of Thoreau even as he is often very sympathetic with Bartleby. But that admiration does not prevent his seeing the absurdity of some of Thoreau's extreme pronouncements in this essay.

Thoreau wishes to choose what he will do and what he will not do. He prefers not to do some things. Let that "preferring not to" become progressively more extended. What then? Moreover, someone makes up for the deficiency. Who paid Thoreau's tax? On whose land did he live? Who acted as his benefactor?

In "Bartleby," Melville has a reference to the notorious New York murder where Colt killed Adams in a fit of imprudent resentment and anger. He then makes the application that even self-interest—if no better reason can be found—demands a charitable attitude. "A new commandment give I unto you, that ye love one another." Even though Melville must have been intrigued by his character Bartleby and admired the self-sufficiency of the man, yet he shows us the implications of such an independent course of action. Bartleby became less and less a man until there was nothing left of him. There can be no such thing as an effective life of aloofness. When Thoreau wrote, "I simply wish to refuse allegiance to the State, to withdraw and stand aloof from it effectually," he was but expressing an absurdity.

Thoreau could write, as he did in his journal for January 16, 1852: "Here was one [Bill Wheeler] who went alone, did no work, and had no relatives that I knew of, was not ambitious that I could see, did not depend on the good opinion of men." If Melville had seen this sentence he would have asked, with a raised eyebrow or a sly wink: "No relatives? Not even a mother? Or a father? No work? On whose efforts does he depend, even if he does not depend on opinions?"

In April of that year before Melville was to write "Bartleby," Thoreau confided to his journal: "Society, man, has no prize to offer me that can tempt me; not one. . . . When I am most myself and see the clearest, men are least to be seen. . . ." "Bartleby" seems to be written in answer to such thought as this. The pathos of "Bartleby" need not blind us to the implications of the story. Try as you will, you cannot cut yourself off from society, and to persist in such a direction can only destroy the individual.

It is possible that Melville, who enjoyed a pun almost as well as he enjoyed enigmas and puzzling allusions generally, may have had a sly reference to Thoreau's extended use of ancient and oriental literature in his suggestion that "Bartleby had been a subordinate clerk in the

Dead Letter Office at Washington, from which he had been suddenly removed by a change in the administration."

Melville had ample opportunity to know a great deal about Henry Thoreau and his various experiments in individualism and in depending on himself. He read some of Thoreau's writing: probably he read the three installments of "A Yankee in Canada," which early in 1853 appeared in *Putnam's Magazine*, the magazine in which "Bartleby" appeared in November of that year. In "Bartleby" he paid his respects to the kind of social attitude represented by Thoreau's two-year "hermitage" by Walden Pond, by his note of withdrawal from organized society, by his refusal to pay his taxes, by his acceptance of a situation in which he lived at the expense of another man, permitting another's paying of his taxes to keep him from jail. "Bartleby" indeed is interesting as a story. It is also interesting as a revelation of Melville's mind and method of writing during 1853. It is an important clue pointing toward Melville's wholesome sanity, his objective searching of social relationships, his active interest in his contemporaries and their writings. In "Bartleby" we see him looking outward, not in any spirit of despairing rebellion searching his own heart.

NOTES

1. The copy of *Aesthetic Papers* which I have in hand for this study, curiously enough, came from the library of Oliver Wendell Holmes, Melville's friend and neighbor in the Berkshires. It is owned by the V. L. Parrington branch of the University of Washington Library.

BILLY BUDD
(HERMAN MELVILLE)

"Billy Budd"
by Milton R. Stern, in *The Fine Hammered Steel of Herman Melville* (1957)

INTRODUCTION

In *Billy Budd*, Melville presents a conflict between moral conscience and the law, one where the innocent Billy Budd is falsely accused. Like Judas in the New Testament, Captain Claggart betrays the Christ-like Budd. But when Billy's stutter keeps him from responding during the investigation Captain Vere performs, Budd lashes out uncontrollably, defying maritime law and becoming the subject of a court martial. In executing Billy, Vere holds fast to the sanctity of law. As this excerpt from Milton R. Stern's *The Fine Hammered Steel of Herman Melville* illustrates, the conflict between conscience and the laws of man are central to understanding Billy Budd's act of civil disobedience.

Translated Cross, hast thou withdrawn,
Dim paling too at every dawn,
With symbols vain once counted wise,
And gods declined to heraldries?

Stern, Milton R. *"Billy Budd." The Fine Hammered Steel of Herman Melville.* Urbana, IL: U of Illinois P, 1957. 206–39.

* * *

The atheist cycles—*must* they be?
Fomenters as forefathers we?

—*Clarel*

Morally, philosophically, emotionally, socially, Melville's search for the complete man is not the search for the knightly hero, but for the Governor. The Governor must repress man's anarchic atheism and must reorient man's frantic activities.

The quester is an atheist because he denies history and thereby rejects man's only possible God. The quietist is an atheist because he denies human commitments and thereby rejects possibility itself. The banded world is an atheist because it denies reality and thereby rejects the true nature of God and of man's potentialities. All these confidence men-atheists have one denial in common: they reject man. They deny man because they cannot recognize the importance of man-self and the subordinate position of one-self; they cannot recognize anything by means of the naturalistic perception wherein the importance of man's morality shrinks on a cosmic scale, and the importance of man's morality grows on the social and historical scale. Thus they all perpetuate a crazy history of crime and error. Sacrifice of self to ideal is not self-sacrifice at all, Melville has suggested, but rather it is that indulgence of self which is the ultimate romantic selfishness. What is needed is a tactically wise, if often distasteful and unspectacular, sacrifice of self to the historical moment. Except for King Media, Melville so far has given us no one willing or able to practice this particularly contemporary, larger-and-smaller-than-traditional sacrifice. In *Billy Budd* he does.

The nature of the governor and the nature of the sacrifice demand an emphasis not on individualism, certainly, or self-expression per se, but on control—which is at the center of Melville's political classicism.

Melville introduces the need for planning by slyly setting the reader at ease with a promise of "that pleasure which is wickedly said to be in [literary] sinning." With such a sin Melville announces that he is "going to err into . . . a bypath" which turns out, after all, to be the direct road into the center of this "inside narrative." Enticed into the bypath, "anybody who can hold the Present at its worth without being inappreciative of the Past," finds in "the solitary old hulk at

Portsmouth, Nelson's *Victory*" a symbol of the conditions of victory, of good government, and of the ruler who recognizes the need for altruistic yet impersonal self-sacrifice to the realities of history.

There are some, perhaps, who while not altogether inaccessible [to the beauty of the past] ... may yet on behalf of the new order, be disposed to parry it; and this to the extent of iconoclasm, if need be. For example, prompted by the sight of the star inserted into the *Victory*'s quarter-deck designating the spot where the Great Sailor fell, these martial utilitarians may suggest considerations implying that Nelson's ornate publication of his person in battle was not only unnecessary, but not military, nay, savored of foolhardiness and vanity. They may add, too, that at Trafalgar it was in effect nothing less than a challenge to death; and death came; and that but for his bravado the victorious admiral might possibly have survived the battle, and so, instead of having his sagacious dying injunction overruled by his immediate successor in command he himself when the contest was decided might have brought his shattered fleet to anchor, a proceeding which might have averted the deplorable loss of life by shipwreck in the elemental tempest that followed the martial one.

Well, should we set aside the more disputable point whether for various reasons it was possible to anchor the fleet, then plausibly enough the Benthamites of war may urge the above.

But the *might have been* is but boggy ground to build on. And certainly in foresight as to the larger issue of an encounter, and anxious preparation for it—buoying the deadly way and mapping it out, as at Copenhagen—few commanders have been so painstakingly circumspect as this same reckless declarer of his person in fight.

Personal prudence even when dictated by quite other than selfish considerations is surely no special virtue in a military man; while an excessive love of glory, impassioning a less burning impulse the honest sense of duty, is the first. If the name *Wellington* is not so much a trumpet to the blood as the simpler name *Nelson*, the reason for this may perhaps be inferred from the above. Alfred in his funeral ode on the victor of Waterloo ventures not to call him the greatest soldier of all

time, though in the same ode he invokes Nelson as "the greatest
sailor since the world began."

At Trafalgar Nelson on the brink of opening the fight sat
down and wrote his last brief will and testament. If under the
presentiment of the most magnificent of all victories to be
crowned by his own glorious death, a sort of priestly motive
led him to dress his person in the jewelled vouchers of his own
shining deeds; if thus to have adorned himself for the altar and
the sacrifice were indeed vainglory, then affectation and fustian
is each more heroic line in the great epics and dramas, since
in such lines the poet but embodies in verse those exaltations
of sentiment that a nature like Nelson, the opportunity being
given, vitalizes into acts. [pp. 822–24]

The goal at the end of this bypath is a statement of the kind
of heroism that, unlike the quester's courage, may lead to salvation,
and that the reader is led to expect to find in the other Great Sailor,
Captain Vere. Practical recognition of actualities is not attacked in this
brief excursion—"the *might have been* is but boggy ground to build
on." Both cheap hindsight and absolutist evaluations are tossed aside
with the rejection of any should-have-been or might-be or must-be
that does not grow out of the conditioning historical facts which
inevitably become a particular historical result. Hand in hand with
this rejection is the attack on "martial utilitarians," who, in this context,
are the dry tacticians who can see tactics only. Strategy, empiricism,
tactics, Melville says here, while of prime importance, cannot be
divorced from the greatest communal aspirations—"the larger issue."
The fact of the existence of aspiration, and recognition of larger issues,
makes it necessary to reckon with human nobility and heroism as
factors in tactical action. The nonrational gloriousness of which man
is capable cannot be denied—indeed must be depended upon—in
strategy which is to win the greatest human victories. In attacking the
might-have-been and the Benthamites of war, Melville attacks the
function of head minus heart, the power politics minus the informing
vision. And because the informing vision is a social, historical vision,
and because man is at once unbelievably heroic and unbelievably blind
and base, the leader must combine Machiavellian circumspect foresight with the glorious and heartful act. The Machiavellian prudence
channels and controls blind, base man, and the glorious act vitalizes

the controlled and channeled man into the proper acts in which his inspired heroism can victoriously operate. The hero thus is a political and moral administrator. The standing in one's fullest magnificence upon the beleaguered quarter-deck of the state stems not from the personal and pathetically heroic idealism of the quester, but from the social and tactical vision of the leader who recognizes that the historical moment demands the sacrifice of self to the possible victory that the combined head and heart may achieve. Thus the shrewdly heroic Nelson, who deliberately and purposefully went out, in the shining medals of his honor, to tempt death.

Thus too, this modern Nelson-hero-Administrator is, like the quester, self-consuming. But unlike the quester, he consumes himself as an inspiration which will result in victory concerning the larger, social issue. He places himself on the altar of "the honest sense of duty," making his very using up of one-self a man-self triumph which saves rather than destroys the ship. And the difference between the Nelson-Vere-captain and the Ahab-captain exists most centrally in this matter of the empirically, communally, historically centered rather than the idealistically, self-centered predisposition. Indeed, "few commanders have been so painstakingly circumspect as this same reckless declarer of his person in fight," and "while an excessive love of glory . . . is the first . . . special virtue in a military man," Nelson's love of glory was no more motivated by Ahabian glory, or *vain*glory, than his painstaking circumspection was motivated by "personal prudence." The implication is that the gloriousness itself, which was always there, would never have been displayed had it not been the tactical move which resulted in the preservation and triumph of the human community, had it not been the socially conscious, altruistic "exaltations of sentiment . . . vitalized into *acts*." So too, Vere's captaincy is not the glory that leads the Ahab-led Ishmael to utter the Solomonic "All is vanity. ALL." Not at all vain, when Vere is ashore

> in the garb of a civilian scarce any one would have taken him for a sailor, more especially that he never garnished unprofessional talk with nautical terms, and grave in his bearing, evinced little appreciation of mere humor. It was not out of keeping with those traits that on a passage when nothing demanded his paramount action, he was the most undemonstrative of men. Any landsman observing this gentleman not conspicuous by his

stature and wearing no pronounced insignia, emerging from his cabin retreat to the open deck and noting the silent deference of the officers retiring to leeward, might have taken him for the King's guest, a civilian aboard the King's ship, some highly honorable discreet envoy on his way to an important post. But in fact this unobtrusiveness of demeanor may have proceeded from a certain unaffected modesty of manhood sometimes accompanying a resolute nature, a modesty evinced at all times not calling for pronounced action, and which shown in any rank of life suggests a virtue aristocratic in kind. [p. 826]

The preparation for Vere made by the Nelson "divergence" exists in more than the nature of self-sacrifice. Not only must Nelson sacrifice the most gloriously beautiful self in order to insure the historically possible larger issue, but so also must Vere, in the rejection of the might-have-been, do the same. But in addition, just as there is no one left to whom Nelson can delegate the proper conduct of the ship of state ("his sagacious dying injunction overruled by his immediate successor") so there is no one left to whom Vere can delegate the proper power and insight. In the perfectly complete parallel between Nelson and Vere, Melville says that if human society can win a victory over itself, no one man can insure the perpetuity of the outcome. Perhaps the governor must be a community of rule. Perhaps, indeed, lasting victory cannot be achieved from the top down at all. Not only is there the implicit rejection of the great-man theory along with the recognition of the identity of the truly great man, but there is the frustrating irony which places destiny in the hands of the general, common man. Because of his blindness, general, common man cannot be led by his nobility (the administrator's self-sacrifice provides the leadership) and there is no avenue left open to the gregarious advancement, which is the only lasting one. Because in *Billy Budd* Melville comes most closely to grips with the problem of rule, the political alternative to his metaphysical rejections, and because the facts of his experience showed him no solution to the problem, *Billy Budd* has the angry, bitter, frustrated tone which too few readers have noticed in their agreement to call the story a testament of acceptance.

Melville orients the elements of Vere's sacrifice as historically as he does Nelson's. He sets up the conditions of Vere's choice in a specific moment which extends to the general history of order and

community versus anarchic atheism, in Melville's sense, and atom-
istic individualism.

[...]

Vere, like Claggart, must confront Baby Budd with an ultimate
rejection. With pained love rather than with envious hatred Vere
must reject what Budd represents to him. As administrator of the
society whose order Claggart's machinations have threatened, Vere
must condemn the actual as well as the representative Budd. To
Claggart, Billy represents the false appearances of the world and is
a hateful idea. To the Dansker, Billy represents an anomaly and is a
curiosity. To Vere, Billy represents the human heart, and is a beautiful
but inoperative idea. Like all Melvillean lures and doubloons, Billy,
to the reader, is the totality of all the perceptions of the individual
characters. Pragmatically, because he too rejects (albeit reluctantly)
the idea and condemns the man, Vere is Claggart. But this is only a
surface similarity. The sorrowful man whose wisdom was tutored by
experience is also within Vere, so that Claggart, in his *initial* being,
is Vere. It is history that has formed Vere's being. It is Claggart who
represents the history which Vere recognizes in order to destroy it.
Claggart is the reason just as Billy is the reason, that the brass buttons
must take precedence over the primal heart. Claggart is the reason
presented by the evils of history which he finally comes to represent,
the gun which Vere uses because he hates the gun; Billy is the reason
presented by the very definition of the primal heart, the innocence
which must always be at the mercy of the gun and is unable to recognize the evils of history in order to use the evils of history in order
to destroy the evils of history. Thus Budd and Claggart are at once
the idealistic side of the polarities presented in the "Preface." They
are externalizations of Vere, and it is this that makes him the central
character. Billy is associated with Vere's beautifully motivated self;
Claggart is associated with Vere's harshly necessary tactical self. The
difference between Claggart as a being and Claggart as part of Vere
is the difference between self-absorption on the one hand and self-
dissection, self-control, self-subordination on the other. That is, Vere
controls and uses—unlike Claggart he does not become—the hideous
truth that both he and Claggart see. Vere controls and uses—unlike
Billy he does not become—the ideal love and innocence and goodness that both he and Billy know. The war between Claggart and Billy
is the internal war between heart and mind which constantly tears

Vere apart in his merger of the two. He needs both; he loves one and hates the activities of the other. He takes his identity from the recognition of what he and Claggart share in common; yet the motivation for his identity is but the desire for the goodness that is the Billy Budd within him. That is, if there is a continuum, a common denominator in humanity, it is the human heart, which desires goodness. But the goodness is redefined by different conditions, so that understanding of conditions, or tactics, is the only method man has with which to identify himself with his underlying self, his heart. Tactics, historical lessons, identity, must all be relearned in each historical moment by each generation. That is the historical identity that dies, like the individual being. But each generation gives birth to new generations, passing on the mystery of the heart-yearning, the aspiration (which is the idealism that makes Melville partly Ahab), along with the historical conditions which the dead identities have created and from which the new men must gain their identities by learning to cope with them (which is the empiricism and materialism that makes Melville Vere). His heart, along with the consequences of history, Vere inevitably leaves as his human heritage to the future. The human heart and the future are heirs of the history he leaves. His own historical identity he cannot leave: the others are inescapable heirlooms, but this must be earned. And the heart of Vere, the inevitable child that each generation leaves to each next generation as part of being human, the heart is the area of Billy's relationship to Vere.

Vere, "the austere devotee of military duty letting himself melt back into what remains primeval in our formalized humanity may in the end have caught Billy to his heart even as Abraham may have caught young Isaac on the brink of resolutely offering him up in obedience to the exacting behest." Biblical reference of course reemphasizes the fact and nature of Vere's sacrifice. But it also suggests the nature of Billy's relationship to Vere. And Billy, as part of Vere, is suggested in more than the Abraham-Isaac analogy. "Billy Budd was a foundling, a presumable bye-blow, and, evidently, no ignoble one. Noble descent was as evident in him as in a blood horse." And without really introducing anyone else but Claggart, the Dansker, and Vere, Melville hints, "for Billy, as will shortly be seen, his entire family was *practically* invested in himself" [italics mine]. The Dansker is old enough to be Billy's father, but he is not noble. Claggart has a certain nobility, but not the right kind, certainly, and he is only "five-and-thirty" besides.

But Vere is truly noble, Melville points out more than once, and as for age, "he was old enough to have been Billy's father." The possibility that Baby is Vere's own natural offspring, the goodness of Vere's own heart, not only sharpens the significance of Vere's sacrifice, but strengthens the thematic consideration of the administrator as the hero, or the only interested God available to man. And even in the extremity of the only choice open to him, when he is robbed of all that his son symbolizes by all that the Satan-gun-thief symbolizes, Vere forces himself to behave according to the need for preservation of the humanity he commands and for which he alone is responsible. For as Father of the Adam who falls and the Christ who is sacrificed, Vere is the only anthropocentric God. He knows that he must control destinies and decide fates in order to gain the goal of the indestructible human heart, and immediately he reverts to the only means for gaining the proper destiny, and he becomes the tactician. He exercises the proper prudence. He forearms against the possible mutinous effect of the court-martial decision. Realizing that intentions make no difference, Vere succeeds in preventing an undesirable consequence of his act. Claggart met the unanticipated consequence of Billy's fist, for all his misdirected personal prudence. His monomania prevented his seeing the wider symbolism, the social vision, that characterizes Vere's every act, and while Claggart's prudence can only result in chaos, Vere's might result in reformation. In this is the note of affirmation that Melville strikes, finally, in his last book: though intentions make no difference in the consequences of an act, the direction of thought which forms the intentions creates a different kind of act which, in its administration, brings different consequences.

Vere necessarily kills the chronometrical Christ for man's own good, so that the death of the false Messiah may bring a redemptive horological paradise on earth. For if Billy, in the chronometrical act of killing Claggart, were allowed to set the example for the world, the effect would be tacit permission for the mutiny and the spontaneous, individualistic, idealistic, atheistic anarchy which brings chaos again. Baby Christ learned the lesson Father Vere had to teach him. As Billy's beautifully good and heartbreakingly innocent relationship with that paradox, a man-of-war's chaplain, makes clear, he is too much the primitive child to comprehend anything intellectually. His "sailor way of taking clerical discourse is not wholly unlike the way in which the pioneer of Christianity full of transcendent miracles was received long ago on tropic isles by any superior *savage* so called." Robbed of complete innocence by evil, by the fact of the gun (when he lies in the darbies, his glimmering whiteness is now "more or less soiled"), he can only understand what is good and right with the goodness and rightness of his helpless heart. And his "God bless Captain Vere!" is the "I forgive you Father, for you know what you must do," which not only emphasizes Budd's goodness but which also emphasizes Vere's stature. Billy does not stutter now, but makes the one clear and final statement of the chronometrical innocence by which he lived. He is the Christ who still turns the other cheek to the man-of-war world, and, except for his new knowledge, takes his crucifixion as he took his impressment. And Vere, while recognizing that Billy leads to hopelessly inoperative behavior, also recognizes in Billy the heartful goodness of the primal human heritage. And when Billy blesses Vere, at "the pronounced words and the spontaneous echo that voluminously rebounded them, Captain Vere, either through stoic self-control or a sort of momentary paralysis induced by emotional shock, stood rigidly erect as a musket in the ship-armorer's rack." Even the simile works. At the moment that he kills the elemental goodness in man, Vere's reaction is both emotional shock and self-control. On the one hand he has his clearest perception of just what it is he kills, and at the same time realizes that if he had to, he would do it all over again. Necessarily he becomes the appearance not of the primal thing inside him, which he sacrifices, but of the gun, the thief-emblem of the world he must preserve, use, and change in order to preclude the conditions of sacrifice. Indeed, when Billy lies in the chains, he lies on the gun deck, which is given the religious imagery of a cathedral—with the gun-bays as the confessionals. Lest the ironic bitterness be lost even here, Melville hints that it is even as Christ hanging between the two thieves that the Baby is "now lying between the two guns, as nipped in the vice of fate."

When Vere dies, he calls his primal identity, his son-self of the indestructible human heart. Removed finally from the rigors of the gun-bearing world and from the pressures of control and from the self-devouring and self-killing sterility of command, he would relax into the something primeval within him and rejoin the perfection of man's heartfelt aspirations. His historical identity cannot continue. But the human heart does. So Vere goes home. He calls "Billy Budd, Billy Budd." And his call is an exhortation and a welcome. "That these were not the accents of remorse, would seem clear from what the attendant said to the *Indomitable*'s senior officer of marines who as the most reluctant to condemn of the members of the drumhead court, too well knew though here he kept the knowledge to himself, who Billy Budd was." Yet, this quotation reintroduces the bitterness which is the closing note of *Billy Budd*'s irony. On the one hand the officer of marines is a good and heartful man, but a man without Vere's historical identity. There is the possibility that this officer does not know Billy's identity any more than Millthorpe knew Plinlimmon or Pierre. Or there is the possibility that in his very heartfulness, the officer of marines, like some of the other crew members, idolized Billy. In this case too, the cycle would be repeated if the man Vere leaves behind him is an embryonic quester. In any case, probably both ironies are intended, for the net result is the final irony that it is the military officer who bears the memory of the chaos-bringing yet primally good Christ. Thus Melville reintroduces the motif of delegated authority. Man, like the Polynesian, is primarily good and primarily blind. The obscuring smoke of the chaos in which man has seasoned himself and his history must be pierced. But even the true hero, who correctly boards in the smoke, cannot as one man redeem the world, for his own historical identity, with all that is involved within it, is the one thing that can not be delegated in time. And, Melville adds, the effective identity must be ready in advance, for "Forty years after a battle it is easy for a non-combatant to reason about how it ought to have been fought. It is another thing personally under fire to direct the fighting while involved in the obscuring smoke of it. Much so with respect to other emergencies involving considerations both practical and moral, and when it is imperative promptly to act . . . Little ween the snug card-players in the cabin of the responsibilities of the sleepless man on the bridge."

That the lessons are lost and that the cycle continues all over again is evident in three "digressions" tacked on to the end of the "inside" narrative.[1] The first is the section wherein Vere is killed by the ship named—the *Atheiste*. The *Atheiste* continues the wrongs of history, for it takes over from a name which is reminiscent of Isabel's mother and her other-worldly associations: this French ship had formerly been the *St. Louis*. The wrongs of the prerevolutionary nation are translated into the wrongs of the postrevolutionary nation—one kind of atheist becomes another kind of atheist under new name and management.

And those who deny the peace of the world and the true welfare of mankind are those who kill Vere. The paradox is that the seamen of France kill the man whose goals are identical with those for which the tactically misdirected French Revolution had been fought. Vere had always known that men on both sides, wanting but the same goodness for which the human heart hungers, after all, cut each other down in the actualities of all the warfare attendant upon the wrong directions to the common peace and welfare. No final resolution has been effected, for Vere can re-inform so that reformation may be possible; but he himself, limited by time, cannot regenerate.

The second "digression" is the *News from the Mediterranean* which appears in an authorized "naval chronicle of the time." The account reports the official version, wherein Claggart is the good but wronged man, and wherein Billy is the villain. Thus appearances for their own sake are preserved. There is even an inversion of origins in the account. Claggart, the alien, is pictured as the true patriot, and Billy, the true-born Englishman, is made suspect of association with all the dimly French origins that actually characterized Claggart. The very basis of proper behavior is inverted. The official account could never admit that the strong arm of order enforcement itself could allow the officer to be the villain and the impressed man the saint. This is order for its own sake, command for the sake of prerogative, appearances for the protection of privilege. This kind of preservation of official appearances is a mindless thing. It is cast and bureaucracy, but it is not the good administration that carries with it the true motives for Vere's siding with official law. The administrator is no God merely by virtue of his position. If he is heartless or mindless, he can offer only official preference, not truth, and he becomes as much a perpetuator of the wrongs of history as was the dictatorial Mrs. Glendinning or the early king Media.

The third "digression" is most basic to the story, and it comprises the conversation of the Purser and the Surgeon together with the ballad of "Billy in the Darbies."

Neither the Purser nor the Surgeon are the men to explain what happened at Billy's execution. The Purser is a ruddy and rotund little accountant of a man who in a few words is presented as a man of no mind, insight, or imagination. The Surgeon is the worst kind of pontificator upon dry facts, being able to cope with experience only in the measurable quantities of what is already known, and avoiding all the very real problems which he cannot explain. Neither of these men are capable of aspiration or of evaluating new experience or of re-evaluating the old. Theirs is the meaningless empiricism of the circumscribed prudential. These two men tell the reader that Billy did not die as hanged men always die. There was no spasmodic movement of the corpse. For neither of these men can Billy be a symbol, be anything but a corpse. It is in the irony of presenting the picture of Billy's death through the eyes of men who cannot evaluate what they see that the suggestion is established that Billy is not a corpse. The meaning of this suggestion is intensified in the Ballad. Members of the *Indomitable*'s crew revere Billy's memory and follow the progress of the yard on which Billy was hung, for "to them a chip of it was as a piece of the Cross." Billy's memory is perpetuated in a kind of Passion-hymn which is narrated in the first person, as if from Billy's point of view. The narrative action of the Ballad seems to be taking place in Billy's mind while he lies in the darbies, just before the execution. But the last two sentences bring the shock of recognition of a type, the realization that this is the voice of the "dead" man in the deep . . . dormant . . . waiting.

> . . . Sentry, are you there?
> Just ease these darbies at the wrist,
> and roll me over fair.
> I am sleepy, and the oozy weeds about me twist.

Billy never died. The aspiring yearning and goodness of man's heart is indestructible. So too, as Vere's defeat indicates, is history. Either heartfulness will continue in a new history made by men like Vere, or history will remain unchanged and heartfulness will continue as the chaos of the French Revolution or as the predisposition which will prompt another quester. The furious hopefulness of the work is in the indestructibility of human aspiration. The furious hopelessness of the work is that nothing but the wrong channels for that aspiration remain. So the human heart will continue to be the trap of the lure, the primitive perfection, the chronometrical Adam-Christ, who still exists in the deeps of human history and experience, mired by the oozy weeds and events of the man-of-war world. As lure, it can do nothing to pave the mire and raze the weeds, can be nothing but that which the quester will follow, at which the Satan will spring, by which the ship-world's common "people" will be deceived, and the cycle will continue . . . and continue . . . and continue.

This last book is not an "acceptance" either of God or of expediency for its own sake. *Billy Budd* accepts only what all the books before it accepted: that if history is the determinant of society, so too society is the determinant of history; that if man is not the cosmic creator and killer, he is at least his own social and individual creator and killer. *Billy Budd* accepts not an absolute fate to which man must bow, but rather it offers the bitterness of the proposition that man may never create the kind of fate that he can place at his own disposal. But for the method for attaining the yearnings of the heart, even in defeat, Melville could easily be entirely characterized by the bitter fatalism which characterized his civil war poem, "The Conflict of Convictions," in which he wrote,

> Power unanointed may come—
> Dominion (unsought by the free)
> And the Iron Dome,
> Stronger for stress and strain,
> Fling her huge shadow athwart the main;
> But the Founder's dream shall flee.
> Age after age shall be
> As age after age has been,
> (From man's changeless heart their way they win);
> And death be busy with all who strive—
> Death with silent negative.
> YEA AND NAY—
> EACH HATH HIS SAY;
> BUT GOD HE KEEPS THE MIDDLE WAY.
> NONE WAS BY
> WHEN HE SPREAD THE SKY:
> WISDOM IS VAIN, AND PROPHESY.

Melville was not able to deduce a changed history from the facts of his times, and therefore could not create a Captain Vere who was in charge of not one ship but all of society—for having then created the proper leader, he would have had to create the picture of the Utopian good society, a task for which in his history and his realism Melville could find no justification. It is the mass of men, the society, that holds the choice of fates; so Vere, as hero, could not be allowed to triumph, and he had to die. As an artist Melville was too honest a symbolist—too honest a liar—too realistically immersed in the destructive element of reflection upon truth to create a shallow happy ending of the universally reformed society, which would be a deception to the facts of his world and time. Like Joyce, Melville was trying to create the uncreated conscience of his human race. And he could find that conscience properly directed only in a man like Vere, for the conscience, the morality, and the act could not be divorced one from the other. It is only the Vere who can lead the Jarl and Samoa and Lucy and Starbuck and Bulkington through the correct courses of conscious and heartfelt action, no matter how official and heart-denying those actions might appear to be. It is this implicit prescription for behavior, together with the God-time-zero which facelessly puts forth the face of all the infinite possibilities of phenomena, that accounts for the dualities and "ambiguities," in all their modifications, in the enormous world of Herman Melville.

Notes

1. My "digressions" are not arranged as Melville lists his. After the "digressions" of the conversation between the Purser and the Surgeon, and the sea burial of Billy, the narrator goes on to say that the further "digressions" of the sequel to the story can be told in three additional short chapters.

BRAVE NEW WORLD
(ALDOUS HUXLEY)

"State versus the Individual:
Civil Disobedience in *Brave New World*"
by Jake Pollerd, Queen Mary,
University of London

At the time of writing *Brave New World* (1932), Aldous Huxley feared industrial capitalism would "standardize the human individual":

> Physically and mentally each one of us is unique. Any culture which, in the interests of efficiency or in the name of some political or religious dogma, seeks to standardize the human individual, commits an outrage against man's biological nature. (*Brave New World Revisited* 36)

In *Brave New World* Huxley creates just such a place, a place where a global federation of World Controllers force genetically engineered, behaviorally conditioned, and narcotically controlled citizens into conformity. In such a place, to think and act independently is to commit civil disobedience. Against this background of human homogeneity and conformity, Huxley's chief characters—Bernard Marx, Helmholtz Watson, and John the Savage—assert their individuality and challenge the insipid values the World State enshrines. All three defy civil order. And, whether they succeed or fail in their efforts, they proffer resistance, becoming models of civil disobedience.

In the opening chapters, Huxley deftly sketches out the sinister new methods of human manufacture practiced in the World State. The Director of Hatcheries and Conditioning explains to a group of students how ova are harvested, fertilized, and subjected to Bokanovsky's Process, whereby an embryo is made to divide not once (which would result in twins) but many times, yielding up to ninety-six identical human beings. In conjunction with Podsnap's Technique (which radically accelerates the ripening process), a single ovary can be made to produce on average "eleven thousand brothers and sisters in a hundred and fifty batches of identical twins." The "principle of mass production," the Director tells his students, has been "applied to biology" (5). In the year A.F. 632, the bible or foundational text on which the state is based is *My Life and Work* (1922) by the industrialist Henry Ford (A.F. stands for After Ford). Huxley was appalled by the dehumanizing new efficiency schemes pioneered by Ford and Frederick Winslow Taylor, which sought to lash men to the Procrustean bed of the shop-floor or machine, so that each worker was given, in the words of Ford, "not a square inch, and certainly not a square foot, more than he requires" (*My Life and Work*, quoted in Sexton 90). Huxley takes Ford's aim to its logical extreme in *Brave New World*, wherein not only are human beings biologically engineered to meet the physical requirements of the job they are predestined to perform (hence the embryos of "chemical workers" are "trained in the toleration of lead, caustic soda, tar [and] chlorine" (13)), but also the lower castes are specifically manufactured to fit the machines with which they will work. For instance, in the helicopter lighting-sets factory:

> One hundred and seven heat-conditioned Epsilon Senegalese were working in the foundry. Thirty-three Delta females, long-headed, sandy, with narrow pelvises, and all within 20 millimetres of 1 metre 69 centimetres tall, were cutting screws. In the assembling room, the dynamos were being put together by two sets of Gamma-Plus dwarfs. The two low work-tables faced one another; between crawled the conveyor with its load of separate parts; forty-seven blond heads were confronted by forty-seven brown ones. Forty-seven snubs by forty-seven hooks; forty-seven receding by forty-seven prognathous chins. (138)

After the embryos mature and are "decanted," the resultant infants are raised by the state, which subjects them to a rigorous process of psychological conditioning, thereby ensuring that its citizens are perfectly satisfied with their caste and unthinkingly uphold the values of the World State. In spite of these comprehensive precautions, a few individuals, such as Bernard Marx, slip through the net. Due to the presence of alcohol in his blood-surrogate (that at any rate is the rumor) the Alpha Plus Bernard has the physique of a diminutive Gamma, which leaves him feeling painfully self-conscious and inadequate, since Alphas are conditioned to be tall and muscular. "Hence the laughter," the narrator notes,

> of the women to whom he made proposals, the practical joking of his equals among the men. The mockery made him feel an outsider; and feeling like an outsider he behaved like one, which increased the prejudice against him and intensified the contempt and hostility aroused by his physical defects. Which in turn increased his sense of being alien and alone. (55–56)

Bernard's individuality leads him to adopt several heretical practices, such as spending time alone, refusing to take *soma* (the state-sponsored drug), and shunning conventional leisure pursuits (such as Centrifugal Bumble-puppy and Musical Bridge). As a sleep-teaching specialist, Bernard perceives the extent to which people are "enslaved by [their] conditioning" (78). For instance, the moral imperative to be sexually promiscuous largely derives from having had the hypnotic proverb "everyone belongs to everyone else" drummed into the unconscious of every child sixty-two thousand times (34).

The World State is so constituted that its citizens need not live in fear of strong emotion, since the causes—namely the family, monogamous relationships, sickness, old age, religion, and art—have been eradicated in the name of social stability. The World Controller Mustapha Mond explains that without technology half the present population would starve to death, therefore the wheels of the machine "must keep on turning," and there "must be men to tend them . . . sane men, obedient men, stable in contentment," rather than men deranged by love, guilt, and the Oedipus complex (36).

Recognizing that "[f]eeling lurks in that interval of time between desire and its consummation," the World State places a moral premium on infantile self-indulgence (37). Hence the would-be rebel Bernard Marx tries his hand at self-denial by attempting not to sleep with Lenina on their first date. Bernard finds that while the spirit is willing the flesh is weak; however, he has the presence of mind to sulk about it afterward: "I want to know what passion is," he tells Lenina, "I want to feel something strongly" (81).

The only person who understands him is his friend, Helmholtz Watson, who lectures at the College of Emotional Engineering. But while Bernard's resentful sense of isolation derives from his failure to conform, Helmholtz is a Renaissance man whose sexual, social, and athletic success sets him apart from his fellow Alphas. Despite their differences, "[w]hat the two men shared was the knowledge that they were individuals" (58). Perhaps unsurprisingly, Helmholtz proves to be more successful at self-denial than Bernard, and he reports that his newfound chastity has led him to believe that he has "something important to say and the power to say it" (59). The problem is that in A.F. 632 there's no such thing as art or literature, and Helmholtz cannot express his latent violence and originality by writing "an article about a Community Sing, or the latest improvement in scent organs" (60). Nonetheless, Helmholtz writes a poem about solitude and reads it to his scandalized students, who report him to the Principal.

For Huxley, art was the apotheosis of individualism, and he was consequently concerned that art and literature were being standardized by new technologies, such as the cinema, which relied on the principles of mass production. "The higher the degree of standardization in popular literature and art," writes Huxley in "The Outlook for American Culture" (1927),

> the greater the profit for the manufacturer. The economic policy of the mass-producers of spiritual goods is to secure the greatest number of buyers for the fewest possible products. Their tendency, therefore, is to disseminate ideas and art of lowest quality. (*Aldous Huxley: Complete Essays, vol. 3* 190)

This development was as regrettable for the guardians of high art as it was for the passive consumers of popular culture. In "Pleasures" (1923), Huxley noted that:

The working hours of the day are already, for the great majority of human beings, occupied in the performance of purely mechanical tasks in which no mental effort, no individuality, no initiative are required. And now, in the hours of leisure, we turn to distractions as mechanically stereotyped and demanding as little intelligence and initiative as does our work. (*On the Margin* 50–1)

The egregious vulgarity of the mechanized amusements in *Brave New World*, such as sexophone music, the feelies and the scent organ, reflect Huxley's anxieties about the future of art. Furthermore, in A.F. 632, not only is literature incompatible with the Fordian culture of mass consumption—"You can't consume much if you sit still and read books," observes Mustapha Mond (42)—the stultifying blandness and moronic happiness of the World State has rendered it incomprehensible. You "can't make tragedies," Mond affirms,

without social instability. The world's stable now. People are happy; they get what they want, and they never want what they can't get. They're well off; they're safe; they're never ill; they're not afraid of death; they're blissfully ignorant of passion and old age; they're plagued with no mothers or fathers; they've got no wives or children, or lovers to feel strongly about; they're so conditioned that they can't help behaving as they ought to behave. (193–194)

Thus while the poet in Helmholtz Watson admires the language of *Romeo and Juliet*, he finds the extravagant emotions of the play inherently rise and fall. Moreover, it is only subversive ascetics such as Helmholtz who attempt to write poetry, since art demands the sublimation of the instincts, whereas the World State is predicated on a culture of instant gratification (Firchow 314).

The most uncompromising individual in *Brave New World* is undoubtedly the Savage. When Bernard meets him in the "Savage Reservation" he feels a strong affinity with him, since John, by virtue of his complexion (both his parents are Brave New Worlders), is even more of an outsider in Malpais than Bernard is in the World State; and just as Bernard secretly longs to conform to his society, so John wishes to participate in the rituals and rites from which he is excluded. John's values have been shaped by his exposure to *The Complete Works of William Shakespeare* and the polytheistic religion practised in Malpais, in which Jesus Christ is worshipped alongside Zuni gods, such as Awonawilona, and the Navaho deity Estsanatlehi. He is therefore appalled by the empty hedonism promoted by the Fordian state and its mass-produced automatons. After witnessing the grotesque Gammas and Deltas employed at the helicopter lighting-sets factory, John recalls the eponymous quote from *The Tempest* ("O brave new world that has such people in it") that he had uttered before leaving Malpais, thinking that the New World would be filled with morally spotless beauties like his idealized love object, Lenina, and the mocking gap between his innocent expectations and the sordid reality causes him to be sick (139).

It is perhaps ironic that the numerous people who have campaigned to have *Brave New World* removed from the school curriculum in the United States have alleged that the book advocates sexual promiscuity and attacks marriage, religion, and the family. While Huxley unabashedly exploits the comic potential of a society in which "everyone belongs to everyone else," he cannot be accused of endorsing its values. In "Personality and Discontinuity of Mind" (1927), Huxley writes:

> the youngest of our contemporaries seem to be entirely uncivilized. And they admit their savagery in these matters, they abandon themselves to it. "Savagery" is perhaps the wrong word; for savages are co-ordinated within a rigid framework of taboos. Our modern savages have no taboos of any sort. They copulate with the casual promiscuousness of dogs; they make use of every violent emotion-producing sensation for its own sake, because it gives a momentary thrill. (*Proper Studies* 258–259)

Hence the Savage, whose morality is grounded both in tribal taboos and a version of Christianity (marriage is practised in Malpais), is more civilized than the savages of the World State. In the same essay, Huxley disparages the modern "unifying principle" of "social efficiency," which has replaced the old religious ethics, and which prizes those qualities, such as avarice, which are associated with material wealth (253–255). In *Brave New World*, Huxley imagines the moral fallout of a society in which Fordism has replaced religion: "All crosses," says Mustapha Mond in his history lesson, "had their tops

cut and became T's" in order to commemorate the T-model Ford (45).
The Solidarity Services are necessary substitutes for religion and are
administered in the same instrumental manner as a Violent Passion
Surrogate. Huxley is not lampooning the Eucharist when he depicts
Bernard's group passing "the loving cup of strawberry ice-cream
soma," rather he is mocking the poverty of the ceremony the state
has contrived to take its place (70). In the appendix to *The Devils of
Loudun* (1952), Huxley writes that man has always felt the urge to
transcend his personality, and that in the absence of "upward self-
transcendence" through religion, he has readily embraced the path of
"downward self-transcendence" through music, dance, sex, and drugs.
Given that the Brave New Worlders worship Henry Ford, they must
make do with Community Sings, casual sex, and *soma*.

Rather than succumbing to the customs of the New World, John
holds himself aloof. For instance, he refuses to take *soma*, and, despite
his passion for Lenina, he spurns her sexual advances. The tension
between John's stubborn individualism and the "swarming indistin-
guishable sameness" he sees in the World State is thrown into sharp
relief by Linda's death (183). On a guided tour of Eton, the Provost
informs John: "Death conditioning begins at eighteen months. Every
tot spends two mornings a week in a Hospital for the Dying," where
they are desensitized to death with the aid of sweets and toys (142).
But for John death is a "sacred mystery," and he is therefore outraged
by the intrusion of a Bokanovsky group of Deltas into the ward where
his mother, who has been on a continuous *soma* holiday since her
return from Malpais, lies dying:

> an interminable stream of identical eight-year-old male twins
> was pouring into the room. Twin after twin, twin after twin,
> they came—a nightmare. Their faces, their repeated face—for
> there was only one between the lot of them—puggishly stared,
> all nostrils and pale goggling eyes. Their uniform was khaki. All
> their mouths hung open. Squealing and chattering they entered.
> In a moment, it seemed, the ward was maggoty with them. They
> swarmed between the beds, clambered over, crawled under, peeped
> into the television boxes, made faces at the patients (177).

When the Savage weeps over Linda's death, the nurse is aghast at
his "disgusting outcry—as though death were something terrible,

as though anyone mattered as much as all that!" (181). Her reaction is a result of there being neither love nor families in A.F. 632: in a communal society such as theirs there are no individuals (notwithstanding exceptions to the rule such as Bernard and Helmholtz) and therefore everyone *is* replaceable.

As John watches the hospital employees queuing up for their *soma* ration, he reflects that "Linda had been a slave," both a slave to *soma* (the large doses she'd been taking had shortened her life), and a slave to her conditioning, and that in order to avenge her death he must empower others to "live in freedom" (185). He stages his revolt by interrupting the work and exhorting the bewildered Deltas to throw off the shackles of *soma* and become free and human as opposed to enslaved insects. By the time Bernard and Helmholtz arrive at the hospital, John has precipitated a riot by throwing the *soma* rations out of the window. Although the police quickly quell the uprising, it equates to a rite of passage for John (who has been unable to prove his manhood in Malpais) and Helmholtz, who rushes to his side, while the cowardly Bernard is reduced to shouting for help.

For their part in the revolt, as well as their unorthodox behaviour, Bernard and Helmholtz are exiled to the Falkland Islands, where they can associate with other individuals unfit for conformity. Thoreau might well have regarded these islands of individualism as a congenial environment, for in "Civil Disobedience" he dreams of a state that recognizes the value of the "individual," one that "would not think it inconsistent with its own repose, if a few were to live aloof from it, not meddling with it, nor embraced by it" (242–243). Although John petitions the World Controller to join his friends, he is forced to remain in England to continue the "experiment" (214). The famous debate between the Savage and Mustapha Mond illustrates the fundamental incompatibility between the former's ethical beliefs, which are founded on religion and art, and the amoral technocracy of the World State, which has sacrificed religion and art on the altar of stability and happiness. It's not that John objects to happiness *per se*, it's more that, as an individual, he reserves the right to be unhappy if he so desires, rather than having happiness imposed from above. He balks at being coddled by the state, which simply eliminates danger, sickness, and all potential causes of unhappiness, such as romantic and familial love, rather than allowing its citizens to choose. "I want God," he tells Mond, "I want poetry, I want real danger, I want freedom, I want goodness. I want sin" (211).

It should not be imagined, however, that Huxley wholeheartedly endorses the Savage's worldview; it is merely the lesser of two evils. In his 1946 foreword to the book, he notes that if he were to rewrite the novel, he would include a "third alternative" to the existing choice between the "insanity" of utopia in the New World and the "lunacy" of primitivism in the Savage Reservation, namely a small-scale mystical community along the lines of Pala, the utopia he was to describe in his final novel, *Island* (1962). John is not meant to represent, as some critics have claimed, the noble savage. This concept became popular in the eighteenth century, when a number of philosophers, such as Claude Helvétius and John Locke, posited that man was innately virtuous, as opposed to originally sinful (the orthodox Christian position), and argued that inequality was the product of environment. Huxley, on the other hand, believed that inequality, such as the demonstrable differences in intelligence, had more to do with heredity, and disagreed with William Godwin and Percy Shelley, who held that the original nobility and virtue of primitive man had been corrupted by civilization (see Huxley's essays "Inequality" and "The Future of the Past"). Hence in *Brave New World* there is nothing innately virtuous or noble about the savages of Malpais: The men treat Linda (John's mother) like a prostitute, the women whip her for sleeping with their men, and John is ostracized by their children. Moreover, as already noted, both John's parents come from the World State, and, in addition to being partially educated by Linda, he has been exposed to the civilizing influence of Shakespeare, and therefore he cannot be regarded as a savage.

Furthermore, Huxley objected to the primitivism of people such as D.H. Lawrence, who advocated a reversion to noble savagery as an antidote to mechanistic modern life. In "Science and Civilization" (1932), Huxley argues that since applied science has "allowed the world's population to double itself in about three generations," the answer is not, as Tolstoy and Lawrence suggest, to abandon science and return to nature, but to have more "science, well applied." Science, he notes, is a morally neutral tool: In the hands of humanists, it will be employed to realize "the highest human aspirations," as can be seen in *Island*, in which science plays a beneficent role, whereas in the hands of capitalists science will be used "to make the world safe for political economy—to train up a race, not of perfect human beings, but of perfect mass-producers and mass-consumers," and this is precisely what has happened in *Brave New World* (*The Hidden Huxley* 106–108).

In an effort "to escape further contamination by the filth of civilized life" (218), John retreats to the country to live as a hermit. In an abandoned lighthouse in Surrey, he attempts to create a Walden-esque life of self-sufficiency: "By next spring, his garden would be producing enough to be independent of the outside world" (218). Indeed, John is an instinctive transcendentalist who senses the divine in the English countryside. It is a noteworthy feature of the New World that even among the upper castes (who are not conditioned to hate the country), the natural world is perceived as uncanny. In order to move closer to God, John embarks on a course of physical austerities. The would-be censors of *Brave New World* often invoke the Savage's self-flagellation as an example of the book's immorality, but as Huxley points out in *Heaven and Hell* (1956), self-flagellation was an orthodox form of penance in the medieval and Early Modern eras, and helped to induce "visionary and mystical experience" in its practitioners (120). But the Brave New Worlders, being ignorant of the very concepts of God and sin and atonement, cannot help but interpret the practice in a sexual light, and shatter John's solitude by arriving *en masse* after having witnessed him whipping himself in *The Savage of Surrey*. In the face of their collective will—they surround him chanting "Orgy-porgy," dancing, and "beating one another in six-eight time" (228)—John is unable to maintain his individuality, and, abandoning the path of upward self-transcendence, he gives in to the state-approved road of *soma*, herd intoxication, and group sex. Overcome with remorse at having betrayed the religious and romantic ideals that rendered him an individual, both in England and Malpais, he commits suicide. Here, as Albert Camus does in *The Myth of Sisyphus*, Huxley asks what makes a life worth living. While for Camus choosing to live means forever pushing a rock and accepting life as fundamentally absurd, for Huxley living means choosing, creating, performing—all the acts and gestures that make us unique. And, at least for the three questioning protagonists caught in a social world where voice, expression, and individuality are denied, in electing to either assimilate or die they defy what tyrants dictate. In an inhumane world such as the dystopia Huxley creates, we find little chance of exercising foundational human rights and little toleration of the attempts made at civil disobedience.

Works Cited

Firchow, Peter. "Science and Civilization in Huxley's *Brave New World*."
    Contemporary Literature 16.3 (Summer 1975): 301–316.

Huxley, Aldous. *Brave New World*. London: Vintage, 2004.

———. *Brave New World Revisited*. London: Chatto & Windus, 1972.

———. *The Devils of Loudun*. London: Vintage, 2005.

———. "The Future of the Past." *Aldous Huxley: Complete Essays*. Edited by
    Robert S. Baker and James Sexton. Vol. 2, 1926–1929. Chicago: Ivan R.
    Dee, 2000. 90–93.

———. *Heaven and Hell*. London: Grafton, 1977.

———. *Island*. London: Vintage, 2005.

———. *On the Margin: Notes and Essays*. London: Chatto & Windus, 1948.

———. "The Outlook for American Culture: Some Reflections in a Machine
    Age." *Aldous Huxley: Complete Essays*. Edited by Robert S. Baker and
    James Sexton. Vol. 3, 1930–1935. Chicago: Ivan R. Dee, 2001. 187–193.

———. *Proper Studies*. London: Chatto & Windus, 1927.

———. "Science and Civilization." *The Hidden Huxley: Contempt and
    Compassion for the Masses 1920–36*. Edited by David Bradshaw. London:
    Faber & Faber, 1994. 106–114.

Sexton, James. "*Brave New World* and the Rationalization of Industry." *Critical
    Essays on Aldous Huxley*. Edited by Jerome Meckier. New York and
    London: G.K. Hall & Co., 1996. 88–100.

Thoreau, Henry David. "Civil Disobedience." *Walden and Civil Disobedience*.
    Edited by Owen Thomas. New York: Norton & Co., 1966. 224–243.

"Civil Disobedience"
(Henry David Thoreau)

"Writing in the Dark"
by Alfred Kazin, in *Henry David Thoreau: Studies and Commentaries* (1972)

Introduction

In "Writing in the Dark," Alfred Kazin discusses Thoreau's essay "Civil Disobedience" and its relation to his life and works. Kazin provides many insights into Thoreau's distinctly literary mode of living, which he calls one of the "most tragic examples in history of a man trying to live his life by writing it." Kazin argues that Thoreau's belief in his ability to construct life through words rests upon a strong faith in the "spiritual power" and sovereignty of the individual. This spiritual power, according to Kazin, is what guides Thoreau's civil disobedience. Ruminating on the significance of "Civil Disobedience" in the age of the modern, "All-Demanding State," Kazin concludes that Thoreau's example " . . . does not help us in the face of the state power which we both need for our welfare and dread for its power over lives."

Kazin, Alfred. "Writing in the Dark." *Henry David Thoreau: Studies and Commentaries*. Edited by Walter Harding et al. Rutherford, NJ: Fairleigh Dickinson UP, 1972. 34–52.

In the Morgan Library in New York one can see the box that Thoreau built to hold his journals. This work runs to thirty-nine manuscript volumes and fourteen published volumes. It contains nearly two million words, more than 7000 printed pages. I do not know if it is the longest journal ever kept; probably not, for Thoreau, who kept it assiduously from the time he was twenty, died before he was forty-five, probably of the struggle I am about to describe. But of one thing about this journal I am sure; it is one of the most fanatical, most arduous, most tragic examples in history of a man trying to live his life by writing it—of a man seeking to shape his life, to *make* it, by words, as if words alone would not merely report his life but become his life by the fiercest control that language can exert.

The greatest part of Thoreau's life was writing, and this is probably true of many writers, especially in our time, when so many writers are interested not merely in composing certain books but in making a career out of literature. But what makes Thoreau's case so singular, and gives such an unnatural severity to his journal itself, is that the work of art he was seeking to create was really himself—his life was the explicit existence that he tried to make out of words. The act of writing became for him not a withdrawal from life, a compensation for life, a higher form of life—all of which it has been for so many writers since Romanticism identified the act of composition with personal salvation. It became a symbolic form of living, a way of living, *his* way of living. Writing was this close to living, parallel to living, you might say, because the only subject of Thoreau's life was himself. He transcribed his life directly onto paper—by which I do not mean that he reported it actually, but that he sought to capture experience in just one form: the sensations and thoughts of a man walking about all day long. To this commonplace daily round he was restricted by his own literal experience, for he did not wish in the slightest to invent anything and was incapable of doing so. But he was also restricted by the fact that he had no experience to report except being a writer and looking for topics. Thoreau never married. Wherever possible, as one can tell from his most famous book, he lived alone; but since this was in fact not always possible, for many members of his family kept together by not marrying and also had the family's pencil business to keep them together, he went about alone and became a naturalist in his own idiosyncratic style, an observer who could find material on every hillside, a "self-appointed inspector of snow-storms and rain-storms." He had his favorite classics to quote from in his journal, books that he used as quotations because they were of the greatest practical use to him; he had this large family, full of eccentrics like himself whom he needed to get away from, and he had a few friends—associates of his ideas rather than intimate friends—notably his employer and sometime patron, Emerson, with whom his journal records the endless friction that was so necessary in his relation with even the most forbearing individualists in New England. Otherwise Thoreau might have felt that he was betraying his ideal life, the life that nobody would conceive for himself but himself, that he lived only in the epiphanies of his journal, that nobody could live except with himself alone.

Since books were really personal instruments, and friends were invariably, sooner or later, to betray his design for life, this left for subject matter, in a book of two million words, what one might call the American God, the only God left to these wholly self-dependent transcendentalists in the New England of the 1840s—Nature. Thoreau told Moncure Conway that he found in Emerson "a world where truths existed with the same perfection as the objects he studied in external nature, his ideals real and exact." Nature, by which Emerson meant everything outside the writer for him to explore and to describe—Nature for Thoreau became the landscape, mostly around Concord, that he could always walk into. It served as the daily occasion of Thoreau's journal, the matter that tied Thoreau to the world outside, that became the world, and that safely gave him something to write about each day. Nature gave him the outside jobs he took as a surveyor from time to time to get some money and to keep him in some practical relation to his town and his neighbors. Nature even made him a "naturalist," a collector of specimens and Indian relics, a student of the weather and of every minute change in the hillsides that he came to know with the familiarity that another man might have felt about the body of his wife.

But above all Nature was himself revealed in Nature, it was the great permissiveness in which he found himself every day. Nature was perfect freedom, Nature was constant health and interest, Nature was the perfection of visible existence, the ideal friend, the perfect because always predictable experience—it was ease and hope and thought such as no family, and certainly no woman, would ever provide. Nature was God, because God to Thoreau meant not the Totally Other, what is most unlike us—but perfect satisfaction.

That is what God had begun to mean to Emerson and other proud evangels of the new romantic faith that God lives *in* us and *as* us—that God is manifested by the power and trust we feel ourselves. Emerson was the oracle of a faith that only he could fully understand, because it rested on his gift for finding God in and through himself. Emerson's faith was pure inspiration; without his presence to give testimony, the intuition's access to the higher mysteries, or what Coleridge had called "reason," had to be painfully approximated by secondary faculties like the "understanding." Emerson was thus the unique case among modern writers of a spiritual genius whose role was essentially public, such as the founders of religion have played. Without his incomparable face, his living voice, Emerson on the printed page was never to inspire in later generations what the magnetism of his presence had created in his own day—a grateful sense on the part of many of his auditors that here was the founder, the oracle, the teacher of his tribe. Emerson, a very gifted writer, was first of all the appointed leader who comes in at the beginning, sounds a new hope and purpose, out of himself passes spiritual strength to the people.

Thoreau's life was entirely private and was lived, you might say, for himself alone. Except for his explosive political concern about the growing power of the slave interest, which was getting such an influence over the United States government that Thoreau properly discerned in it a threat to *his* absolute freedom as well as an affront to his wholly personal Christianity, he was, of course, not merely indifferent to the State but contemptuous of it. He was interested in "society" only as an anthropologist of sorts taking notes on his Concord neighbors and their peculiar ways. His God was private to himself and really not to be taught to, or shared with, anyone else. You might say it was imaginative pure power, Henry Thoreau's most perfection acquisition, in a narrow life that sought only a few acquisitions, and these the brightest and purest—pure morality, pure love, pure creation in the pages of his journal he rewrote each night from the notes taken on his walks.

God was not a person; He was the meaning you caught in the woods as you passed. But of course other poets of nature were saying this in the first half of the nineteenth century in England, Germany, and the United States. What Thoreau was saying, in prose of exceptional vibration, was that he had this God, this immanence in the woods, for and to himself whenever he wanted to; that he had only to walk out every afternoon (having spent the morning rewriting his field notes for his formal journal), to walk into the woods, to sit on the cliffs and look out over the Concord River and Conantum hills, for the perfect satisfaction to return again. As late as 1857, he could write in his journal: " . . . cold and solitude are friends of mine . . . I come to my solitary woodland walk as the homesick go home. This stillness, solitude, wildness of nature is a kind of thoroughwort or boneset, to my intellect. This is what I go out to seek. It is as if I always met in those places some grand, serene, immortal, infinitely encouraging, though invisible companion, and walked with him."

The satisfaction lay first of all in the daily, easy access to revelation, for sauntering—a word which Thoreau playfully derived from *à la sainté terre*, to the holy land—his mind dreamily overran what he saw even when he was most assiduously playing the inspector of snowstorms and rainstorms, overran it and filled up the spaces with evidence of design, growth, meaning. If you constantly note the minute changes in plants and animals, you create the figure of Nature as a single organism with the irresistible tendency to explain herself to you. The visible surface of things then shines with the truth of the evolutionary moral that Emerson had so contentedly taken away from his visit to the Botanical Garden in Paris on July 13, 1833, of which he wrote—"Not a form so grotesque, so savage, nor so beautiful but is an expression of some property inherent in man the observer,—an occult relation between the very scorpions and man. I feel the centipede in me,—cayman, carp, eagle, and fox. I am moved by strange sympathies; I say continually 'I will be a naturalist.'" Thoreau's sympathies with the rough and the wild were so intense that he hauntingly identified himself with other forms of life, but they also dumbly and pleasingly arranged themselves to an eye that could not have been more unlike the professional naturalist's disinterestedness and experimental method. Thoreau sought ecstasy.

This perfect satisfaction could not always be found; there were inevitable days of bleakness, dissatisfaction, and weakness. But Thoreau, using nature and God as instruments of personal power and happiness, was able to create on paper his own life of satisfaction, to retain in words the aura of some bygone ecstasy he had found through nature. He was able, thus, to make a life by writing it. This was his great instrument, a prose that always took the form of personal experience, a prose created wholly out of remembrance and its transfiguration, a prose in which the word sought not only to commemorate a thing but to replace it. What had been lost could always be found again on the page, and what had merely been wished for could be described as if it were remembered. Memory was Thoreau's imagination to the point where it relived the original so intensely that it replaced it as style. The dreaming mind of the writer, remembering his life, created it.

But this called for the most relentless control over life by style, by an attentiveness to the uses of words that quite wore him out, by calculated epigrams, puns, paradoxes, plays on words, ingenuities, quotations, that, as he complained in his journal of 1854, were his faults of style. He had practiced these "faults of style" so long that he had become weary of his own strategy, for even the most devoted reader of Thoreau is likely to see through his literary tricks. But these "tricks," or "faults of style," are the essence of Thoreau's genius and the reason for his enduring appeal. They have an extraordinary ability to evoke the moment, the instant flash of experience, to give us the taste of existence itself. They give us the glory of a moment—single, concrete, singular.

Thoreau was always, I think, a young man, and certainly oriented, as Thornton Wilder put it, to childhood. He addressed his most famous book to "poor students," and his most admiring readers, whether they are young or not, always recognize the inner feeling of youth in his pages—the absoluteness of his impatience with authority and his all too conscious revolt against it, the natural vagabondage, the faith in some infinite world just over the next horizon. Students recognize in Henry Thoreau a classic near their own age and condition.

All his feelings are absolutes, as his political ideals will be. There is none of that subtlety, that odd and winning two-handedness, that one finds in Emerson's simultaneous obligation to both his deepest insights and to the social world he thinks in. Thoreau wrote in his journal for 1851 that "no experience which I have today comes up to, or is comparable with, the experiences of my boyhood . . . As far back as I can remember I have unconsciously referred to the experiences of a previous state of existence . . . Formerly, methought, nature developed as I developed, and grew up with me. My life was ecstasy. In youth, before I lost any of my senses, I can remember that I was all alive, and inhabited my body with inexpressible satisfaction."

This happiness is what Thoreau's admirers turn to him for—it is a special consonance of feeling between the pilgrim and his landscape. And it was not so much written as rewritten; whatever the moment originally was, his expression of it was forged, fabricated, worked over and over, soldered together, you might say, from fragmentary responses, to make those single sentences that were Thoreau's highest achievement, and indeed, his highest aim. For *in* such sentences, and not just *by* those sentences, a man could live. Transcendentalism rested on style. Each of Thoreau's sentences is a culmination of his life, the fruit of his hallucinated attachment to the visible world; each was a precious particle of existence, existence pure, the life of Thoreau at the very heart. Each was victory over the long, unconscious loneliness; and how many people, with far more happiness in others than Thoreau ever wanted or expected, can say that their life is all victory? how many can anticipate a succession of victories? In the end was the word, always the word:

> When I was four years old, as I well remember, I was brought from Boston to this my native town, through these very woods and fields, to the pond. It is one of the oldest scenes stamped on my memory. And tonight my flute has waked the echoes over that very water. The pines still stand here older than I; or, if some have fallen, I have cooked my supper with their stumps, and a new growth is rising all around, preparing another aspect for new infant eyes. Almost the same johnwort springs from the same perennial root in this pasture, and even I have at length helped to clothe that fabulous landscape of my infant dreams, and one of the results of my presence and influence is seen in these bean leaves, corn blades, and potato vines.

A student once wrote in a paper on Thoreau: "This man, too honest, too physically aware to fashion an imagined scene, ... searched to exhaustion a scene that sometimes appeared empty." But another student, as if to answer this, noted that after writing *Walden* Thoreau could look about him, as we do today when we visit Walden Pond, with the feeling that this environment had been changed by his writing the book. Thoreau did create and recreate Walden Pond; the total attachment to that bit of land, from the hut which became for him, Ellery Channing said, the wooden inkstand in which he lived—this attachment is as total and single in its all-absorbing attentiveness as a baby's to its mother, as a prisoner to his cell. *Walden* is

the record of a love blind to everything but what it can gather from
that love, to everything but the force of its will. That is why those to
whom their own will still stands supreme, to whom freedom is the
freedom of *their* will, solitary but sovereign, can recognize in *Walden*
the youthful climate of feeling that is touched by doom but not by
tragedy—to whom death seems easier than any blow whatever from
the social compact.

For youth the center of the world is itself, and the center is bright
with the excitement of the will. There is no drama like that of being
young, for then each experience can be overwhelming. Thoreau knew
how to be young. He knew, as he said, how to live deep and suck
all the marrow out of life. "I went to the woods because I wished to
live deliberately, to front only the essential facts of life, and see if I
could not learn what it had to teach, and not, when I came to die, to
discover that I had not lived. I did not wish to live what was not life,
living is so dear; nor did I wish to practise resignation, unless it was
quite necessary." That is youth speaking, for only youth thinks that it
can live by deliberation, that a man's whole happiness can be planned
like a day off, that perfect satisfaction can be achieved without any
friction whatever, without friends, without sex, with a God who is
always and only the perfect friend, and all this in relation to a piece of
land, a pond, practicing the gospel of perfection. Yet only youth ever
feels so alone, and being alone, burns to *create* its life—where so many
people merely spend theirs. Thoreau's greatness lies in his genius for
evoking the moment, in sentence after sentence each of which is like
a moment. For only the individual in the most private accesses of his
experience knows what a moment is; it is a unit too small for history,
too precious for society. It belongs only to the private consciousness.
And Thoreau's predominating aim was to save his life, not to spend
it, to be as economical about his life as his maiden aunts were about
the sugar in the boarding house they ran. He wanted to live, to live
supremely, and always on his own terms, saving his life for still higher
things as he went.

Here is where the State comes in. Nature, as we know, Thoreau
could always transcendentalize. No storms or solitude or discomfort
could turn him out of his fanatical control there. He felt at home in
the world of savages. If he was in any sense the scientist he occasion-
ally wanted to be, it was when he felt superior and untouched by
dumb things in nature. The only object in nature that seems genuinely

to have frightened him was Mount Katahdin in Maine. Describing the night he spent on the summit, he significantly confessed: "I stand in awe of my body, this matter to which I am bound has become so strange to me. I fear not spirits, ghosts, of which I am one ... but I fear bodies, I tremble to meet them. What is this Titan that has possession of me? Talk of our life in nature—daily to be shown matter, to come in contact with it—rocks, trees, wind on our cheeks! the *solid* earth, the *actual* world! the *common sense*! Contact! *Contact*! Who are we? *where* are we?"

Still, he could always get off that mountain and return to the village of which he said, "I could write a book called Concord," and which he began to see wholly as the book he was writing in his journal. But the State, which to begin with was represented by other men he could not always ignore—this was to become the Other that he could not domesticate as he did God, Nature, and other men's books. In chapter 8 of *Walden*, "The Village," he describes his arrest (July, 1846) as he was on his way to the cobbler's. He was arrested for not paying the poll tax that in those days was still exacted by the state in behalf of the church. Thoreau's father had been enrolled in the church, and Thoreau's own name should not have been on the roll. He spent a peaceful, dreamy night in jail. In "Civil Disobedience" he reports that "the night in prison was novel and interesting enough ... It was like travelling into a far country, such as I had never expected to behold, to lie there for one night ... It was to see my native village in the light of the Middle Ages, and our Concord was turned into a Rhine stream, and visions of knights and castles passed before me." At the suggestion of the Concord selectmen, he filed a statement after he had demanded that his name be dropped from the church rolls: KNOW ALL MEN BY THESE PRESENTS THAT I, HENRY THOREAU, DO NOT WISH TO BE REGARDED AS A MEMBER OF ANY INCORPORATED SOCIETY WHICH I HAVE NOT JOINED. The experience was not a traumatic one, and on being released he "returned to the woods in season to get my dinner of huckleberries on Fair Haven Hill." But he says truly, "I was never molested by any person but those who represented the State."

In *Walden* Thoreau was to say of his prison experience that it showed the inability of society to stand "odd fellows" like himself. In the essay "Civil Disobedience," 1849, he was to say in a most superior way that the State supposed "I was mere flesh and blood and bones, to be locked up," and since it could not recognize that his immortal spirit was free, "I saw that the State was half-witted, that it was timid as a lone woman with her silver spoons . . . and I lost all my remaining respect for it, and pitied it."

But what gives "Civil Disobedience" its urgency is that between 1846, when he was arrested for a tax he should have paid in 1840, and 1848, when he wrote it, the State had ceased to be his friend the Concord sheriff, Sam Staples, who so pleasantly took him off to the local hoosegow, but the United States government, which, under the leadership of imperialists like President James Polk and the Southern planters who were determined to add new land for their cotton culture, was making war on Mexico and would take away half its territory in the form of California, Texas, Arizona, and New Mexico. The Mexican War was openly one for plunder, as Lincoln and many other Americans charged. But it was the first significant shock to Thoreau's rather complacent position that the individual can be free, as free as he likes, in and for himself, though his neighbors think him odd. Oddity, however, was no longer enough to sustain total independence from society. Despite Thoreau's opposition to slavery in principle, he knew no Negroes, had never experienced the slightest social oppression. He was a radical individualist very well able to support this position in Concord; he had a share in the family's pencil business, but was not confined by it, and he was indeed as free as air—free to walk about all day long as he pleased, free to build himself a shack on Walden Pond and there prepare to write a book, free to walk home any night for supper at the family boarding house. Up until the Mexican War—and even more urgently, the Fugitive Slave Law of 1850 and finally John Brown's raid on Harpers Ferry in 1859—Thoreau's only social antagonist was the disapproval, mockery, or indifference of his neighbors in Concord. He never knew what the struggle of modern politics can mean for people who identify and associate with each other because they recognize their common condition. Thoreau was a pure idealist, living on principle—typical of New England in his condescension to the Irish immigrants, properly indignant about slavery in far-off Mississippi, but otherwise, as he wrote *Walden* to prove, a man who proposed to teach others to be as free of society as himself.

"Civil Disobedience" is stirring, especially today, because of the urgency of its personal morality. As is usual with Thoreau, he seems to be putting his whole soul into the protest against injustice committed by the state. He affirms the absolute right of the individual to obey his own conscience in defiance of an unknown law. But despite his usual personal heat, he tends to moralize the subject wholly and to make it not really serious. He makes a totally ridiculous object of the State, he turns its demands on him into a pure affront, and is telling it to stop being so pretentious and please to disappear. This is certainly refreshing. But anyone who thinks it is a guide to his own political action these days will have to defend the total literary anarchism that is behind it. And it is no use, in this particular, identifying Gandhi with it, for Gandhi, as a young leader of the oppressed Indians in South Africa, was looking for some political strategy by which to resist a totally oppressive racist regime. There were no laws to protect the Indians. Thoreau's essay is a noble, ringing reiteration of the highest religious individualism as a self-evident social principle. The absolute freedom of the individual like himself is his highest good, and the State is not so much the oppressor of this individual as his rival. How dare this Power get in my way? For Thoreau the problem is simply one of putting the highest possible value on the individual rather than on the state. This is urgent because we are all individuals first, and because it is sometimes necessary to obey oneself rather than the State. But for the greatest part, Thoreau is not aware that the individual's problem may be how to resist his state when he is already so much bound up with it. He can hardly just turn his back on it.

The significantly political passages in the essay have to do with what Thoreau calls slavery in Massachusetts. He of all people could not grant that property is the greatest passion and the root of most social conflicts and wars. But he insisted "that if one thousand, if one hundred, if ten men whom I could name—if ten *honest* men only—ay, if *one* Honest man, in this State of Massachusetts, *ceasing to hold slaves*, were actually to withdraw from this co-partnership, and be locked up in the county jail therefor, it would be the abolition of slavery in America." With his marvellous instinct for justice, for pure Christianity, for the deep-rooted rights of the individual soul, he said "Under a government which imprisons any unjustly, the true place for a just man is also a prison." But morally invigorating as this is, it would perhaps not have helped the fugitive slave, and the Mexican prisoner on parole, and the Indian come to plead the wrongs of his race when, as Thoreau said, they came to the prison and found the best spirits of Massachusetts there. Thoreau estimated the power of individual example beyond any other device in politics, but he did not explain how the usefulness of example could communicate itself to people who were in fact slaves, and not free.

By 1850 the fury of the coming war could already be felt in Massachusetts. The Fugitive Slave Law was made part of the compromise of 1850, and now Thoreau really exploded. "There is not one slave in Nebraska; there are perhaps a million slaves in Massachusetts." With all his uncompromising idealism he attacked every possible expediency connected with politics, and wrote: "They who have been bred in the school of politics fail now and always to face the facts. They put off the day of settlement indefinitely, and meanwhile, the debt accumulates." The "idea of turning a man into a sausage" is not worse than to obey the Fugitive Slave Law. Rhythmically, he pounded away at the State, the Press, the Church, all institutions leagued, as he felt, by this infamous conspiracy to send runaway slaves back to their masters. He mimicked the attitude of the timorous, law-obeying citizen: "Do what you will, O Government! with my wife and children . . . I will obey your commands to the letter . . . I will peaceably pursue my chosen calling on this fair earth, until perchance, one day, when I have put on mourning for them dead, I shall have persuaded you to relent." Each sentence is, as usual, an absolute in itself; each is a distillation of Thoreau's deepest feelings. Yet it is impossible to imagine the most passionately anti-Vietnam writer saying today that, in the face of such evil, "I need not say what match I would touch, what system endeavor to blow up . . ." We have all lived too much under the shadow of the Bomb to be persuaded by the violence of language.

Thoreau's greatest affirmation in politics (something different from a great political utterance) is, I think, *A Plea For Captain John Brown*, delivered in the Concord Town Hall on the evening of October 30, 1859. Emerson's son Edward, who heard Thoreau deliver this, said that he read his speech as if it burned him. There is nothing quite so strong elsewhere in Thoreau's work; all the dammed-up violence of the man's solitary life has come out in sympathy with Brown's violence. It is clear that Brown's attack on Harpers Ferry roused in Thoreau a powerful sense of identification. Apocalypse had come. John Brown's favorite maxim was: "without the shedding of blood there is no remission of sins." Brown's raid was exactly the kind of mad, wild, desperate, and headlong attack on the authority of the United States, on the support it gave to the slave system, that Thoreau's ecstatic individualism sympathized with. It was too violent an act for Thoreau to commit himself; he had long since given up the use of firearms, and was more or less of a vegetarian. But Brown represented in the most convulsively personal way the hatred of injustice that was Thoreau's most significant political passion—and this was literally a *hatred*, more so than he could acknowledge to himself, a hatred of anyone as well as anything that marred the perfect design of his all-too-severe moral principles.

All his life, Thoreau had been saying that there are two realms. One is of grace, which is a gift and so belongs only to the gifted; the other is of mediocrity. One is of freedom, which is the absolute value because only the gifted can follow it into the infinite where its beauty is made fully manifest; the other of acquiescence and conformism, another word for which is stupidity. One is of God, whom His elect, the most gifted, know as no one else can ever know Him; the other is of the tyranny exacted by the mediocre in society. John Brown, whom all the leading historians, judges, lawyers, and respectable people solidly denounced as mad; John Brown, who indeed had so much madness in his background, nevertheless represented to Thoreau the gifted man's, the ideal Puritan's, outraged inability to compromise between these two realms. Nothing is worse than evil except the toleration of it, thought John Brown, and so he tried to strike at evil itself. This directness proved his moral genius to Thoreau. Then, as the State of Virginia and the Government of the United States rallied all its forces to crush this man and to hang him, it turned out, to Thoreau's horror, that this exceptional man was not understood. The State, which would do nothing to respect the slave's human rights, and had in deference to Southern opinion acknowledged its duty to send back every runaway slave, would indeed obliterate John Brown with an energy that it had never showed in defense of helpless human beings.

It was this that roused Thoreau to the burning exaltation that fills *A Plea For Captain John Brown*. He had found his hero in the man of action who proclaimed that his action was only the force of the highest principles. Thoreau's "plea" indeed pleads principle as the irresistible force. The pure, vehement personalism that had been Thoreau's life, in words, now sees itself turning into deeds. The pure love of Christ, striking against obstinately uncomprehending, resisting human heads, turns into pure wrath. God has only certain appointed souls to speak and fight for Him, and that is the secret of New England. "We aspire to be something more than stupid and timid chattels, pretending to read history and our Bibles, but desecrating every house and every day we breathe in ... At least a million of the free inhabitants of the United States would have rejoiced if he had succeeded ... Though we wear no crape, the thought of that man's position and probable fate is spoiling many a man's day here at the North for other thinking. If anyone who has seen him here can pursue successfully any other train of thought, I do not know what he is made of. If there is any such who gets his usual allowance of sleep, I will warrant him to fatten easily under any circumstances which do not touch his body or his purse." But for himself, Thoreau added, "I put a piece of paper and a pencil under my pillow, and when I could not sleep I wrote in the dark."

He wrote in the dark. Writing was what he had lived for, lived by, lived in. And now, when his great friend was being hanged in Charlestown prison, he could only speak for. The word was light, the word was the Church, and now the word was the deed. This was Thoreau's only contribution to the struggle that was not for John Brown's body but for righteousness. He called the compromisers "mere figureheads upon a hulk, with livers in the place of hearts." He said of the organized Church that it always "excommunicates Christ while it exists." He called the government this most *hypocritical* and *diabolical* government, and mimicked its saying to protesters like himself: "What do you assault me for? Am I not an honest man? Cease agitation on this subject, or I will make a slave of you, too, or else hang you." He said, "I am here to plead this cause with you. I plead not for his life, but for his character—his immortal life; and so it becomes your cause wholly, and is not his in the least. Some eighteen hundred years ago Christ was crucified; this morning, perchance, Captain Brown was hung. These are the two ends of a chain which is not without its links."

There was nothing Thoreau could do except to *say* these things. Brown, who was quite a sayer himself, had said to the court: "Had I so interfered in behalf of the rich; the powerful, the intelligent, the so-called great ... it would have been all right ... I am yet too young to understand that God is any respecter of persons. I believe that to have interfered as I have done—as I have always freely admitted I have done—in defense of His despised poor, was not wrong but right."

Yet we in our day cannot forget that Brown was punished for a direct assault on the Government, for seeking to stir up an actual insurrection. By contrast, *our* martyrs, in the age of the Big State, the Totalitarian State, the All-Demanding State, have been innocent children like Anne Frank, who died in concentration camps simply because they were Jews; isolated German soldiers like Franz Jägerstätter, beheaded because they would not kill; theologians like Dietrich Bonhoeffer, executed because they openly opposed killing; the Polish priest Maximilian Kolbe, who took another man's place in one of the "starvation cells" at Auschwitz and died after weeks of agony. If we have any moral heroes and imminent martyrs today, it is not men of violence, no matter how holy the cause seems to them, but Russian writers and poets who are locked up for years in Arctic camps for sending their manuscripts out of the country; American scientists who refuse to aid in the destruction of Vietnam and its people; young students who believe in peace, live by peace, and act for peace. Thoreau said that "the cost of a thing is the amount of what I will call life which is required to be exchanged for it," and the cost of nonviolence itself is sometimes so great in the face of the powerful twentieth-century state that Thoreau, who identified power only with individual spiritual power, does not help us in the face of the state power which we both need for our welfare and dread for its power over lives.

Thoreau did not anticipate the modern state. He distrusted it even more absolutely than did Jesus in the days when Rome was the greatest power on earth. Jesus counseled—Render unto Caesar the things that are Caesar's. Not only would Thoreau not compromise with the State; he would not recognize it. Near his end, when the Civil War broke out, he advised an abolitionist friend to "ignore Fort Sumter, and old Abe, and all that; for that is just the most fatal, and indeed, the only fatal weapon you can direct against evil, ever . . ." In short—"Be ye perfect, even as your Father in Heaven is perfect." That was all the power Thoreau knew and believed in, outside of the writer's power that he lived by. He would not have believed it possible that the United States would be reading and applauding Thoreau without any sense of irony. The greatest irony is that this American government has become just as self-righteous as Thoreau thought the individual should be.

CRIME AND PUNISHMENT
(FYODOR DOSTOEVSKY)

"Crime and Punishment Draws the Line"
by Claudia Verhoeven, George Mason University

In *Crime and Punishment*, Rodion Romanovich Raskolnikov, a college dropout living in Saint Petersburg, Russia, commits a brutal double murder, but finds he cannot bear the burden of the ensuing guilt. Exhausted and half-mad, he turns himself in to the authorities, who then sentence him to seven years in Siberia. It took Dostoevsky a little less than two years to write what is considered the first of his major works, and it was published in a literary journal called the *Russian Messenger*, in monthly installments, over the course of 1866.

Eighteen sixty-six was not just any year. That spring, the Russian revolutionary movement suddenly exploded into violence when Dmitry Vladimirovich Karakozov—also a college dropout—attempted to assassinate Tsar Alexander II. This historical context is crucial when interpreting *Crime and Punishment*, especially because the assassin uncannily resembled Raskolnikov. Karakozov and Raskolnikov shared age, background, psychological profile, beliefs, and ideas. In one important respect, though, they seemed to differ: Karakozov's crime was public and political, while Raskolnikov's was private and philo-sophical. Precisely because they are so similar, this difference sticks out all the more suspiciously. Karakozov's political violence makes us think twice about the nature of Raskolnikov's crime, and ultimately allows us to see that Dostoevsky deliberately depoliticized the motive of his famous protagonist.

On a first reading, it can seem that there are no politics in *Crime and Punishment* at all. This is because Dostoevsky expressly wrote it as an act of resistance against civil government. Quite literally, the novel is an artistic expression of the political idea that Dostoevsky's contemporaries should not challenge their station in life, and that Russia should remain an autocracy, governed by divine right. How does *Crime and Punishment* make this political argument, and make it so successfully, all the while not appearing to make it at all? What Dostoevsky did—through a series of strategies that will be discussed below—was to take the most revolutionary ideas of his time, but present them in such a distorted way that they end up appearing not political, but grotesque. Below the surface the novel actually teems with politics.

Dostoevsky had not always been a political conservative. In his midtwenties—during the repressive reign of Nicholas I—he had held progressive views and associated with radicals, so much so, in fact, that he was sent to Siberia for a ten-year spell. Whether his only crime had been to read out loud to a group of literary enthusiasts Belinsky's famous letter to Gogol (in which the former admonishes the latter for political conservatism and religious obscurantism) or, rather, to participate in a conspiracy against the autocracy is still not known. What is known, however, is that in Siberia Dostoevsky underwent a religious conversion and was ever after a changed man.

He returned from exile on the eve of the so-called era of Great Reforms. A war had been lost, the old tsar had died, and the new tsar, Alexander II, had begun to implement a series of reforms—of the press, universities, courts, local government, military, and, most importantly, serfdom—to modernize the empire. Lamentably, the "Tsar-Reformer" refused to relinquish his own absolute right to rule (thereby inadvertently radicalizing the revolutionary movement), but what resulted, nevertheless, were "the sixties," one of the most interesting and innovative periods in Russian history. Critical reason, enlightenment, and techno-scientific progress were celebrated; new media brought a communications revolution; literature and criticism had a golden age; class distinctions were trampled underfoot; gender relations questioned; fashions outrageous; etc. It was a decade so remarkable, in short, that it may rightfully be compared to its extraordinary counterpart in the twentieth century.

Dostoevsky, however, was rather an odd man out in this atmosphere. He was older now, and he was a religious man in the midst of a popular culture that embraced nihilism. Nihilism was a concept that functioned as shorthand for all sorts of cultural disobedience ever since the term had been popularized in Turgenev's *Fathers and Sons* (1862). Somewhat more specifically, it may be said to refer to a combustible mixture of democratic and, for the most part, anti-religious political ideologies (e.g., socialism). The heroes of the young generation were the literary critics Chernyshevsky, Dobroliubov, and Pisarev (all ridiculed—directly or indirectly—in *Crime and Punishment*), and they were radicals. Dostoevsky was not.

Sensing in the spirit of the sixties a threat to the order of things, Dostoevsky waged war against its incarnations in his literary works. His favorite method was to imitate and then parody the enemy: He would create characters that embraced the ideas of the sixties, and who then, ostensibly as a result of their sixties attitude, would find themselves entangled in tragicomic situations. Dostoevsky played this game of devil's advocate so well, in fact, that it often seems as if these dire situations follow *logically* from the ideas of the sixties. Indeed, it has often been said that Dostoevsky was uniquely capable of thinking these ideas through to their inevitable conclusion. Really, however, what Dostoevsky did was place his characters inside an invisible grid of religious truth and then measure their ideas by *its* standards, so that the end is not a logical, but a foregone conclusion.

This is precisely the trick Dostoevsky plays with Raskolnikov in *Crime and Punishment*. The intention is already evident in an early proposal he sent to Mikhail Katkov, publisher of the *Russian Messenger*, to secure publication for *Crime and Punishment*:

> The action is contemporary, this year. A young man, expelled from the university, petit-bourgeois by social origin, and living in extreme poverty, after yielding to some strange, "unfinished" ideas floating in the air, has decided . . . . (*Complete Letters* 174)

He first presents an exemplar of a well-known social type of the sixties (young, educated, alienated, and poor, meaning a member of the petit bourgeois intelligentsia) who is affected by the *Zeitgeist* ("ideas floating in the air"). Then, as a direct result of this *Zeitgeist*, comes the plot:

> He has resolved to murder an old woman. . . . He decides to murder her and rob her in order to make his mother, who

lives in the provinces, happy; to deliver his sister, who lives as a hired companion for certain landowners, from the lascivious attentions of the head of the landowner household—attentions that threaten her with ruin; and to finish the university, go abroad, and then for his whole life long to be honest, firm, unswerving in fulfilling his "humanitarian duty to humanity," whereby, of course, "the crime will be expiated," if in fact crime is the term for that action against a deaf, stupid, malicious, and sick old woman who does not know why she is alive herself and who perhaps would have died on her own in a month. (174)

Raskolnikov, in short, rationalizes murder through utilitarianism: Since so much social use will come of this killing, the end justifies the means (note the references to sixties dogma Dostoevsky finds especially ridiculous: "humanitarian duty to humanity," etc.). Dostoevsky goes on to explain that the young man gets away with it, but then, suddenly,

God's justice, earthly law, comes into its own, and he finishes by being *compelled* to denounce himself. . . . The law of justice and human nature have come into their own. (175)

God's justice, earthly law, and *the law of justice and human nature*: While hardly an argument, these sentences are the novel's Archimedean point. Raskolnikov's fate unfolds against the background of these "truths": However he struggles, he is always already on the way to Golgotha—because there is no resurrection without the cross. The distinctly Christian narrative of punishment and redemption that animates the novel is summed up succinctly by Dostoevsky in the third of his notebooks for *Crime and Punishment*:

THE IDEA OF THE NOVEL
1.
THE ORTHODOX POINT OF VIEW,
WHAT ORTHODOXY IS
There is no happiness in comfort. Happiness is bought with suffering.

Man is not born for happiness. Man earns his happiness, and always by suffering. (*Notebooks* 188)

This is really the crux of the novel, and the crux of Dostoevsky's argument with his ideological opponents, who held that improvements in material conditions (comfort) might lead to an overall increase in human happiness, and that it was worth fighting for this. Not so for Dostoevsky, for whom man never lives by bread alone.

The fact that Dostoevsky uses his novels to score points for his political agenda has long ceased to offend or trouble anyone. There is a long-standing line of argument in Dostoevsky criticism that holds that, in the end, Dostoevsky the artist always won over Dostoevsky the ideologist. This idea goes back to the work of the great and enormously influential literary critic Mikhail Bakhtin, who argued that whatever convictions Dostoevsky himself might have held, the ideas of his characters were always given a fair hearing: Dostoevsky creates "*free* people capable of standing *alongside* their creator, capable of not agreeing with him and even of rebelling against him." (Bakhtin 6) This is true in *Crime and Punishment*. After Raskolnikov has already confessed and been exiled, for example, Dostoevsky still permits that he "did not repent of his crime" (544). And even after his conversion ("something seemed to pierce his heart," etc.), Raskolnikov remains hesitant about religion: "Can [Sonya's Orthodox] convictions not be my convictions now?" (548; 464). But it is also true—and this applies especially to *Crime and Punishment*—that, nevertheless, Dostoevsky's authorial position remains dominant.

Dostoevsky is not tolerant of everything, and he has a number of effective techniques for demonstrating his distaste for progressive ideas and their revolutionary potential. One tactic is to ridicule and belittle, such as when he names a filthy tavern in the slums of Saint Petersburg "The Crystal Palace," after Victorian England's most accomplished architectural feat and the bourgeois century's premier symbol of progress. Or when Luzhin is praised for being enlightened (when in fact he is not) because he would not mind (when in fact he would) "if in the very first month of marriage Dunechka [his fiancé, Raskolnikov's sister] should decide to take a lover" (365). Or, finally, when utilitarianism is put down by having the novel's representative man of the sixties, Lebeziatnikov, claim that cleaning cesspits is an activity that is "much higher than the activities of some Raphael or Pushkin, because it's more useful" (371).

A second tactic is the frontal attack. As an example, take the narrator's description of Lebeziatnikov.

He was one of that numerous and diverse legion of vulgarians, feeble miscreants, half-taught petty tyrants who make a point of instantly latching on to the most fashionable current idea, only to vulgarize it at once, to make an instant caricature of everything they themselves serve, sometimes quite sincerely. (365)

It is important to note that this description is the narrator's (rather than one of the novel's characters), for this ostensibly lends it more objectivity. Auxiliary support, however, comes from having the book's most reasonable character, Razumikhin (his name derives from 'razum,' reason), exclaim apropos of the ideas discussed by Lebeziat-nikov, Luzhin, etc.:

[All] this gratifying chatter, this endless stream of commonplaces, and all the same, always the same, has become so sickening after three years [presumably meaning since the publication of Chernyshevksy's influential 1863 novel *What Is to Be Done?*] that, by God, I blush not only to say such things, but to hear them said in my presence. (149)

Razumikhin is not above making money off this "chatter," because he works as a translator for a bookseller who has "hooked onto the trend" and publishes books that peddle the cult of science. "[And] how they sell!" he exclaims. "The titles alone are priceless!" (112). To help him make money, Razumikhin farms out to Raskolnikov a translation of a German text called *Is Woman a Human Being?*, describing it as "the stupidest sort of charlatanism" (112).

Finally, *Crime and Punishment* pushes the idea that scientific knowledge (whether natural or social) is suspect. Dr. Zosimov's interest in psychology ("he's gone crazy over mental illnesses"), for example, is cause for laughter throughout the novel, and the courts—and mind, these are the *reformed* courts—are entirely blind to the truth of Raskolnikov's crime (191).

But Dostoevsky's masterstroke is the one he pulls off when he transforms Raskolnikov's violence into something grotesque, something so misshapen that it becomes difficult to characterize. As initially presented (both in the proposal sent to Katkov and in the early chapters of the book), it is difficult to see how Raskolnikov's crime is not political: He will kill and rob an economically exploitative witch of a woman, then redistribute her money and do good for humanity (it is a crime, in fact, quite on the level with Karakozov's plan to kill the tsar in order to redistribute his power among the people). The only law that could conceivably counter Raskolnikov's logic is the Divine law: "Thou shalt not kill." But even this, it seems, is too weak here, for no one—no character, no reader—ever shed a tear for the murdered moneylender. To provoke abhorrence for Raskolnikov's crime, Dostoevsky had to introduce a second and even a third victim: Lizaveta—and her unborn child. The moneylender herself won't do, and so it is exactly right, what is said about her: "What does the life of this stupid, consumptive, and wicked old crone mean in the general balance?" (65).

The fact that Russia needed someone to do it some good, moreover, is clear from *Crime and Punishment*'s sketches of reform-era Petersburg:

> It was terribly hot out, and moreover close, crowded; lime, scaffolding, bricks, dust everywhere, and that special summer stench known so well to every Petersburger who cannot afford to rent a summer house ... The intolerable stench from the taverns, especially numerous in that part of the city, and the drunkards he kept running into even though it was a weekday, completed the loathsome and melancholy coloring of the picture. (4)

This environment produces few upstanding citizens. Take the novel's major characters. Raskolnikov is a murderer. Svidrigailov is a murderer, a debaucher, and probably a rapist. Raskolnikov's love interest, Sonya, is a prostitute. Raskolnikov's sister, Dunya, by agreeing to enter a loveless marriage for financial gain, no less so (albeit a more socially acceptable sort). Raskolnikov's mother, meanwhile, thinks it no sin to sell her daughter for the sake of her son. Sonya's father, Marmeladov, does think it sinful to sell Sonya, but he does it anyway, because he is a drunkard. Dunya's fiancé, Luzhin, is a petty despot, a miser, and a liar. Raskolnikov's doctor, Zosimov, is "a philanderer ... and a dirty one" (208). Even the "kind" and "virtuous" Razumikhin had "some little turns laid to his account ... not really dishonest, but all the same!" (344; 211–212). About the investigator Porfiry Petrovich "there is nothing to like," he himself admits, and of course the moneylender is an evil parasite. Finally there is Lizaveta: tragically pregnant at the

time she was killed, yes, but beyond that, in fact, "constantly pregnant ..." (64). The minor characters are not much better, and as for
the general background: Every time Raskolnikov ventures onto the
streets, the only people he encounters are alcoholics, prostitutes, tricks,
tramps, and suicides. Sinners, every last one of them—yet who would
cast the first stone?

In this respect, it is highly significant that Raskolnikov finally
decides that he will kill the moneylender immediately upon reading
the letter from his mother that informs him that she will permit his
sister to sell herself for his sake. Whatever other reasons Raskolnikov
may have had, he is first of all plainly a man in revolt against the order
of things.

Of course, later in the novel, Raskolnikov suddenly says: "I did
want to help my mother, but that's not quite right either ..." (413).
And this is why: Dostoevsky rethought Raskolnikov's motive while
writing *Crime and Punishment*. As his notebooks have been preserved,
it is possible to track the novel's compositional history, and of the fact
that Dostoevsky made over Raskolnikov's motive, the third one bears
precise evidence:

> [Raskolnikov's] idea: assume power over this society. ~~so as to do~~
> ~~good for it~~ Despotism is his characteristic trait. (*Notebooks* 188)

It is as if Dostoevsky first took the professed "so as to do good for it"
at face value—he still spotlighted it in the proposal sent to Katkov
and in the early part of the book—but then dug himself a tunnel into
his subject's psyche and hunted its twisted curves for the true motive;
evidently, only upon reemergence from below did he know the real
reason Raskolnikov committed his crime. Retracing this excavation,
the latter parts of *Crime and Punishment* slowly strip Raskolnikov's
utilitarian logic of its humanitarian veneer until it stands revealed,
stark naked, as what has come to be known as the Napoleonic Idea.

The Napoleonic Idea has humanity divided into ordinary and
extraordinary people: The first follow the law, the latter break and
remake it—they have "the right to crime," including, in the most
extreme cases, the right to kill (261). The extraordinary criminals are,
first of all, "the lawgivers and founders of mankind" (mentioned are
Lycurgus, Solon, Muhammad, and, naturally, Napoleon): "all of them
to a man were criminals," Raskolnikov says, "from the fact alone that

in giving a new law they thereby violated the old one" (260). But the category also includes genius innovators like Newton, and "even those who are a tiny bit off the beaten track, that is, who are a tiny bit capable of saying something new" (260). So when Raskolnikov confesses to Sonya, "You see, I wanted to become a Napoleon, that's why I killed," he has this in mind: to raise himself above the rest, to become an extraordinary man (415). "Freedom and power, but above all, power!" Dostoevsky has him say (330).

Raskolnikov's motive is thus transformed into *will to power* and *might makes right*. This not only robs him of any moral high ground he might have had, but also makes him ridiculous—and he knows it. With the new motive, there appears an insurmountable disproportion between the content and the form of his crime: "Napoleon, pyramids, Waterloo—and a scrawny, vile registrar's widow, a little old crone, a moneylender with a red trunk under her bed [. . .] would Napoleon, say, be found crawling under some little old crone's bed!" (274). Repeatedly, Raskolnikov grasps that his real problem is one of aesthetics: "Eh, an aesthetic louse is what I am, and nothing more" (274). So Porfiry Petrovich in fact gets it right when he says, "there are bookish dreams here": Raskolnikov is a spiritual brother of Don Quixote, whose imagination was similarly out of proportion with his circumstances, but who had the good fortune to have read himself crazy with tales of chivalry rather than with the nihilistic theories of the 1860s, and whose goodness saved him from the grotesque results that Dostoevsky prepared for his proud antihero (456). Thus Raskolnikov is tut-tutted for his idea. "A so-so theory," Svidrigailov calls it, and Porfiry Petrovich says, "He came up with a theory, and now he's ashamed because it didn't work, because it came out too unoriginally!" (491; 459).

But why is it not enough to expose Raskolnikov's crime as being rooted in despotism? Why must it also be grotesque? The Napoleonic Idea contains at its core a radical democratic thrust and, indeed, a theory of civil disobedience, and this is Dostoevsky's real target. Obscured by the way the division between ordinary and extraordinary people is naturalized in the novel (people are thus divided, says Raskolnikov, "according to the law of nature," making it seem like the extraordinary are a quasi-Nietzschean or proto-Nazi "race" of supermen), it is easy to overlook a crucial statement Raskolnikov makes about the latter: "For the most part they call, in quite diverse declarations, for the destruction of the present in the name of the better" (261). Most generally, that is, extraordinary people are revolutionaries, and so it is for revolutionaries that Raskolnikov's theory conquers the right to crime. Which is to say: the right to rebel against the order of things for the sake of higher justice.

Raskolnikov's Napoleonic Idea thus supports and in fact approximates the political radicalism of the sixties, which likewise blurs the distinction between crime and civil disobedience. The socialist views of crime are summed up in the novel, as "protest against the abnormality of the social set-up." So, once society is restructured, crime will disappear (256). This is anathema to Dostoevsky, and so he has Razumikhin—again, ostensibly as the novel's voice of reason, but really as the author's mouthpiece—deliver a diatribe against socialism, whose designs for a better society are deemed an offense to "nature," "the living process of life," "the living soul," and "life's mystery" (256–7). Once more, the same strategy as in Dostoevsky's letter to Katkov, where similar terms purport to prove that nihilism replaces life with logic and is, to put it bluntly, against God.

One can place God against "Nihilism," or modernity's political culture, but—and Dostoevsky knew this well enough—God is a point of view, not an argument. There is only one possible proxy for this argument, and that is art, and of that Dostoevsky had plenty. In the same way he once noted that *The Brothers Karamazov* as a whole was "an answer" to the devastating logic of Ivan Karamazov's Legend of the Grand Inquisitor, so all of *Crime and Punishment* was conceived as a counterpoint to the nihilism of the sixties as embodied in Raskolnikov (*Polnoe sobranie sochinenii* 27:48). It is testimony to Dostoevsky's brilliance as an artist that the persuasive powers of *Crime and Punishment* continue to convince readers that Raskolnikov's double murder is the logical conclusion of nihilism, that the Napoleonic Idea is grotesque, and that socialism goes against the grain of human nature.

Nevertheless, it is also true that in spite of Dostoevsky's religiously motivated intentions, *Crime and Punishment* does not suspend disbelief, and God remains dead for the modern mind. Raskolnikov earned a place in the pantheon of literary creations not as an exemplary repentant and Orthodox convert, but as one of the great modern rebels. And beneath Raskolnikov's Napoleonic ego, there is enough compassion for the world to remind readers that the residents of the modern age have not only the right, but also the responsibility to rebel against injustice.

WORKS CITED

Bakhtin, Mikhail. *The Problem of Dostoevsky's Poetics*. trans. Caryl Emerson. Minneapolis: University of Minnesota Press, 1984.

Dostoevsky, Fyodor. *Crime and Punishment*. trans. Richard Pevear and Larissa Volokhonsky. New York: Vintage Classics, 1992.

———. *Complete Letters, vol. 2: 1860–1867*. trans. David A. Lowe. Ann Arbor: Ardis, 1989.

———. *The Notebooks for Crime and Punishment*. ed. and trans. Edward Wasiolek. Chicago: University of Chicago Press, 1967.

———. *Polnoe sobranie sochinenii v tridtsati tomakh*. Vols. 7 and 27. Leningrad: Nauka, 1973 and 1984.

THE CRUCIBLE
(ARTHUR MILLER)

"Civil Disobedience in
Arthur Miller's *The Crucible*"
by Joshua E. Polster, Emerson College

Arthur Miller's 1953 production of *The Crucible* was a creation of the Cold War, the period that reignited the Red Scare and the actions of the House Un-American Activities Committee (HUAC), which was established in 1938 to investigate subversive Communists and Fascists, and later helped initiate the Hollywood Blacklist. Miller—who went before HUAC and was convicted of contempt of Congress for refusing to reveal names of alleged Communist writers—wrote that one can "tell what the political situation in a country is" when *The Crucible* is performed and "is suddenly a hit" (*Timebends* 348). It therefore was no surprise to Miller when his play successfully returned to Broadway just after the introduction of the USA Patriot Act (2001). Arthur Miller's *The Crucible* provided and continues to provide an essential space for disobeying government ideology and exposing and disrupting corrupt ideologies. The relationships of Arthur Miller, Elia Kazan, and Molly Kazan against the strategies of governing power created a countrywide dispute that fractured the United States at a personal and national level on the issues of civil liberties and national security, a dispute that continues today.

From the Salem witchcraft trials to the HUAC hearings to the military tribunals implemented by the USA Patriot Act, there have always been efforts to compromise civil liberties in the name of national security. The tension between civil liberties and national security has not been resolved. It was not solved in 1798 with the Alien and Sedition Acts; in the Civil War when Abraham Lincoln suspended habeas corpus; or in the Second World War when Franklin Roosevelt sent Japanese Americans to internment camps. Still today the ideological war between civil liberties and national security has not been reconciled, and the consequence is a national anxiety that is performed on our public, private, and artistic stages. *The Crucible* has been and continues to be a powerful participant in this cultural anxiety, an act of civil disobedience that challenges the discourse of the dominant power structures in society.

In the mid-twentieth century, there was a strong peak in anti-Communist hysteria. The Communist Party had taken control in China; Communist North Korea had invaded South Korea, bringing the United States into the Korean War; and the Soviet Union had tested its first atomic bomb. Civil defense preparations for a Soviet atomic bomb strike were going on throughout the U.S. The HUAC testimonies of self-confessed spies Louis Budenz and Elizabeth Bentley and the conviction of the Rosenbergs perpetuated the fear of an extensive espionage network operating in the United States. President Truman issued Executive Order 9835, a loyalty and security program within the federal government that initiated a published blacklist of alleged subversives. FBI Director J. Edgar Hoover, who had made the uncompromising connection between affiliations to the Communist Party and Soviet espionage, kept thousands of files on people believed to be members of the Communist Party. In this political climate, the Republican Party was gaining strength against the Democratic administration that had been in place since Franklin Roosevelt. Republicans declared the Communist takeover of China and infiltration within the United States a failure of the Democratic administration. In the Senate, Joseph McCarthy was made chair of the Committee on Government Operations, where he investigated Communism in the government. In the House, John Parnell Thomas chaired HUAC, whose members included a young Richard Nixon. HUAC investigated Communism in U.S. society, in particular the entertainment industry for its celebrity appeal and mass public influence.

It was in this cultural context when, in April of 1952, there was a conversation that would go down in theatre history. Elia Kazan phoned Arthur Miller and asked if Miller could visit Kazan at his country home. Miller immediately suspected that his old friend, who had inspired him as an actor with the Group Theatre and as the director of his plays *All My Sons* (1947) and *Death of a Salesman* (1949), was in trouble with HUAC. As he drove to Kazan's house on a gray rainy New England morning, Miller recalled Kazan's brief membership in the Communist Party in the 1930s—a membership that was not and never had been illegal in the United States—and feared that Kazan had decided to cooperate with the Committee. Miller grew angry, not at Kazan—whom he considered a brother—but at HUAC, which he saw as "a band of political operators with as much moral conviction as [New York mobster] Tony Anastasia" (*Timebends* 332).

When Miller arrived at Kazan's house, the rain briefly stopped, so he and Kazan took a walk in the woods, not far from where several girls had danced and spoken of witchcraft centuries earlier. Kazan spoke of how he was subpoenaed by the Committee and had refused to cooperate, but then changed his mind and returned to testify about his Party membership and to name seven former members of the Group Theatre. Kazan explained to Miller his need to confess to the Committee, so that he, at the height of his creative powers, could continue to make films:

> [I'd] told Art I'd prepared myself for a period of no movie work or money, that I was prepared to face this if it was worthwhile. But that I didn't feel altogether good about such a decision. That I'd say (to myself) what the hell am I giving all this up for? To defend a secrecy I didn't think right and to defend people who'd already been named or soon would be by someone else? I said I'd hated Communists for many years and didn't feel right about giving up my career to defend them. (*A Life* 460)

Kazan, at the time, was one of the most successful and highly paid directors on Broadway and in Hollywood. Kazan had no desire to be among those on the Hollywood Blacklist—the "unfriendly witnesses" of HUAC and those listed in the anti-Communist pamphlet *Red Channels* (1950), which accused affiliates of the entertainment industry, such as Miller, of being members of subversive and Communist organizations. Kazan had good reason to fear being blacklisted. The president of Twentieth Century Fox, Spyros Skouras, had told Kazan the company would let him go unless he satisfied the Committee. To confess was to survive, and Kazan had always told Miller that he had come from a family of survivors.

As Miller listened to Kazan on that April day, he grew cool thinking of how he too could be "up for sacrifice" if Kazan knew that he had attended meetings of Communist writers years ago and, at one such meeting, delivered a speech (*Timebends* 334). In response to Kazan, Miller felt "a bitterness with the country that [he] had never even imagined before, a hatred of its stupidity and its throwing away of its freedom" (*Timebends* 334). If Kazan had invited Miller to his home that day for validation for his cooperation with HUAC, he did not get it. The playwright could only say that he thought this dark time would pass and that it had to pass or it would destroy the country.

It began to rain again, so Miller returned to his car. Before he could leave, he was approached by Kazan's wife, Molly, who previously served as an editor of *New Theater* magazine and play reader for the Group Theatre. She bluntly asked Miller if he realized that Communists controlled the United Electrical Workers union. Molly then pointed to the road ahead and told the playwright that he no longer under-stood the country—"everybody who lived on that road approved of the Committee and what had been done" (*Timebends* 335). Molly may have been partially acting out of interest for her husband—to save his name and career—but she was also a firm supporter of HUAC. Molly believed, as did many, that Communism was a real and present threat to the nation, and cooperating with the Committee was a necessary responsibility of each citizen, even at the expense of civil liberties.

Miller, feeling the gap widen between him and Molly, responded that he could not agree with the actions of the Committee. He believed in the right of one's own convictions, even of unpopular beliefs such as Communism. Standing in the rain, Molly then asked where he was going. Miller said that he was going to do some research in the town of Salem. She instantly understood Miller's intention. Her eyes flashed open with apprehension and anger. "You're not going to equate witches with this!" (*Timebends* 335). Miller said he was not sure and, with a grim wave, drove away.

Miller did write of witches. *The Crucible* premiered at the Martin Beck Theatre in New York, less than one year after his meeting with Kazan. It tells the story of Salem in 1692, when the town was seized by a fear of witchcraft. The fear of witchcraft quickly grew to hysteria and paralyzed the judicial faculties of the townspeople and those in authority. Rumors of witchcraft turned into suspicions, which then turned—in the minds of the townspeople—into facts. Neighbor accused neighbor of allegiance to the devil; witchcraft trials were established to verify the charges, and those who refused to confess, atone for their sins, and name other conspirators were executed by public hanging. Only a few town members, such as protagonist John Proctor, stood up against the growing hysteria but then failed to convince the accusers and authorities. Eventually, even the most respected members of the community—like John Proctor and his wife, Elizabeth—were indicted. Proctor was given the chance to save his life by confessing to witchery and naming names, but, in an act of civil disobedience, he chose death over betraying his integrity and the townspeople. *The Crucible* disparages the informer and advocates taking a stand to preserve civil liberties against tyranny.

The Crucible demonstrates how ideology is used as a means to attain and confirm power in society. In a Marxist view, ideology and power, in general, are created, rehearsed, and sustained in society by repressive structures (such as judicial courts, prisons, police forces, armies) and ideological structures (political parties, press, schools, media, churches, families, art). Salem is presented as a society inundated with the images, myths, and ideas of those in power that use repressive and ideological structures within the courtroom, political parties, churches, and families to suppress divergent thought and action. This, in turn, brings the townspeople to be dominated by consent, where they govern themselves and thus maintain the status quo. Reverend Hale, for example, carries "*half a dozen heavy books,*" books that are "weighted with authority" (33–34).

> Here is all the invisible world, caught, defined, and calculated. In these books the Devil stands stripped of all his brute disguises. Here are all your familiar spirits—your incubi and succubi; your witches that go by land, by air, and by sea; your wizards of the night and of the day. Have no fear now—we shall find him out if he has come among us, and I mean to crush him utterly if he has show his face! (36)

These books contain the rules that instruct Salem's perceptions, thoughts, and ethics. Instead of being skeptical of Hale and his books, the townspeople consent to his authority. Parris, for instance, says to

Hale, "It is agreed, sir—it is agreed—we will abide by your judgment" (35). Salem, Miller reminded his readers in the play notes, was "an autocracy by consent, for they [the townspeople] were united from top to bottom by a commonly held ideology whose perpetuation was the reason and justification for all their sufferings" (4).

The Crucible unveils the ideological discourses of power and demonstrates their use of force in society. Reverend Hale, for instance, threatens, "We shall find him [the Devil] out if he has come among us, and I mean to crush him utterly if he has shown his face" (36). *The Crucible* also demonstrates how these discourses of power try to reinforce their perspective on what is happening in society and allow no alternative perspectives. Reverend Hale, for example, says, "Now let me instruct you. We cannot look to superstition in this. The Devil is precise; the marks of his presence are definite as stone" (35).

Miller used *The Crucible* as a political weapon, a means to scrutinize ideology and transform society by arousing the spectators' capacity to make decisions and take actions against oppressive powers. The audience of *The Crucible*, therefore, is not intended to be passive, but to be an instrument of social disruption and change. There were, however, audience members, such as Molly Kazan, who were not pleased with Miller's comparison of those who believed in witches in Salem to those who believed in Communist spies in the United States. Her instant reaction against the Salem analogy, according to Miller, was that "there are Communists, but there never were any witches" (*Timebends* 339).

In response to *The Crucible*, Molly Kazan retaliated with her play *The Egghead* (1957). It clearly presents the side of those who believed in a dangerous Communist espionage network that thrived under "soft liberalism." The play, also set in a small town of New England, centers on Professor Parson, a militant "egghead" liberal (most likely based on Miller), who sanctimoniously defends a former student against the FBI charge of Communism. Throughout the play, the professor thunderously chastises FBI agents, shouts at and humiliates his family, disobeys the college president, and puts his classroom at risk by allowing the former student to present a lecture. The final act shows the professor duped—the former student is revealed as a dangerous propagandizing Communist set to undermine the country. In his article "Broadway in Review," John Gassner described *The Egghead* as a "dramatic investigation of the failure of naïve liberalism in a world menaced by contemporary Communism" (311).

Elia Kazan also struck back with his film *On the Waterfront* (1954), which presents the side of the informer, who is seen as both scapegoat and hero for protecting people's safety. It concerns ex-fighter Terry Malloy who works for Johnny Friendly on the gang-ridden New York waterfront. "Malloy," observes theatre scholar Brenda Murphy, "defies the 'Deaf & Dumb' code of the longshoremen to testify against the corrupt union-boss Johnny Friendly for having killed Joey Doyle, who had been about to testify, and Terry's brother Charley, who had refused to turn Terry over to Friendly's thugs. Terry is ostracized by the men until he leads them to see that it is Johnny who is the betrayer" (212). At the end of the film, Malloy righteously exclaims, "I'm glad what I done—you hear me?—glad what I done! ... I was rattin' on myself all them years and didn't know it" (Schulberg 132).

Elia Kazan also took out a full-page advertisement in the *New York Times*—written, in fact, by Molly—urging other liberals to "speak out," insisting, "secrecy serves the Communists" ("A Statement" 7). This fracture between Miller and the Kazans represents the fracture within the country.

Beyond the Kazans, Miller saw alienation among friends and strangers as they turned on each other to save their professional careers from the Communist blacklists. "People were being torn apart, their loyalty to one another crushed ... common human decency was going down the drain" (*Arthur Miller and Company* 81). To Miller, the similarities between Salem in 1692 and the United States in 1953 were obvious; this did not escape the attention of HUAC when Miller was called before them:

> Mr. Arens: Are you cognizant of the fact that your play *The Crucible*, with respect to witch hunts in 1692, was the case history of a series of articles in the Communist press drawing parallels to the investigation of Communists and other subversives by Congressional Committees?
> Mr. Miller: The comparison is inevitable, sir.
> HUAC Hearings, 21 June 1956 (Murphy 133)

It is true that Miller wrote about what was in the air, but he had intended *The Crucible* to have a much broader significance, and not only refer to McCarthyism. The hegemonic barrage of McCarthyism headlines—from both the Left, who praised or critiqued the play's assumed portrayal of the HUAC hearings, and the Right, who viciously attacked the play in order to maintain its position of power—dominated the readings of *The Crucible*. According to Miller, this "deflected the sight of the real and inner theme, which . . . was the handing over of conscience to another, be it woman, the state, or a terror, and the realization that with conscience goes the person, the soul immortal, and the *name*" (Martin 153).

Miller saw how "a political, objective, knowledgeable campaign from the far Right was . . . creating not only a terror, but a new subjective reality, a veritable mystique which was gradually assuming even a holy resonance" (Martin 153). Miller wanted to reveal through *The Crucible* that the world was deeply coded, structured, and manipulated by aggressive dominating powers that enforce their particular viewpoints as natural in order to create and enforce their dominance at the expense of civil liberties. These are the aspects of *The Crucible* that make the play an immutable classic, give it a life beyond its cultural context, and allow it to speak to numerous countries and periods about the dangers of tyranny and the need to perform civil disobedience. Miller said, "When [*The Crucible*] gets produced in some foreign country, especially in Latin America . . . it's either that a dictator is about to arise and take over, or he has just been over-thrown. I'm glad something of mine is useful as a kind of a weapon like that. It speaks for people against tyranny" (Martine 14). Its relevance continued in the United States after the terrorist attacks of September 11, when civil liberties were considered, once again, to be compromised for the benefit of national security.

Forty-five days after the September 11 attacks, the USA Patriot Act (2001) was passed with little debate. The Patriot Act expanded the authority of U.S. law enforcement agencies to fight terrorism in the United States and abroad. In *The USA Patriot Act: Preserving Life and Liberty (Uniting and Strengthening America by Providing Appropriate Tools Required to Intercept and Obstruct Terrorism)*, the U.S. Department of Justice emphasizes the "key part" of the Patriot Act in protecting national security:

> Since its passage following the September 11, 2001 attacks, the
> Patriot Act has played a key part—and often the leading role—in
> a number of successful operations to protect innocent Americans
> from the deadly plans of terrorists dedicated to destroying

America and our way of life. While the results have been important, in passing the Patriot Act, Congress provided for only modest, incremental changes in the law. Congress simply took existing legal principles and retrofitted them to preserve the lives and liberty of the American people from the challenges posed by a global terrorist network. (http://www.aclu.org)

However, according to the American Civil Liberties Union (ACLU), civil liberties were substantially compromised for the benefit of national security, as was the case during the McCarthy era.

There are significant flaws in the Patriot Act, flaws that threaten your fundamental freedoms by giving the government the power to access your medical records, tax records, information about the books you buy or borrow without probable cause, and the power to break into your home and conduct secret searches without telling you for weeks, months, or indefinitely. (http://www.aclu.org)

The ACLU recorded many acts of injustice initiated by the Patriot Act, including the interrogation of immigrants based solely on religion or ethnicity; the holding of thousands—including American citizens—in secretive federal custody without charges or access to lawyers; the barring of the press and public from secret immigration court hearings; the government monitoring of conversations between federal detainees and their lawyers; the spying of the FBI on organizations and individuals without evidence of wrongdoing; and the creation of military commissions that can convict non-citizen terrorist suspects based on hearsay and secret evidence by only two-thirds vote (http://www.aclu.org).

The most recent Broadway production of *The Crucible* went on just after the introduction of the USA Patriot Act (2001). Director Richard Eyre connected the Salem witch trials and the HUAC hearings "in which all dissent [was] construed as opposition" to the post 9/11 atmosphere of the United States (http://www.aclu.org). In Eyre's view, the culture that enforced the actions of HUAC and created *The Crucible* resonated with the culture that created the Patriot Act. In his article in *The Guardian*, "Why the Big Apple Was Ripe for Miller's Return," he wrote:

> After the introduction of the USA Patriot Act in November
> (which relaxed many of the rules that protect people suspected
> of crime from unfair investigation and prosecution) and the
> introduction of military tribunals, John Ashcroft, the attorney
> general, said that civil-rights activists who question or oppose
> the legislation are giving aid and comfort to the terrorists.
> (http://www.aclu.org)

To Eyre, Ashcroft closely resembled the character of Danforth, the deputy governor in *The Crucible* who proclaims that, "a person is either with this court or he must be counted against it, there be no road between" (90). Danforth's proclamation is also strikingly similar to President George W. Bush's warning to French president Jacques Chirac: "You're either with us or against us in the fight against terror" (http://archives.cnn.com/2001/US/11/06/gen.attack.on.terror/). President Bush's "axis of evil" (his term for governments accused of sponsoring terrorism) reinforces the binary opposition between the forces of "Good" and the forces of "Evil." This also strongly resonates with Danforth's perspective of the time:

> This is a sharp time, a precise time [. . . when one can] live no
> longer in the dusky afternoon when evil mixed itself with good
> and befuddled the world. Now, by God's grace, the shining sun
> is up, and them that fear not light will surely praise it. (90)

This type of conceptualization helped empower the Patriot Act, which today continues to restrict civil liberties in the name of national security.

Eyre saw the Patriot Act as a political campaign from the far Right, a campaign that was creating mob fear and provocation similar to that found in Salem during the witch trials and across the U.S. during the Red Scare. In his article in *The Guardian*, Eyre illustrated a dangerous consequence of the Patriot Act. During a recent production of *Kiss Me Kate*, a man telephoned a booking agent for tickets. He asked the agent about the size of the theatre and the location of his seats before giving his credit card information, which included his Arab surname. When the man arrived at the theatre, he was met by four FBI agents and arrested as a suspected terrorist (Eyre 1).

Productions of *The Crucible* continue to be used as spaces for civil disobedience to resist repressive strategies of those in power. To many, *The Crucible* speaks as clearly now as it did over fifty years ago about the tense relationship between civil liberties and national security. The United States continues to be divided at a national and personal level. *The Library Journal*, for instance, reports that the nation's public librarians are sharply divided over how to protect their patrons' privacy. "Those responding [to a survey] split almost evenly on whether they had complied with requests for voluntary coopera- tion with law enforcement" asking librarians to require identification from patrons that use the Internet, to monitor their online research, and to report suspected terrorist activity (http://www.libraryjournal. com/article/CA271369.html).

As for Arthur Miller and the Kazans, nothing was ever the same. Miller never bridged his relationship with Molly Kazan, who died in 1963; and he never regained his close friendship with Elia Kazan. Kazan wrote, "I would never really feel toward him what a friend should feel. Nor, I imagine, he toward me." For many years, the two men only spoke to each other through their work—Miller with *The Crucible* and *A View from the Bridge*, another play that disparaged the informer, and Kazan with *On the Waterfront*. Before both men died, Kazan in 2003 and Miller in 2005, they released their autobiogra- phies one year apart—each still fighting, as the country continues today, in the ideological battle over how best to govern the country in dangerous times.

WORKS CITED AND CONSULTED

American Civil Liberties Union. *The USA Patriot Act and Government Actions that Threaten Our Civil Liberties*. New York: American Civil Liberties Union, 11 Feb. 2003 http://www.aclu.org.

CNN. "You're Either With Us Or Against Us In The Fight Against Terror." 6 Nov. 2001. 15 Jan. 2008 http://archives.cnn.com/2001/US/11/06/gen. attack.on.terror/.

Eyre, Richard. "Why the Big Apple was Ripe for Miller's Return." *The Guardian*. 16 March 2002. 15 Jan. 2008 http://www.guardian.co.uk/ saturday_review/story/ 0,,668040,00.html.

Gassner, John. "Broadway in Review." *Educational Theatre Journal*. 9.4 (1957): 311–320.

Kazan, Elia. *A Life*. New York: Da Capo Press, 1988.

Kazan, Elia. "A Statement." *New York Times*. 12 April 1952: 7.

"New Survey: Librarians Divided Over Privacy Issues." *Library Journal*. 21 Jan. 2003. 15 Jan. 2008 http://www.libraryjournal.com/article/CA271369. html.

Martin, Robert. Ed. *The Theater Essays of Arthur Miller*. New York: Da Capo Press, 1978.

Martine, James. Ed. *The Crucible: Politics, Property, and Pretense*. New York: Twayne Publishers, 1993.

Miller, Arthur. *The Crucible*. New York: Bantam Books, 1963.

Miller, Arthur. *Timebends*. New York: Grove Press, 1987.

Murphy, Brenda. *Congressional Theatre*. Cambridge: Cambridge University Press, 1999.

Schulberg, Budd. *On the Waterfront*. Carbondale, IL: Southern Illinois University Press, 1980.

United States. Department of Justice. *The USA PATRIOT Act: Preserving Life and Liberty (Uniting and Strengthening America by Providing Appropriate Tools Required to Intercept and Obstruct Terrorism)*. Washington: GPO, 15 Jan. 2008 http://www.lifeandliberty.gov/highlights.htm.

FAHRENHEIT 451
(RAY BRADBURY)

"'And the Leaves of the Tree Were for the Healing of the Nations': Reading and Civil Disobedience in Ray Bradbury's *Fahrenheit 451*"
by Alina Gerall and Blake Hobby,
University of North Carolina at Asheville

Ray Bradbury opens *Fahrenheit 451* with an epigraph by Juan Ramón Jiménez: "If they give you ruled paper, write the other way." This short command to perform an act of disobedience mirrors the defiant action Guy Montag, *Fahrenheit 451*'s protagonist, and a group of rebels take as they seek to preserve human culture and, in doing so, defy the law of the land. Montag and company rebel against a totalitarian government by doing something most of us take for granted, something we tend to view as a passive activity that provides intellectual growth and a respite from our day-to-day lives. They read. As we turn the pages of Bradbury's dystopic novel, we occupy a close space with Montag, who comes to see the inadequacies of the civil order, ignores the totalitarian state's prohibitions, and encourages others to become literate. By the end of this story about literacy, censorship, and the power of the word in resisting civil authority, we and Guy Montag see books as mirrors for self-understanding, repositories of culture and myth, and ultimately tools with which to build a new society.

In *Fahrenheit 451*, a totalitarian state suppresses critical thought by banning and burning books. The novel follows Guy Montag, a *fireman*—a book burner—who, rather than putting out fires, sets them, incinerating what the state has prohibited for "the good of humanity." After meeting Clarisse McClellan, however, Montag begins to question what he has done; as he prepares to torch more books, Montag begins to read:

> Books bombarded his shoulders, his arms, his upturned face. A book lit, almost obediently, like a white pigeon, in his hands, wings fluttering. In the dim wavering light, a page hung open and it was like a snowy feather, the words delicately painted thereon. In all the rush and fervor, Montag had only an instant to read the line, but it blazed in his mind for the next minute as if stamped there with fiery steel. Montag had time to read one of the lines and it said, "Time has fallen asleep in the afternoon sunshine." He dropped the book. Immediately, another fell into his arms. (37)

Significantly, the line Montag reads comes from Alexander Smith's *Dreamthorp: Essays Written in the Country* (1863). In *Dreamthorp*, Scottish poet Alexander Smith describes a mythical world through which he articulates his ideas about the role poetry and the prose essays can play in edifying human life. Ultimately, he turns to happiness in general, the good life, and the need human beings have to understand themselves, the very things Montag weighs throughout Bradbury's novel:

> There is no happiness in the world in which love does not enter; and love is but the discovery of ourselves in others, and the delight in the recognition. Apart from others no man can make his happiness; just as, apart from a mirror of one kind or another, no man can become acquainted with his own lineaments. (http://www.gutenberg.org/files/18135/18135–8.txt)

Here Smith outlines the ways in which others can fulfill a human life, and the way a "mirror of one kind or another" helps human beings understand themselves. For Smith, Bradbury, and for Guy Montag, self-understanding and the social order depend upon learning through reading and studying books. In *Fahrenheit 451*, not only do Granger, Montag, and company remember as much literature as they can to preserve it, but also, in working to preserve the past and create a better future, they resist civil authority and seek an end to civil strife, each breaking the law and performing acts of civil disobedience.

While many contradictory definitions for the term exist, especially in contemporary political theory and law studies, where thinkers often argue over what civil disobedience is and is not, the term is generally understood in literary studies as it was practiced and written about by two key figures, Henry David Thoreau (1817–1862) and Mahatma Gandhi (1869–1948), two pacifists who practiced nonviolent protest as a means of objecting to laws that violated foundational human rights. Both Gandhi and Thoreau believed in the possibility of changing the governmental machine through nonviolent means. In *Civil Disobedience*, Henry David Thoreau proclaims, "The mass of men serve the state thus, not as men mainly, but as machines . . . In most cases there is no free exercise whatever of the judgment or of the moral sense . . ." (229). For Thoreau, serving the state in this fashion means strengthening the government's tyrannical hold and failing to develop the capacity for judging, deciding and choosing associated with the cultivation of the moral sense. Thus, he challenges citizens to do everything possible to end governmental intervention in private lives. For Thoreau, freedom can only exist when individual autonomy is honored: "There will never be a really free and enlightened State, until the State comes to recognize the individual as a higher and independent power, from which all its own power and authority are derived, and treats him accordingly" (246). Following Thoreau, Mahatma Gandhi coined the term *satyagraha* to describe his philosophy of nonviolent civil resistance, a philosophy he used to mobilize Indian people and the world to see the injustice of British colonialism. Yet acts of civil disobedience can be seen as early as in Aristophanes' play, *Lysistrata*, where women upset the social order by withholding sex, ultimately gaining power through a nonviolent act. Thus, while Thoreau articulates what most Americans have come to understand as nonviolent protest, this concept can be traced from the literary tradition of antiquity to contemporary political philosophy to the civil rights era and the ideals of Martin Luther King, Jr. As with others seeking to change not only ideas but also actions, what is at stake for Bradbury is the denial of free speech and the eradication of cultural memory, the things that necessitate civil disobedience in *Fahrenheit 451*. Free speech and freedom from censorship are both essential human rights that, according to Bradbury, are necessary for creating a humane society. In *Fahrenheit 451*, reading is a subversive act capable of undermining the social order; those who fight the totalitarian government seek an end to oppression and mass ignorance. Rather than bear arms, they bear books. One of those books, significantly, is by Thoreau (76, 153). As a work much like Thoreau's *Civil Disobedience*, *Fahrenheit 451* challenges the institutions that define how a human life might flourish and demonstrates literature's ability to cultivate human autonomy. Bradbury divides his novel into three sections that mark the development of the main character's sense of identity and capacity for individual thought. The three sections of Bradbury's narrative track the progression of Montag's civil disobedience, from questioning his own ignorance to taking action against oppression.

The first section of the story, "The Hearth and the Salamander," describes the steps Montag takes as he first realizes not only the confines of his own life, but also the role he has played in confining others. At the onset of the novel, he is satisfied with his life. The opening chapter describes the "pleasure" he derives from watching "things eaten, to see things blacken and changed." Montag senses the power he wields and is proud of his position in society. He is a man to be respected, a defender of the peace. This is important because it illustrates the seduction of complacency; Montag is rewarded for his unexamined obedience. However, it takes only a few encounters for Montag's world to unhinge. During his initial conversation with Clarisse, Montag takes his first steps away from an imprisoning world where free speech is denied and free thought, exemplified in the act of reading, amounts to civil disobedience. He begins to question the world around him. His faith in the system fails, and he is forced to confront his own discontent.

The section title refers to two connotative images of fire. A hearth is the floor of a fireplace, one that signifies home life. There, before the fire's flames, families gather for warmth and traditionally have regaled one another, especially before the advent of electricity, with stories. It is an ideal space for experiencing not only the sort of community that storytelling creates, but also it provides needed light for reading. With this familiar image, Bradbury frames the novel. The second image, the salamander, is often associated with fire and resisting fire. Montag wears a salamander patch on the shoulder of his uniform, a symbol of his job as a fireman, one who incinerates books. As a fireman, Montag holds a position of power and prestige; he is both respected and feared by those who see him in uniform. The salamander however, does not affect Clarisse, a liberated seventeen-year-old woman who is Montag's neighbor. As she speaks to Montag, she comments: "So many people are. Afraid of firemen, I mean. But you're just a man, after all" (7). Here, and throughout the book, Bradbury questions what constitutes humanity. For Clarisse, being human means having weaknesses, faults that lead others to disrespect autonomy, the desired attribute that Clarisse embodies. After Clarisse makes this matter-of-fact observation, Montag begins to move outside of himself and comes to understand how he has neither considered how other people might see him nor questioned the actions that make him complicit in denying fundamental human rights. As in Alexander Smith's *Dreamthorp*, the issue at hand is the good life: the way a human life may flourish and the way a just society may cultivate human autonomy. With such concerns in mind, Montag begins questioning the very civil order he has enforced. In making this turn from policing to defying the state, Montag breaks the law, and, in telling others about what he has read and in encouraging them to use the written word as a means of passive resistance, he commits acts of civil disobedience.

The second section of the novel, "The Sieve and the Sand," chronicles Montag's attempts to subvert the system of oppression from within. The section title refers to a childhood trick played on Montag that leaves him desperately trying to fill a sieve with sand. In the context of the second section, the sieve and sand serve as a metaphor for the mind's limits. As beings with finite understanding, all truth, knowledge, and happiness are but sand hastily shoveled into the permeable sieve of intellect. The futility of the task is overwhelming. As Montag faces the depth of his ignorance, he begins to question whether there is any point in thinking on his own at all: Submitting to prescribed boundaries might be much easier, and safer, than participating in the arduous life of the inquiring mind. Montag has arrived at the core issue; Bradbury points to the trend in his own time to rely more and more heavily upon convenience. A child of the Depression and a skeptical adult of the fifties, Bradbury thought an unchallenged imagination made for a more controllable population. And people were all too often taken in by the conveniences of gadgetry and the simple hum of the television. But, as Bradbury explicitly and implicitly suggests throughout the narrative, it is in the struggle to discern meaning that the human mind finds purpose. With every thousand ideas that pour through the sieve, a hundred may stick. The task of the individual is to challenge the limits of the mind. Faber, the man Montag seeks out to be his teacher, explains that this level of depth need not come from books alone: "It's not books you need, it's some of the things that once were in books." While existing forms of media like television and radio could be used to stoke the mind, the society no longer demands or even allows for it. Reading is an exercise that illustrates what has truly been lost: independent thought. In the world of *Fahrenheit 451* the individual is the enemy.

Montag's wife Mildred seems to think so, clinging to her "family" of soap opera characters on television and rejecting the attempts Montag makes to include her in his rebellion. There is security in her superficial existence when compared to the peril of reading books, a point Mildred emphasizes when she observes to Montag: "if Captain Beatty knew about those books . . . he might come and burn the house and the 'family.' That's awful!" (73). Mildred's security comes with a price though, expressed in her repeated suicide attempts. By acquiescing to the will of the larger society, she must repress her individual mind to the extent that the only act of disobedience left to her is self-destruction. The fact that she does not seem to recall her actions further serves to illustrate the dysfunction of her conformity. Mildred is never able to make a break with her addiction to mind-numbing media, and through her Bradbury shows us how dangerously easy, and common, it is for an oppressive social order to get its people to submit. But he also shows us the cost of that submission. Mildred is ultimately inconsequential. We do not truly get to know her or her motivations because there is nothing left to know. The ultimate conflict will occur between Montag and his boss, Captain Beatty, who represents the social order itself; Mildred is merely one of its drones.

Beatty is a book burner, but he is also very literate. He is able to quote literature and has a grasp of history. As a manager of the system, he seems to hold himself to a different standard; and it is difficult to discern whether he even believes in the rhetoric he spouts. Beatty is our way into the philosophy behind the totalitarian structure of their society. He provides the history of the firehouse, how books came to be banned and "the word intellectual . . . became the swear word it deserved to be." Beatty tells Montag that the trouble with books started when special interest or minority groups began to find certain passages or works offensive and sought to remove them. He describes a world of growing populations and with them, increasing numbers of minority groups living in ever-closer proximity to each other: "The bigger your market, Montag, the less you handle controversy, remember that!" Here Beatty raises the challenge of living in a diverse culture. He suggests that the differences between these splintered groups are petty; nonetheless they are significantly disruptive to the harmony of the mass population. He highlights the fact that people's demand for uncontroversial easy entertainment made literature obsolete well before it was prohibited. The result, Beatty claims, is a peaceful and happy culture. The trouble is that what Beatty calls "peace" and "happiness" is a form of obedience and complacency we find in Homer's Land of the Lotus Eaters. By de-emphasizing authorship and ideas, and instead supporting the proliferation of mass media, the establishment has chosen to numb people to their differences rather than teaching people to work with them. By committing his first act of disobedience, Montag has already broken with the state, and he resolves not to submit to Beatty's authority.

In the third and final section of the novel, "Burning Bright," Montag emerges as a rebellious figure poised to challenge conformity. Montag's reticence to abandon, and perhaps destroy, all that he has known is at odds with his desire to combat social ills. This ethical impasse is mirrored by the fractured nature of a simultaneous conversation Montag has with Beatty and Faber. Standing in front of his own house, Montag discusses with Beatty the duties of a fireman, while also trying to covertly speak with Faber by way of a radio concealed in his ear. Each figure represents a path—obedience or rebellion—and Montag must ultimately choose which to follow. Beatty eventually discovers the earpiece, forcing his hand. He turns his flamethrower on Beatty and destroys his link to the social order. Beatty's murder, by far the most public and violent act of Montag's rebellion thus far, makes him an outcast and a fugitive.

When Montag sees that the task of awakening others is greater than one man can take on, he flees to the wilderness. Outside of the city limits, Montag meets a wandering band of homeless academics led by Granger, who introduces Montag to a new form of rebellion. Rather than agitating from within the system, as Montag has attempted, these academics defy the government by preserving the textual remnants of a creative culture that honors autonomy. Granger explains: "All we want to do is keep the knowledge we think we will need intact and safe" (152). Because the academics remain passive, "the cities don't bother [them]" (154), and the academics are free to continue with their endless task of memorization and preservation. The text-preservation project of the academics, though imperfect, will ultimately enable future generations to rebuild a new and better society from the pages of past efforts.

The final section title returns the reader to the image of fire, but in a sense of illumination, burning bright, as if to read by and see more clearly, and also to cleanse. We see from a distance the death of an entire community rife with censorship and ignorance. The society and all of Montag's connections to it simply evaporate in a mushroom cloud; what remains is the potential of a new society from within the ranks of the homeless academics, a society of people with inquiring minds that learn from the past. At this juncture, where Montag and the reader are able to reflect on past societies and those to come, Granger compares humanity to the phoenix, the mythical bird who builds a pyre, bursts into flame, and is reborn every hundred years. Granger has hope not just for this incarnation of society, but also for all future human beings:

> We know the damn silly thing we just did. We know all the damn silly things we've done for a thousand years and as long as we know that and always have it around where we can see it, someday we'll stop making goddamn funeral pyres and jumping in the middle of them. We pick up a few more people that remember every generation. (163)

While *Fahrenheit 451* begins as a dystopic novel about a totalitarian government that bans reading, the novel ends with Montag relishing the book he has put to memory. As Granger discusses how these memorized books are, at that very moment, in the safekeeping of small, isolated communities to be "written again," the only specific texts he mentions by name are Thoreau's *Walden* and the essays of noted philosopher and outspoken pacifist Bertrand Russell (152). Here Bradbury seems to suggest the centrality civil disobedience and self-reliance have in our efforts as a species to become more civilized. Though Granger is pragmatic to the point of pessimism—"we'll set it up in type until another Dark Age, when we might have to do the whole damn thing over again"—both Bradbury and his characters are assured of their own civil disobedience and its ability to redeem society (152). In the final lines of the novel, Montag thinks of the words he will leave until noon: "the leaves of the tree were for the healing of the nations" (172).

Guy Montag disobeys the civil order by reading. He refuses to uphold the rule of law, stops starting fires and burning books, and memorizes works of literature. Doing so, he works to preserve human culture. As Bradbury's band of social pariahs journey to the city, where it is conceivable they will influence others, they form a community predicated upon civil disobedience, a community invested in teaching others and future generations about the power of the word. Fighting for justice, decrying tyrannical institutions and, perhaps most importantly, forming an autonomous self through the act of reading, Guy Montag lives according to the word, seeking to commit the book of Ecclesiastes to memory. As Bradbury's work comes to a close, Montag prepares to memorize a specific Bible passage about the tree of life, whose leaves "were for the healing of the nations." For Montag and for all who have stepped away from the world, read a book, returned to their station in life changed, and then desired to affect the social world, reading is personal and communal, private and public. It offers a means of sustaining the self and of opening out to the world that always stands just beyond the page. As a book about books that challenges readers to see the value of human creativity and the moral agency found in the power of the word, *Fahrenheit 451* is by nature polemical. But, like Thoreau's *Civil Disobedience*, Bradbury's novel cultivates the mind while encouraging the autonomous self, a necessary work of fiction.

WORKS CITED

Bradbury, Ray. *Fahrenheit 451*. New York: Random House, 1953.

———. *Bradbury Classic Stories 1: From* Golden Apples of the Sun *and* R Is for Rocket. New York: Spectra, 1990.

Rawls, John. *A Theory of Justice*. Cambridge: Harvard UP, 1971.

Thoreau, Henry David. "Civil Disobedience." *Walden, Civil Disobedience, and Other Writings*. New York: Norton, 2008.

THE POETRY OF LANGSTON HUGHES

"Langston Hughes: Rhetoric and Protest"
by Margaret A. Reid, in
The Langston Hughes Review (1984)

INTRODUCTION

In her discussion of Langston Hughes's poetic style, Margaret Reid explains how the poet crafted his works to "depict the social evils of America, to prick the conscience of Americans, and to exhort Black Americans to protest." Christening him a "forerunner of the militant poets of the Sixties," Reid examines how Hughes utilizes irony, ambiguity, unconventional poetic structure, as well as the "Negro folk idiom" to satirically protest the social conditions of Blacks in Harlem (which she calls Hughes's "synecdoche of America") and the Jim Crow South. Hughes's innovative deviation from accepted poetic convention "adds to the poignancy of the theme of despair" in his works. Thus, Hughes depicts the injustices of racism and evokes the despair of its victims, calling for acts of civil disobedience.

Reid, Margaret A. "Langston Hughes: Rhetoric and Protest." *The Langston Hughes Review* 3.1 (1984 Spring): 13–20.

Given the kinds of social, economic, political and physical abuse that Blacks suffered from slavery through the 1920's, it is inevitable that the Black poet as the voice of the masses would react in protest. There were those who heard the clarion call for protest. There were those who found a voice in spite of the fact that often the publication of their literary efforts was dependent upon White patronage. The poets often had to write their poetry in such a way that it would be understood by Blacks but not always understood by Whites. They made much use of irony and ambiguity. Some of these Harlem Renaissance poets couched their protest in Standard White English using conventional imagery, but many also used the folk idiom to protest the social issues of the period. Their themes as well as their poetic styles gave the poems their universal appeal.

As the poets experimented with their verse forms and poetic language, there evolved unconventional forms and language. These unconventional techniques which emerged during the Twenties were not as radical as those of the Sixties, but there were those poetic techniques which deviated from the traditional mode. Such techniques sometimes included a break from the standard poetic forms such as the ballad, sonnet, ode, and other styles. For these poetic innovators, rhyme, rhythm, and meter were not always the prime prerequisites that they were for the traditionalist. In contrast to metrical verse, free verse was used quite frequently during the Harlem Renaissance.

Another trend was the linguistic style. As the Black poet chose to write about the harsh realities of Black life, he began to use the idiom of his people. Although the unconventional techniques were not the norm of the period and were employed by few of the poets, one can definitely see a trend slowly developing that was to reach its height in the Sixties.

The most avant-garde of these poetic innovators during the Harlem Renaissance was Langston Hughes. When he published his *Weary Blues* in 1926, the literati saw a new trend developing in Black poetic forms. Hughes had used the Black idiom, Black themes, and the blues and spiritual forms from the folk art tradition. Although Hughes used the folk forms in a more sophisticated fashion than James Weldon Johnson or Paul Laurence Dunbar, Hughes was criticized for using these folk sources. The Black intelligentsia did not want its "uncultured," "unsophisticated" and "illiterate" side exposed. In contrast, Whites were fascinated by this primitivism and exoticism, and at night hundreds of Whites went to Harlem to view it firsthand. Hughes alludes to this exoticism in his "Negro Dancers" and "Cat and the Saxophone 2 A.M." Nevertheless, writing about such realities in the language of the folks who experienced these realities made Hughes the poetic innovator that he came to be. As Hughes and others after him were to discover, the rhymed abstractions of the classical poetic tradition were not always suited to the portrayal of the concrete hardships borne by the oppressed Negro. The conventional, often stilted, literary, language often lacked emotional power. To find the exact word—*le mot juste*—the poet resorted to the rich folk idiom.

Hughes borrowed his language from the Negro folk idiom, his poetic form from the spiritual and blues tradition, and his themes from the life and experiences from the common Negro. Using this blues form, Hughes, wrote of the social tragedies in ways that would allow the Negro to see himself and laugh to keep from crying. That is what the blues songs were about. Concealed in Hughes' portraits of the Negro experience was a protest that was sometimes subtle and often satiric: Hughes' free-flowing lyrics gave the Negro something to smile about in spite of his adversities. Furthermore, these poetic portraits gave back images that Waring Cuney's dishwater did not give back.

Although Hughes wrote about the fun-loving Harlemites, he was still protesting their social conditions. (Harlem served as a synecdoche for America.) Very often Hughes did not hide his protest; it was glaringly obvious. One such poem is "The South" published in his anthology *The Weary Blues* in 1926.

The unconventional poetic style of Langston Hughes adds to the poignancy of the theme of despair. His style seems to suggest the chaos which causes the hopelessness of the Negro. Though Hughes uses an unconventional poetic structure, he relies heavily on conventions such as antithesis, irony, hyperbole, personification, and syntax to make his satiric comment about the South. His poem "The South" is written in an un-rhyming, free-verse style with varying line lengths ranging from dimeter to tetrameter. Such free verse style can be suggestive of the chaos that the South stands for, but Hughes' language is very controlled. The free verse style also suggests that the poets wished their people to be free from the bonds of servitude. Every metaphor works to make a haunting accusation about the South's mistreatment of Negroes. Each metaphor helps to tell the history of Southern brutality. "The South" with its myriad personifications is likened to "a beast," "an idiot" and is

> Beautiful, like a woman
> Seductive as a dark-eyed whore,
>> Passionate, cruel,
>> Honey-lipped, syphilitic—
>> That is the South.[1]

One of the ironies of the poem is that though the persona focuses on the ugly deeds of the cruel South, Hughes also describes the scenic beauty of the South, for the South is also symbolic of

> Cotton and the moon
> Warmth, earth, warmth,
> The sky, the sun, the stars,
> The magnolia-scented South.

This positive image of the South set in opposition to the negative image makes the South just that much more objectionable. These four lines of positiveness are incidental since the dominating themes of the remaining twenty-four lines depict the cruelty of the South. In spite of these four lines, the opening lines with the contrasting images set the tone for the poem:

> The lazy, laughing South
> With blood on its mouth.
> The sunny-faced South, . . .

Finally, the poem progresses to its paradoxical climax. Regardless of how the South has mistreated the Negro, the persona expresses an unrequited love for her:

> And I, who am black, would love her
> but she spits in my face,
> And I, who am black,
> Would give her many rare gifts
> But now she turns her back upon me.

The persona then sings lamentingly the swan song that was so typical of Southerners during the great Migration of the Twenties. The poem closes with this irony:

> So now I seek the North—
> The cold-faced North,
> For she, they say,
> Is a kinder mistress,
> And in her house my children
> May escape the spell of the South.

The "cold-faced North" was more than wintry cold. She was coldly indifferent to the plight of the Negro who still had to contend with racial discrimination, regardless of how covert it may have been. So with this closing ironical statement, Hughes satirizes the North as well as the South.

The two contrasting themes, hope and despair, and the contrasting styles, conventional and unconventional, indicate the shifting mood in Black poetry during the Harlem Renaissance, especially at the beginning. Most Negroes were tired of waiting. They had been waiting for three hundred years, and even the Emancipation Proclamation had not brought them what they had hoped for. Consequently, the time for being humble had passed; now some began to protest with indignation. One of the factors which caused great anguish and which provoked the poet to raise his voice in thunderous wrath was lynching.

Hughes, who was the most prolific writer of the Harlem Renaissance, was considered—along with Claude McKay—the most rebellious poet of the period. Thus, it is Hughes' poem "Silhouette" which protests lynching. The poet relies on ambiguity, contrast, paradox, and irony to make his satiric attack on lynching—a prevalent theme in Black literature. He gives the poem its ironic impact by having the persona say

> Southern gentle lady
> Do not swoon.
> They've just hung a black man
> In the dark of the moon.[2]

The underlying implication of this poem is that the Black man was probably hanged because of an alleged rape of a white woman. Ironically, Hughes poeticized that the hanging is "how Dixie protects / Its white womanhood." And it is possible that the victim is innocent as were the nine Black boys in the infamous Scottsboro case of 1931.

There are three questions that arise from the use of "swoon" which means "to faint" or "to feel strong, especially with rapturous emotion." First, is the "Southern gentle lady" fainting at the sight of this ghastly, mutilated body of a Black man hanging from a tree? Second, is she swooning at the loss of her illicit lover? Or, is the sight of the Black man's manhood causing her to swoon? This "lady" may have been the town's whore who made false accusations against her illicit lover when the two of them were caught. If she is not a lady, then the poet admonishes her to become one in his closing lines:

> Southern gentle, lady,
>   Be good!
>   Be good!

If "good" is to be translated to mean either "respectable," "morally sound," "virtuous," or "well-behaved," then the poem closes with the same sarcasm with which it began. Such ambiguity in "lady" and "good" increases the irony.

As a matter of fact, the title is ironic in that the Black man has allegedly committed a crime against a white woman. This contrast is the basis of "silhouette" which is defined as "any dark shape or figure seen against a light background." This black/white contrast is advanced more by the line "In the dark of the moon." This line also provides a paradoxical element since there is no light; yet by "the dark of the moon / the world [is] to see / How Dixie protects / Its white womanhood." The dark moon symbol also portends the evil and sinister things that lurk in the night—lynchers.

Hughes has presented a very complex situation in a thirteen-line poem. Those thirteen lines signify all of the bad luck or ill-feelings that existed in the South.

Illicit sex and/or miscegenation between the races was one of the moral blemishes which was bitterly frowned upon during the Twenties. However, the real tragedy of such a liaison was that the mulatto off-spring not only suffered taunts and abuse but, even worse, felt the lack of a real identity—being neither Black nor White.

Hughes satirizes the mulatto theme in "Mulatto." Irony, metonymy, personification, oxymoron, repetition, paradox, and syntax—along with his unconventional poetic style—give the poem its satiric thrust as it reiterates the mulatto theme. (Claude McKay wrote a similar poem by the same title in 1925.) The acerbity of Hughes' poem is more overwhelming than McKay's "Mulatto." McKay's poem opens with a statement of humility:

> Because I am the white man's son—his own,
> Bearing his bastard birth-mark on my face,
> I will dispute his title to the throne,
> Forever fight him for my rightful place.[3]

A subordinate clause as an opening line diminishes the forceful impact that an opening should have when the theme is such a forceful one. McKay's poem does build in intensity as the poem progresses, but Hughes does not delay any action. In stark contrast to McKay's opening, Hughes opens with an emphatic declaration: "I am your son, white man!" Note how the poet punctuates his pronouncement with under-lining as well as the exclamation point. These two rhetorical strategies along with the repetition of key images, short simple sentences—often fragmented—stress the tension and bitterness in this dialogue between the bastard son and his white father. Just as forceful as the mulatto's pronouncements are the denials of the father which are interspersed throughout the poem.

In very straightforward language, the father retorts:

> You are my son!
> Like hell!
> Naw, You ain't my brother.
> Niggers ain't my brother.
> Not ever.
> Niggers ain't my brother.[4]

The contradictions of these accusations and denials are heightened by the picturesque setting that the poet describes. (The romantic setting is reminiscent of the scene in "The South.")

> Georgia dusk
>
> The moon over the turpentine woods.
> The Southern night
> Full of stars,
> Great big yellow stars.
> Silver moonlight everywhere.
> The bright stars scatter everywhere.
> Pine wood scent in the evening air.

Despite the romantic setting the occasion is not a romantic one. The epithets "nigger wenches," "nigger night," "Bastard boy," "nigger joy," negate the otherwise romantic setting. As a matter of fact, the phrase "turpentine wood" is not very romantic either. Turpentine wood makes excellent fire wood—excellent for the funeral pyre of a lynching victim.

The two oxymora "juicy bodies" and "sweet birth" further promote the contrast in this caustic attack on one of America's moral blemishes. Though these two images are not placed near each other in the poem, the images are interrelated and, therefore, reflect off each other, such as "juicy" and "sweet" and "birth" and "bodies." Then note the poignancy of yet another contrast in the second line:

> Dusk dark bodies
> Give sweet birth

> To little yellow bastard boys.

Every image and every rhetorical strategy that Hughes uses attest to the cruelty of the South. The contemptuous disregard that the White South has for Black women is summed up in the two rhetorical questions of the poem: "What's a body but a toy?" and "What's the body of your mother?" Perhaps the poet makes a prediction that such uncivilized cruelty may cause the barbaric civilization to crumble when he states:

> Georgia dusk
> And the turpentine woods.
> One of the pillars of the temple fell.

Of course, it is also obvious that the last line refers to one of the town's officials who committed this dastardly deed. So Hughes has made a double satiric play with just one line. His constant repetition of "star" to illumine the romantic setting may also have a satiric allusion to the "star" that presided over an unusual birth two thousand years ago.

In "Mulatto" Hughes garnered those rhetorical and poetic devices necessary for creating the intensity of his protest. The unusual way that he separates his lines just might be symbolic of the separation of the races. So with all these techniques, the bitterness of the protest is brought full circle as the poem closes with the opening line: "I am your son, white man!" But there is some added venom: "A little yellow / Bastard boy."

As it was previously mentioned, Langston Hughes was to be the forerunner of the militant poets of the Sixties who poeticized their protests about the moral blemishes that scarred America's sense of justice. As with the poetry of the Harlem Renaissance, the poetry of the Revolutionary Sixties used as its objective correlative these social and moral blemishes. One such blemish that was not considered in poetry during the Harlem Renaissance is drug addiction. Drug addiction in the earlier part of the century was a little-known problem, and then it was most prevalent among musicians. But seemingly after each war or military conflict that America enters, drug addiction becomes rampant, with its widespread use becoming a national problem after the Vietnam conflict. Langston Hughes alludes to this fact in his poem "Junior Addict." Note the references to war:

> Quick, sunrise, come—
> Before the mushroom bomb
> Pollutes his stinking air
> With better death
> Than is his living here,
> With viler drugs
> Than bring today's release
> In poison from the fallout
> Of our peace.[5]

Langston Hughes, who began writing poetry in his teens, had his first volume of poetry published in 1926 and continued to write poetry that reflected the times until his death in 1967. His volume, *The Panther and the Lash*, which was published posthumously contains poems that are reflections of the Sixties. In his last poetry, Harlem is still the synecdoche for America.

As it was very typical of the poetic style of the Sixties, plain and direct language replaced metaphorical language. Although Hughes was a poetic innovator among the traditional group, for the most part his linguistic style does use the metaphor—"sunrise;" but his main strategy lies in his syntax and punctuation. Written in free verse as is most of Hughes' poetry, "Junior Addict" tells a sad story:

> The little boy
> who sticks a needle in his arm
> and seeks an out in other worldly dreams,
> who seeks an out in eyes that droop
> and ears that close to Harlem screams . . . .

There is no indirection in this poem. The poet paints a dismal picture of a young addict's world of despair. The word "despair" has a two-fold purpose in that the despair of the social situation has probably caused the youth to turn to "the drug / of his despair" which then intensifies the addict's desperation. The addict

> cannot know, of course,
> (and has no way to understand)
> a sunrise that he cannot see
> beginning in some other land—

"Sunrise" is the metaphor of hope in this poem. But there is little hope for a better future "to one who will not live." Yet the persona pleads frantically in the coda:

> Quick, sunrise, come!
> Sunrise, out of Africa,
> Quick, come!
> Sunrise, please come!
> Come! Come!

In spite of the desperation of the situation, the poem ends on the optimistic note that there is still hope. But this hope is to come out of Africa, the ancestral homeland which is not yet tainted by this scourge of western civilization—drug addiction.

The urgency felt in the coda with the use of the word "Quick" is aided by the use of the exclamation points and the rapidity of the five staccato lines. These five lines range from monometer to trimeter with a spondaic beat. Also, the poem found this urgency to be achieved better with the one and two syllabic words. "Africa" is the only three-syllable word in the five lines. But with the initial vowel being a slack syllable, "Africa" is not a full-fledged three-syllable word.

The sentence structure at the beginning of the poem suggests the mood of the poem. The urgency that is climaxed in the end by the use of the short exclamatory sentences is also sensed in the long complex sentences of the first and second verses. Additionally, the two very long complex sentences are indicative of the complexities of an addict's life such as the causes and the effects of his addiction. One such complexity is mentioned in this poetic soliloquy:

> "It's easier to get dope
> than it is to get a job."
>
> Yes, easier to get dope
> than to get a job—
> daytime or nighttime job,
> teen-age, pre-draft
> pre-lifetime job.

The poem is void of esoteric images. With direct and simple language, the poem makes a social commentary on drugs, war, and unemployment. Hughes, who always used the folk idiom of his people, has written a poem which reflects the concerns of his people.

Thus, it was with Langston Hughes who throughout his prolific literary career felt the urgent necessity to depict the social evils of America, to prick the conscience of Americans, and to exhort Black Americans to protest. Allen Prowle adequately summarizes Hughes' protest poetry when he affirms that "protest is the dominant theme of his poetry—a protest expressed in varying degrees of intensity, but which is always at the root of his creativity."[6]

NOTES

1. Langston Hughes, *The Weary Blues* (New York: Alfred A. Knopf, Inc., 1926), p. 54.

2. M. Graham, *Anthology of Revolutionary Poetry* (New York: Active Press, 1929), pp. 208–9.

3. Wayne Cooper, *The Passion of Claude McKay: Selected Poetry and Prose, 1912–48* (New York: Schocken Books, 1973), p. 126.

4. Langston Hughes, *Fine Clothes to the Jew* (New York: Alfred A. Knopf, 1927), pp. 71–72.

5. Langston Hughes, *The Panther and the Lash* (New York: Alfred Knopf, 1967), pp. 12–13.

6. Allen D. Prowle, "Langston Hughes," in *The Black American Writer: Poetry and Drama*, Vol. II, edited by C. W. E. Bigsby (Baltimore: Penguin Books, Inc., 1971), p. 78.

INVISIBLE MAN
(RALPH ELLISON)

"Where Is the Civil in the Invisible Man's Disobedience?"
by Brian E. Butler, University of North Carolina at Asheville

There are no instances of civil disobedience in *Invisible Man*. This omission, far from being an oversight, actually follows from Ellison's understanding of the relative position of law in *Invisible Man*'s society. Ultimately, the lack of civil disobedience in *Invisible Man* follows the lack of recognition and the legal invisibility of African Americans in the United States of the 1930s.

John Rawls, in *A Theory of Justice*, defines civil disobedience as "a public, nonviolent, conscientious yet political act contrary to law usually done with the aim of bringing about a change in the law or policies of the government" (Rawls 364). He goes on to state that

> civil disobedience is a political act not only in the sense that it is addressed to the majority that holds political power, but also because it is an act guided and justified by political principles, that is, by the principles of justice which regulate the constitution and social institutions generally. (365)

For Rawls, it is important to note that in the case of civil disobedience, "The law is broken, but fidelity to law is expressed by the public and nonviolent nature of the act, by the willingness to accept the legal consequences of one's conduct" (366). It is illuminating to examine how this conception of civil disobedience relates to *Invisible Man*.

Often the perceived disobedience of the unnamed narrator of *Invisible Man*, hereafter referred to as the Invisible Man, is unintentional. For example, at the university his dismissal comes about not because of any conscious insubordination to Bledsoe, but because of his all-too-slavish wish to please the school's white trustee, Mr. Norton. Another example is that the Invisible Man makes speeches trying to raise interest in the Brotherhood only to be told he is not staying close enough to the party line.

One of the central acts of the Invisible Man's disobedience is not seen by anyone; the narrator and his grandfather do not consider this act as disobedience at all. In fact, why this clandestine act (to be described below) is disobedience at all is never clarified, though it is a very central type of disobedience repeated throughout the novel. The supreme disobedient act? Full agreement. In the first scene of Chapter 1, the Invisible Man is present at his grandfather's deathbed when his grandfather tells his father that,

> . . . our life is a war and I have been a traitor all my born days, a spy in the enemy's country ever since I give up my gun back in the Reconstruction. Live with your head in the lion's mouth. I want you to overcome 'em with yeses, undermine 'em with grins, agree 'em to death and destruction, let 'em swoller you till they vomit or bust wide open. (16)

Here, acting out full agreement when really disagreeing is seen as a subversive act.

But there are some notable events where the narrator engages in conscious and conspicuous disobedience. For starters, there is the eviction speech in Chapter 13. This event begins as the Invisible Man is walking along with his head down to avoid some fumes from a small fire. He notices a pile of what looks like discarded junk in the street. Counteracting this impression is the fact that surrounding the junk is a crowd intensely watching white men carrying furniture, more junk, out of a building. The junk, we realize, contains the contents of an old black couple's apartment; the complete physical contents of their long lives are being removed from the building and unceremoniously dumped on the street. They are being evicted. The crowd, while hostile, at first seems content to grumble amongst themselves, both about the eviction, but also about the shamefulness of the old couple's poverty. As the old woman being evicted tries to wrest her bible from one of the men, she moans, "These white folks, Lord. These white folks," and while her husband tries to calm her, she continues, "It's all the white folks, not just one. They all against us" (263). With this, the crowd gets more vocal and angry. When the old woman tries to go back into the apartment to pray she is disallowed because, as is stated, "You were legally evicted." But the old couple tries to enter nevertheless and is pushed backward. The crowd appears ready to attack. This moves the Invisible Man to action. He runs to the front of the crowd and yells, "Black men! Brothers! Black Brothers! That's not the way. We're law-abiding. We're a law-abiding people and a slow-to-anger people." He continues, "We're angry, but let us be wise." Members of the crowd, though, are angry and want action. Our narrator then starts describing the contents of the junk and the life of the old couple to the crowd, emphasizing their history and years of work. Someone shouts angrily that the couple has been dispossessed. The Invisible Man replies, ironically, that they could not be dispossessed because the "Great Constitutional Dream Book" that the old couple lived by is "all cataracted like a cross-eyed carpenter and it doesn't saw straight" (273). More directly, they cannot be dispossessed because they never were allowed to have, to really rightfully possess, anything in the first place. The Invisible Man then looks toward the leader of the group of white men performing the eviction. He states,

> ... but remember that we're a wise, law abiding group of people. And remember it when you look up there in the doorway at that law standing there with his forty-five. Look at him, standing with his blue steel pistol and his blue serge suit, or one forty-five, you see ten for every one of us, ten guns and ten warm suits and ten fat bellies and ten million laws. *Laws*, that's what we call them down South. Laws! (271–272)

About this time the crowd grows angry and inpatient, attacking the white men despite, and possibly because of, the Invisible Man's oration. In the ensuing scuffle the Invisible Man once again finds his voice and convinces the people to bring the contents of the apartment back inside. During this activity the police arrive. After briefly taunting the police by claiming that the group was only cleaning the streets of litter, and laughing to himself, the Invisible Man is overwhelmed by the scene and makes a rooftop escape, leaving the others to face the impending arrival of the riot police.

Another moment of implied disobedience is during Clifton's funeral. The funeral arises out of an act of disobedience. Ultimately it turns into an event premised upon injustice and aimed at recognition. A favorite community leader in the Brotherhood, the semisecret organization that recruits the Invisible Man after he shows leadership in the eviction speech, Clifton disappears from the organization and then resurfaces selling dancing Sambo dolls on the street. Clifton is next seen being harassed by a police officer. While the police officer marches Clifton along, Clifton turns violently and punches him. Though it is a strong blow that knocks the officer to the ground, the police officer manages to shoot Clifton and he dies in the street. As a witness to this scene, the Invisible Man seizes on this as an opportunity to "put his [Clifton's] integrity together again" and attract members to the Brotherhood (441). Clifton's funeral becomes a huge spectacle with a drum corps, a thirty-piece band and a large group of attendees. The Invisible Man's speech, while not technically against the law (especially the law as a set of written texts), centers on the nature of the relationship between blacks and the police (the real "law").

> "Listen to me standing up on this so-called mountain!" I shouted. "Let me tell it as it truly was! His name was Tod Clifton and he was full of illusions. He thought he was a man when he was only Tod Clifton. He was shot for the simple mistake of judgment and he bled and his blood dried and shortly the crowd trampled out the stains. It was a normal mistake of which many are guilty: He thought he was a man and that men were not meant to be pushed around. But it was hot downtown and he forgot his history, he forgot the time and the place. He lost his hold on reality. There was a cop and a waiting audience but he was Tod Clifton and cops are everywhere. The cop? What about him? He was a cop. A good citizen. But this cop had an itching finger and an eager ear for the word that rhymed with 'trigger,' and when Clifton fell he had found it. The Police Special spoke its lines and the rhyme was completed . . ." (450)

The Invisible Man tells the crowd to teach the police to think, "when they call you *nigger* to make a rhyme with *trigger* it makes the gun backfire" (451). He then concludes, "I do not know if all cops are poets, but I know that all cops carry guns with triggers. And I know too how we are labeled. So in the name of Brother Clifton beware of the triggers" (451).

One of the most powerful images of disobedience is a short incident within the very intricate and surreal riot described in Chapter 25. Here, our narrator is following a group of men he met for the first time during a race riot in Harlem ostensibly caused by outrage over Clifton's death. Instead of joining the random looting and pillaging going on all around him, the Invisible Man becomes part of a group that appears to have a specific aim and a well-thought-out plan with which to carry it out. Dupre, the leader of the group, directs them to a hardware store where they fill buckets with oil. With full buckets in hand the group walks in deliberate fashion to a "huge" tenement building where, we learn, two of the men the Invisible Man is with, Dupre and Scofield, live. Dupre intends to burn it down, but is very methodical in bringing about his plan. He states, "look here y'all . . . I wants all the women and chillun and the old and the sick folks brought out" (536). After making sure no one is left in the building Dupre continues with a just as careful plan as to how the arson will be carried out. The Invisible Man's response to the successful fulfillment of Dupre's aim is exaltation, at least in part because "They did it themselves . . . planned it, organized it, applied the flame" (540).

And, most dramatically, there is "the bump." While placed in the prologue, the accidental bump incident is, according to the narrator's story, last of all the disobedient acts to happen of those investigated in this paper. In this incident, the Invisible Man is walking on a deserted street when he accidentally bumps into a tall blond and blue-eyed man. The man in response calls our narrator "an insulting name" (4). Because of this, the Invisible Man seizes his coat lapels and demands he apologize. Instead of apologizing, the blond man curses him. The Invisible Man head butts the man's chin, which results in blood and the tearing of flesh and then, following this, repeatedly kicks him while yelling, "Apologize! Apologize!" The man refuses to do so, and instead continues to utter insults "though his lips were frothy with blood" (4). Finally, the narrator tells us: "I got out my knife and prepared to slit his throat . . . when it occurred to me that the man had not *seen* me, actually; that he, as far as he knew, was in the midst of a walking nightmare!" (4). With this realization, the Invisible Man decides not to kill, and drops the man down onto the street. His narration continues:

> He lay there, moaning on the asphalt; a man almost killed by a phantom. It unnerved me. I was both disgusted and ashamed. I was like a drunken man myself, wavering about on weakened legs. Then I was amused: Something in this man's thick head had sprung out and beaten him within an inch of his life. I began to laugh at this crazy discovery. Would he have awakened at the point of death? Would Death himself have freed him for wakeful living? But I didn't linger. I ran away into the dark, laughing so hard I feared I might rupture myself. (4)

None of these incidents qualify, at least if we accept Rawls's definition, as civil disobedience. For example, in the eviction speech there is no address to the majority. The Invisible Man addresses only the people in his neighborhood. Further, the only reference to law is that the people he addresses are "law-abiding." There is no belief in law as a source to look to for help or protection. Here the law only commands. In fact, the "Great Constitutional Dream Book" is described as cross-eyed and "all cataracted." If the Constitution cannot see, the law is not available and fidelity to law, another key factor in Rawls's definition, has no place in the event. Further, the idea that the eviction was not seen as a dispossession at all undercuts any literal argument against *unjust* dispossession.

Clifton's funeral, on the other hand, starts with an act of disobedience that ends in Clifton's death due to a police officer's nigger/trigger complex. Here, the Invisible Man's speech clarifies where law fits in all this. The narrator explains that Clifton had made the mistake of judgment in thinking that he was a man because "he forgot his history, he forgot the time and place." To be black in the eyes of the law is to be seen by the "good citizen," in the form of the cop, as not human. Here there is no appeal to change any law as Rawls would require. Further, there is once again no appeal to the majority's sense of justice. Finally, and most tragically, there is no opportunity for Clifton to show a "willingness to accept the legal consequences" of his demand to be treated as a man because the consequences are a little too drastic—immediate death.

These issues are equally clear in the tenement episode and the bumping incident. The tenement torching is clearly a conscious, if not conscientious, act contrary to law. The act, like all of the others investigated here, is not justified or motivated by political principles but rather by moral indignation. Finally, arson is somewhat violent (therefore not satisfying the nonviolent test) and the act, done as it is during a riot, shows no conscious willingness by the group to accept the legal consequences attached to breaking such a law. In fact, it seems that it is only under the cover of general chaos that such an act could be carried out without resistance. Of course, the bumping act is clearly eliminated from Rawls' civil disobedience definition because of its extreme violence. While an act of moral outrage, the fact that in the newspaper it is reported as a mugging shows not only that there is no willingness to note the wrongfulness of the blond man's verbal attack, but also that the Invisible Man's protest is not seen as protest at all. This is very significant. His type is not really allowed a civil space within which to protest.

Upon finishing the narration of the bump episode, the Invisible Man imagines the reader's reaction:

> I can hear you say, "What a horrible, irresponsible bastard!" And you're right. I leap to agree with you. I am one of the most irresponsible beings that ever lived. Irresponsibility is part of my invisibility; any way you face it, it is a denial. But to whom can I be responsible, and why should I be, when you refuse to see me? And wait until I reveal how truly irresponsible I am. Responsibility rests upon recognition, and recognition is a form of agreement. (13–14)

The Invisible Man, and those like him, are not allowed a civil space within which they can be seen as legitimately protesting the injustice of law. The possibility of legitimacy in the face of the law is refused. Rawls explains, "civil disobedience ... arises only within a more or less just democratic state for those who recognize and accept the legitimacy of the constitution" (Rawls 363). But here the Constitution is corrupt. When the Constitution is cross-eyed and all cataracted it should not be trusted.

This thought is played out nicely by Martha Nussbaum in "Invis-ibility and Recognition: Sophocles' *Philoctetes* and Ellison's *Invisible Man.*" Nussbaum claims that, "Like the *Philoctetes*, Ralph Ellison's novel concerns a refusal of acknowledgment, a humanity that has been effaced" (259). *Invisible Man*, according to her, aims to undo the refusal of recognition. The lack of recognition is seen to be "a moral and social defect, but also, more deeply, as a defect of imagination, of the inner eyes with which we look out, through our physical eyes, on the world" (260). Therefore the need is to create the ability, the means, for a broader ability to [re]imagine the place of blacks in American society. Nussbaum thinks that Ellison had to construct commonality between seemingly opposite views of the world. To construct this "idea of common humanity" Ellison has to utilize a very diverse set of strategies:

> We can understand ultimately (again, a controversial presupposition of Ellison's art), but only if we are hectored and confused, shocked and astonished, approached with a bewildering combination of mythic violence, sardonic humor, bizarre narrative, and expressive symbolism. Only such nonrealist devices are adequate to the recording of the inner complexity of a daily life in racially divided America. (Nussbaum 264–265)

This explains why there is so little appeal to law in *Invisible Man*: Ellison appeals to persuasion instead of force, not only because he thinks that this type of appeal is more effective, but really because there is no avenue of appeal to the protection of law; therefore legal force is no solution.

Through Ellison's narrative craft, and the various strategies shown in *Invisible Man*, the reader can join with the narrator in working out the implications of this invisibility, of this lack of recognition. As Danielle Allen puts it, Ellison recognizes and embraces the fact that democracy rests upon sacrifice, especially the sacrifice of minorities who are not fully represented in any particular law but must still be faithful to the law. This works and is just when the sacrifices necessary for civil society are spread around equally, but:

> When sacrifices are not voluntary but demanded, those who give something up for the common good have been treated

as scapegoats and are not sacrificers. And when a sacrifice is
accepted without the honor due to the benefactor and without
eventually being reciprocated, those who gain from their fellow
citizens' losses also abuse them. (Allen 859)

In other words, because blacks are involuntary scapegoats, and because
the society they live within will not see their sacrifice as sacrifice,
the law represents abuse in its most direct and clear manifestation.
Because of this, civil disobedience is impossible.

Allen concludes from this that, "citizens of the post-Reconstruc-
tion American South, habituated to poor standards of citizenly inter-
action, understood something that Fine and political theorists often
had not: The political-juridical world comes to exist out of the social
world, which sets limits on and also facilitates the operations of the
political world" (Allen 886). In other words, in opposition to Watts's
claim that, "should the United States ever advance to the point at
which black jazz musicians and writers are given just recognition for
their accomplishments, it will be the result of some type of political
agitation," it is more nearly the opposite in the areas of the arts as well
as civil rights (Watts 117). As Steven Tracy states:

> . . . at the time of his publication of *Invisible Man*, many whites
> were frequently not ready to acknowledge the contributions of
> African Americans, with *Brown v. Board of Education*, lunch
> counter sit-ins, bus strikes, and civil rights marches not yet
> materialized. It seems more likely, then, that Ellison was merely
> awakening to and illuminating for his audience the artistic and
> intellectual contributions that had been there in front of their
> faces all along. (Tracy 111)

But, as Ellison shows us, seeing another's face right in front of ours,
even when it is threatening us with death, is sometimes beyond
our ability. One is confronted with an urgent problem—how to get
someone who is cross-eyed and cataracted by bias and privilege to
see the invisible, the unrecognized, as worthy of honor and respect.
As Ellison asserts, "it is futile to argue our humanity with those
who willfully refuse to recognize it, when art can reveal on its own
terms more truth while providing pleasure, insight and, for Negro
readers at least, affirmation and a sense of direction" (*Essays* 740).

That recognition is the result of an artistic and creative construction. Before there can be political agitation, one must be seen as a member of the *polis*, as at least potentially a citizen. In this sense, the Invisible Man had to disobey in his way because civil disobedience was not an option. Further, of course, *Invisible Man* can be read as a revelation of sacrifice, of humanity, an aesthetic recreation of the social world so that acts of civil disobedience in a Rawlsian sense can happen. If there is a realm of the civil in *Invisible Man*, it is not in the manner of civil disobedience but in its appeal to the larger (latent) civility in society. It is not the top-down or bottom-looking-up appeal to authority, but a face-to-face appeal to democratic values. Ellison, as effectively as anyone, used the literary imagination to "smuggle the black man into society's machinery in some form" (*Trading Twelves* 223). The Invisible Man must be smuggled into American society so as to be seen.

WORKS CITED AND CONSULTED

Allen, Danielle. "Law's Necessary Forcefulness: Ralph Ellison v. Hannah Arendt on the Battle of Little Rock." *Oklahoma City University Law Review* 26 (2001): 857–95.

Bates, Daisy. *The Long Shadow of Little Rock*. Fayetteville: University of Arkansas Press, 2007.

Benston, Kimberly W. *Speaking for You: The Vision of Ralph Ellison*. Washington: Howard University Press, 1987.

Bloom, Harold, ed. *Ralph Ellison*. New York: Chelsea House, 2003.

Brophy, Alfred L. "Foreword: Ralph Ellison and the Law." *Oklahoma City University Law Review* 26 (2001): 823–837.

Callahan, John F., ed. *Ralph Ellison's Invisible Man: A Casebook*. Oxford: Oxford University Press, 2004.

Cashman, Sean Dennis. *African-Americans and the Quest for Civil Rights: 1900–1990*. New York: New York University Press, 1991.

Ellison, Ralph. *The Collected Essays of Ralph Ellison*. New York: The Modern Library, 2003.

———. *Flying Home and Other Stories*. New York: Random House, 1996.

———. *Invisible Man*. New York: Random House, 1992.

———. *Juneteenth*. New York: Random House, 1999.

———, with Albert Murray. *Trading Twelves: The Selected Letters of Ralph Ellison and Albert Murray*. Edited by Albert Murray and John F. Callahan. New York: The Modern Library, 2000.

Glaude, Eddie S. *In a Shade of Blue: Pragmatism and the Politics of Black America*. Chicago: The University of Chicago Press, 2007.

Jackson, Lawrence. *Ralph Ellison: Emergence of Genius*. New York: John Wiley and Sons, 2002.

Magee, Michael. *Emancipating Pragmatism: Emerson, Jazz, and Experimental Writing*. Tuscaloosa: The University of Alabama Press, 2004.

May, Larry, ed. *Recasting America: Culture and Politics in the Age of Cold War*. Chicago: The University of Chicago Press, 1989.

Meacham, John. *Voices in Our Blood: America's Best on the Civil Rights Movement*. New York: Random House, 2001.

Morel, Lucas E., ed. *Ralph Ellison and the Raft of Hope: A Political Companion to Invisible Man*. Lexington: The University Press of Kentucky, 2004.

Murray, Albert. *The Omni-Americans: New Perspectives on Black Experience and American Culture*. New York: Outerbridge and Dienstfrey, 1970.

Nussbaum, Martha C. "Invisibility and Recognition: Sophocles' *Philoctetes* and Ellison's *Invisible Man*." *Philosophy and Literature* 23.2 (1999): 257–283.

Polsgrove, Carol. *Divided Minds: Intellectuals and the Civil Rights Movement*. New York: W. W. Norton and Company, 2001.

Posnock, Ross, ed. *The Cambridge Companion to Ralph Ellison*. Cambridge: Cambridge University Press, 2005.

Rampersad, Arnold. *Ralph Ellison: A Biography*. New York: Vintage Books, 2008.

Rawls, John. *A Theory of Justice*. Cambridge: Harvard University Press, 1971.

Stephens, Gregory. *On Racial Frontiers: The New Culture of Frederick Douglass, Ralph Ellison, and Bob Marley*. Cambridge: Cambridge University Press, 1999.

Sundquist, Eric J. *Cultural Contexts for Ralph Ellison's* Invisible Man. New York: Bedford Books, 1995.

Tracy, Steven C. "A Delicate Ear, a Retentive Memory, and the Power to Weld the Fragments." *A Historical Guide to Ralph Ellison*. Edited Steven C. Tracy. Oxford: Oxford University Press, 2004. 85–114.

———, ed. *A Historical Guide to Ralph Ellison*. Oxford: Oxford University Press, 2004.

Watts, Jerry Gafio. *Heroism and the Black Intellectual: Ralph Ellison, Politics, and Afro-American Intellectual Life*. Chapel Hill: The University of North Carolina Press, 1994.

JULIUS CAESAR
(WILLIAM SHAKESPEARE)

"Julius Caesar"
by Stopford A. Brooke, in
Ten More Plays of Shakespeare (1913)

INTRODUCTION

In his analysis of *Julius Caesar* Stopford Brooke focuses on the political elements of the play, examining the revolutionary nature of the civil disobedience that leads to Caesar's downfall. For Brooke, the revolution in the play is unsuccessful. Even though Caesar is slain and his despotic reign ended, the play "puts, indirectly, into artistic form the two reasons why revolutions which are in the right do not always succeed against forms of government which are in the wrong: that is, why a struggle for freedom fails against a tyranny, or, if it should succeed for a time, as in the French Revolution, why it finally falls again under the power of a despotism."

The play of *Julius Caesar* is the form into which Shakespeare cast the materials he had collected out of *Plutarch's Lives* of Caesar, Antony, and Brutus. The subject was a common one. Polonius says in *Hamlet*:

Brooke, Stopford A. "Julius Caesar." *Ten More Plays of Shakespeare*. London: Constable and Co., 1913. 58–90.

In the university "I did enact Julius Caesar: I was killed in the Capitol: Brutus killed me." Every one knows how much life Plutarch gave to his characters, but the life which Shakespeare gave them was more full, various, and feeling than Plutarch's power could paint. A multitude of stories interesting as history, a host of philosophic remarks interesting as Plutarch's, illuminate but sometimes overwhelm the presentation of these three men by Plutarch. In Shakespeare's play, the men themselves are the first interest; and only those events and passions are chosen out of the history, which develop the characters, urge on the action of the play, or enliven the scenes into a vivid reality. The political philosophy, of which there is a fair sprinkling in the play, does not seem to proceed from Shakespeare, but from the very nature of each of the characters he has separately individualised. Even when Brutus, Cassius, Casca lay down identical theories, the expression of them is different on the lips and in the mind of each. In all that Plutarch writes of his men we are in touch with Plutarch, but in this play we do not touch Shakespeare, but Brutus, Cassius, Antony, Casca, Cicero, or Caesar. And in this contrast is contained the eternal distinction between the man of talent and the man of genius, between the describer and the creator, between the intellectual man and the poet.

Then, again, a creative genius, having collected his materials, feels his mastery over them, and uses them as he pleases. He is going to make a greater matter than that which actually happened; something that will endure when the historical events have become dreams. Therefore Shakespeare makes what changes he will in the history of Plutarch. He makes Caesar's triumph occur on the same date as the Lupercalia. It really took place six months previously. He brings the murder of Caesar, the funeral speeches, and the arrival of Octavius in Rome, into the circle of one day instead of many. He combines into one the two battles of Philippi, quietly setting aside the interval of twenty days between them. This is the imagination dealing as it pleases with facts. It is possible historians may dislike it, but what talk we of historians when there is such a man as Shakespeare.

Nor does he less show his sense of mastery over his materials when he takes from Plutarch, whenever he thinks them good enough for his purposes, the very words that Plutarch uses or invents. It is true they were in the noble English of North's translation—contemporary English with which Shakespeare was in sympathy—but all the more one would think that he would avoid transcribing whole sentences, almost word for word, out of North's prose into blank verse. Not at all. Genius takes all it wants, and is confident of its right to do this. "I have power to adopt what is good," Genius would say if he were questioned, "because it is better where I place it than it was in its original surroundings."

The play appeared in 1601. Weever's *Mirror of Martyrs*, printed in 1601, refers to Antony's speech in this play, for which there is no original in Plutarch. Hence we know that *Julius Caesar* preceded Weever's book, and probably was written in 1600. It was acted at the beginning of 1601.

The subject-matter of the play was of great interest at this time. Perhaps in 1562, certainly before 1579, and again in 1588, there were plays on the fate of Caesar. In 1589 a play with the title *Julius Caesar* was known, and was acted by Shakespeare's company in 1594. Then, after Shakespeare's play, that is, after 1601, a number of plays represented various portions and views of the same subject. Indeed, the matter has always engaged the thoughts of men, their passion and their genius. It is a political interest;—the natural war which has existed since the beginning of the world between the idea of Liberty and the force of Autocracy; and this play, where the two powers clash, where they are impersonated in Caesar and Brutus, has been, on many a stage, the means of giving expression to the anger and pity of those who, among a people degraded by the gratuities and coaxing of Imperialism, lived and died for the rugged liberties they could not win.

That interest has been seen and felt in this play. What has not been seen and felt in it—at least not to my knowledge—is that it puts, indirectly, into artistic form the two reasons why revolutions which are in the right do not always succeed against forms of government which are in the wrong: that is, why a struggle for freedom fails against a tyranny, or, if it should succeed for a time, as in the French Revolution, why it finally falls again under the power of a despotism.

The first of these reasons is—that the single idea which belongs to all the revolutionists is not kept apart, in each of them, from personal motives. Each man adds to it his own interest or his own passion; and these several interests or passions divide the men from one another. Then unity is lost, and with the loss of unity, force is dispersed. Of all the conspirators, only Brutus had a single aim uninjured by any personal motive. Shakespeare makes that plain. His Cassius, Casca, Cinna, and the rest, had each his own axe to grind, or his own personal envy of Caesar. Not one of them is ever able to conceive the impersonal, the unselfish attitude of Brutus. Brutus—and this is the deep tragedy of the play—far apart from the rest in his own ideal world, thinks, stands, lives, and dies alone. His is a position which has been repeated again and again in the history of revolutions. It was, to give one example from our own time, the position of Délécluze in the story of the Commune. The other conspirators have little bond of union except the desire to slay Caesar; no uniting ideal aim in which their individual selfishnesses are absorbed. Where that is the case, as often it has been in the story of the struggle of Ireland, and, as yet, of the working classes in England and abroad, failure is certain.[1] Even if, for the moment, they act together, as in the slaughter of Caesar, they fall asunder, each to his own interest, when the act is accomplished; and their want of union for one collective, ideal aim ruins their cause. The only thing which binds the conspirators together after the death of Caesar is that they are all proscribed, and have to fight for their lives. It is astonishing how clearly this comes out in *Julius Caesar*. It dominates the play till the death of Caesar. It is not neglected afterwards. Even the great and vital friendship between Brutus and Cassius is imperilled by the personal aims of Cassius. On the eve of the battle which will decide their fate, these two friends all but split asunder.

Again, a still more important reason why revolutions against Imperialism fail, is that their leaders have no settled form of government ready to replace that which they have overthrown; and no men, trained in official work, to use as means for carrying on a government. The consequence is, that after the outburst everything is at sixes and sevens; the various parties devour one another; and in the confusion the mere mob of the violent, unthinking, drifting people get the upper hand. Anarchy, then, makes every kind of human life and effort, and all property, uncertain; and then the steady body of the whole State, sick of disturbance, illegality, change, uncertainty, welcomes despotism again, because it governs. This was the career of the French Revolution.

Shakespeare makes the lesson clear in this play. The pure political idealist, like Brutus, is absolutely at sea the moment he has destroyed the government of Caesar. And Cassius, Casca, Cinna, like Brutus, have nothing ready with which to replace it. They are all left, in ridiculous failure and confusion, face to face with the mob whom the embryo imperialism of Caesar has weakened and degraded by amusements and gratuities. Nothing can be better put than this is by Shakespeare in the blind, futile, inconsequent, disintegrated talk of the conspirators after they have slain Caesar. Brutus, their noblest comrade, is at this crisis the most amazingly foolish of them all. He loses his head. He shouts like an Anarchist. He thinks all Rome is on his side. He is absolutely ignorant of the people he has only conceived in his study. He thinks Rome will govern itself. He takes no measures to set any government on foot. He believes in Antony! He acts like a man in a dream. He makes a speech to the people, hands them over to Antony's seductive tongue, and walks home, as if he had done nothing and had nothing more to do, to talk the matter over with Portia. The inevitable follows; and he flies for his life with Cassius through the gates of the city he has, by his action, handed over to a more organised despotism than Caesar ever exercised.

Imperialism has won, Republicanism has failed, and Shakespeare, in the quiet apartness of the Creator, marks out, through the dramatic action and speech of his characters, what are the main points of the event. He records things as they are, and in the quarrel seems to take no side. This is the proper position of a great dramatist. Yet, as in *Coriolanus*, where Shakespeare's sympathy seems, on the whole, to be on the side of the tribunes, so here, and more probably here than in any other play, the personal sympathy of Shakespeare seems to emerge on the side of Republicanism. He has, as always, his "good-humoured contempt of the mob." But there is a heightening of his phrasing, an intensity of the soul he puts into his words when he speaks of Brutus or makes him speak, which draws me into the imagination that his sympathy was with the thoughts of Brutus, the republican. There is not enough on which to base any definite conclusion, but there is enough on which to base a suggestion. And this sugges-tion of his personal sympathy with the Republicanism of Brutus is perhaps buttressed by the strange and half-contemptuous sketch he makes of Caesar, the great imperialist. It is unlike any other image I know of Caesar. He is represented as subject to superstitions, as wavering to and fro, as led by the nose by his enemies, as vain even to insolence, as having lost his intellectual powers in self-sufficiency, as one who thinks himself separated altogether from his fellow-men. His speeches are almost the speeches of a fool. Shakespeare seems to have gone out of his way to make this representation, this *dénigrante* representation; and it is very curious when we contrast it with the lofty, dignified, and beautiful representation he makes of the man who embodies Republicanism. I do not say that Shakespeare was a republican; that would be absurd. Nobody knows what he was; and he was not likely to openly sympathise with Republicanism, even of the kind then conceived, under the rule of Elizabeth. But he was likely to be opposed to despotism, to maintain the freedom which England had already won. And it is worth saying that when this play was written in 1601, Elizabeth had tried to enforce the Tudor despotism, to impose her own will on Parliament; and was successfully met and defeated by Parliament quietly insisting on its ancient liberties. She yielded with a good grace; but no Londoner, and least of all one of Shakespeare's vast intelligence, could be unaware of this struggle. A great contention of this kind steals into the thoughts and imagination of men, and consciously or unconsciously influences their work, even though the work have nothing to do with the struggle itself. I think it possible, then, that the representation of the contrasted political ideas of Brutus and Caesar, which Shakespeare (to the advantage of Brutus) makes so plain, was indirectly coloured by the struggle between Elizabeth and the Parliament—between the despotic will of the Queen and the ancient liberties of England.

But all this is scarcely an argument, much less an assertion. The common thing to say is that Shakespeare, on debatable matters, such as politics and religion, took no side himself. And one proof of this impersonal attitude is, that even if he sympathised with the political ideas of Brutus, he as plainly did not sympathise with his weakness in action, with his inability to govern or to manage men. His representation of Brutus both before and after the death of Caesar, is of a man totally unfit to handle events or to direct a State. Shakespeare may have thought it right to oppose despotism, but even despotism was better than anarchy. Brutus was a better man than Caesar or Octavius. But Brutus could not govern, Octavius could.

The play is a political play, and of a kind different from that of any other in his works, even from that of *Coriolanus*. It is concerned with affairs of State throughout, and when the ordinary passions of human life enter into it, they come as episodes. The domestic and personal life of Coriolanus is more important for that play than the affairs of the State. But in *Julius Caesar*, on the contrary, the relation between Portia and Brutus, the friendship between Brutus and Cassius, are extraneous; do not affect the dramatic conduct of the drama, or the catastrophe. They are relieving interludes of great charm, and made more charming still not only by the invention of Lucius, who in his happy youth has nothing to do with the storm of events around him, but also by the gentle and gracious relations between the boy and his master Brutus. But none of these things interfere with the main action—with the contest between Caesarism and the old Republicanism of Rome, between a worn-out Past and a living Present. Brutus is defeated; Caesar conquers; and the play is rightly named *Julius Caesar*.

Some have said it ought to be named by Brutus's name, and that he is the true hero of the drama. But great as Brutus is in the drama, and apparent master of its action, Caesar is in reality the cause of all the action and its centre. His spirit dominates the whole. But in the first part it is not the Caesar of the play who dominates, it is the Caesar who *has been*; the life, the doings, the spirit of the Man who in the past has bestrid "the world like a Colossus." What Shakespeare has made of the existing Caesar is what a man becomes who having been great, thinks his will divine, even the master of Fate; and falling into that temper which the Greeks called Insolence, becomes the fool of Vanity and the scorn of the gods who leave him to relentless Destiny. Shakespeare's picture of Caesar resembles the picture drawn by the Greek tragedians of the chiefs who, isolating themselves from their fellow-men, equalised themselves to the gods in their self-opinion, and placed themselves—as the gods did not—above eternal Law. But his present folly does not lessen Caesar's past greatness; and Shakespeare takes pains to show how great he was, and how great he still is in the minds of men. The play opens with his triumph over Pompey. Brutus loves him, while he hates his idea of Empire. Cassius, Casca, while they cry him down, exalt his image in our eyes. When they slay him, they are like men who have murdered a world. Even the starry powers, in Shakespeare's imagination, emphasise his greatness. The whole heaven, when Caesar comes to die, is racked with storm; lions roam the streets, the dead rise from their graves. And when he is dead, all his vanity and folly are forgotten instantly. Rome rises to drive out his assassins. His spirit broods over the rest of the play in executive power. It is Caesar who wins the battle of Philippi, who plants the sword in the heart of Cassius and of Brutus. The theory of government, because of which he died, defeats the theory Brutus held; the new world he initiated disperses to all the winds the old world that Brutus, in vain, tried to reanimate. Caesar is lord of the play; Brutus is in the second place.

Being thus a Drama concerned with Statesmen and State affairs, there is but little in it of human passion at its height. The note of the play is low in sound. There is the passion for liberty in Brutus, but it is the passion of the student, not of the man of action. The same high passion is supposed to be in the other conspirators, but it is really the mean passion of envy which influences them. There is neither loftiness of motive nor depth of wrath for freedom in anything they say or do.

Then, with regard to Brutus, his Stoic nature forbids in him deep emotion; and his personal love for Caesar prevents him from feeling any intensity of indignation against Caesar. His love for Caesar depresses into a still sadness his eagerness for liberty. Moreover, he is not angry with anything Caesar has as yet done. He slays Caesar lest he should do wrong to liberty in the future. This doubt as to whether Caesar will become a tyrant or not (the slaughter of Caesar being only to prevent a possibility) would naturally take all passion out of his thought and act. Scepticism—save vaguely with regard to itself—is naturally unimpassioned, except in a young man like Hamlet. Brutus was a mature man and a Stoic. Sad and earnest then, in quiet Stoicism, without any passion, his mind works, and his hand strikes. His sense of what he thinks himself compelled to do depresses rather than excites him. Therefore, with regard to the passion for liberty, the dramatic note is low and still.

Then, again, the human relations of this play do not reach the high levels of the great emotions. They are chiefly the relations of friend to friend. Antony is Caesar's friend, but his friendship is mixed with his political selfishness. His various speeches over Caesar's body rise now and then into a semblance of passion, but they are calculated. He sees himself rising into power on Caesar's death. He is as cool as an iceberg when he talks with Octavius and Lepidus.

Again, the friendship of Brutus and Cassius is a true friendship but not an equal one. An unequal friendship does not stir into move-ment the deeper waters of feeling. The stronger nature of Brutus has another world in which to live where Cassius cannot come. One feels this apartness again and again in the famous dialogue between them. Even in the reconciliation there is that condescension on the part of Brutus which is incompatible with an impassioned friendship.

[...]

Though the image of Caesar dominates the play, and Caesarism conquers in it, yet its main subject is the working out of the fate of

Brutus as the last hero of Roman liberty; and the fall of Republicanism in his death is the true catastrophe of the Drama. The representation of this might have been made more impassioned. But, even in this, passion was excluded, because Brutus, being a Stoic, his law of life excluded passion. Shakespeare was forced then to keep his representation of Brutus quiet. And nowhere is his careful work as an artist more remarkable, more close to his conception of a Stoic student pushed into the storm of great affairs, than in his slow, restrained, temperate development of the character of Brutus. Again and again we expect a high outburst of poetry. The events seem to call for it from Brutus. But Shakespeare does not choose him to rise above the level of his Stoicism; he does not even permit the tide of his own emotion, as he writes, to erase the stern lines of the character he has conceived. Twice only (after Caesar's slaughter, and during the battle), Brutus is swept out of his self-restraint.

Nevertheless the position of Brutus, though it is marked by this self-quietude, is a noble subject for dramatic poetry. It is the struggle of the hero who belongs to a past world against the victorious pull of the present world. And since Brutus is high-hearted, and his idea morally right, and the world he fought with ignoble and unmoral, his overthrow does not lower him in our eyes. He is conquered by circumstance, but his soul is unconquered. He becomes more fit for lofty tragic poetry when, as the play moves on, he stands alone in his nobleness, apart not only from his enemies, but in the purity of his motives from his friends. And the tragic in him is lifted into splendour of subject when we see clearly that which he did not see till he came to die: that the death of Caesar—the means, that is, which he took in order to bring back to Rome the freedom that he loved—was the very event which riveted on Rome the Imperialism which he hated. Few situations are more poetic. The ghost of Old Rome stands on the threshold of Imperial Rome, and fades before its worldly splendour. But as the phantom fades away, we follow it with praise and honour. It will rise into life again when Imperial Rome shall have fallen into the helpless ruin it deserved. The spirit of Brutus can never die.

In the very first scene (in Shakespeare's preparing fashion), two main elements of the drama are represented. There is, first, the mindless mob, spoilt by the bread and games successive leaders have given to it; which has no care for liberty or any policy, only for entertainment. The second is the division of Rome into violent parties. We see the partisans of Pompey and Caesar, hot with anger; then, in another class, all those who, like the tribunes, hold some office, and are enraged with Caesar who threatens to take all offices into himself. These two elements become as it were two *leit-motifs*, which occur again and again throughout the play. We hear in the first Scene the growl of the popular storm which threatens Caesar. In the next we are in the thick of it. Caesar enters in triumph. A short dialogue, quick and crisp, sketches the pride, the superstition, the *insolentia* of Caesar—the temper of one whom the gods have doomed; the flattery which has brought him to this point of foolishness; the pride which could not conceive that misfortune or death could touch him. When the Soothsayer bids him beware, he cries—

He is a dreamer; let us leave him: pass.

The pageant then passes on, and Cassius and Brutus are left alone. We hear that Brutus has been brooding of late, apart from his friends, in silence. No one knows, not even Cassius, what turn his thoughts have taken on the politics of Rome. Has he even discovered himself what he thinks? There are thoughts in us which we need to hear shaped by another person or by some event before we are conscious that we have had them for a long time; and Brutus is in this condition when Cassius probes him about Caesar—

BRUTUS: Into what dangers would you lead me, Cassius,
        That you would have me seek into myself
        For that which is not in me?

Then the event finishes what Cassius had begun. A shout at a distance forces out of Brutus the dominant and concealed thoughts within him, and crystallises them into expression—

What means this shouting? I do fear, the people
Choose Caesar for their King.

On that Cassius works to win Brutus to his side against Caesar; and at every point of the dialogue the character of Cassius is dramatically divided from the character of Brutus. Brutus only cares for the public weal, for his republican ideal. Cassius is consumed with envy of Caesar; and the bitter hatred of envy appears in the stories he tells of Caesar's physical weakness—anything to degrade the image of the man he hates—as if Caesar's not being able to swim well, or his trembling in a fever, proved that he was not a better man than Cassius or Brutus. This has no effect on Brutus, who is incapable of envy. Brutus scarcely hears him. He is listening for a renewal of the shouts. Then Cassius, seeing that the chord of jealousy and envy does not answer to his touch, changes his attack, and changes its motive three times in the course of his speech until at last he strikes the note which is answered in the soul of Brutus. First, it is discontent with Fate that he touches—"Why should we be underlings and he half a god ?" That note does not touch Brutus. Then he tries ambition—"Why, Brutus, should you not be as great as Caesar ?" That also does not affect him either. At last he sounds the note of the ancient liberty of Rome—

> There was a Brutus once that would have brook'd
> The eternal devil to keep his state in Rome
> As easily as a king.

That echoes in the soul of Brutus; and to develop it further into act, Caesar enters in all his pomp. Shakespeare's pictorial imagination strikes out, as it were in flashes, the outward appearance and the characteristics of the passers-by—

> Look you, Cassius,
> The angry spot doth glow on Caesar's brow,
> And all the rest look like a chidden train:
> Calpurnia's cheek is pale, and Cicero
> Looks with such ferret and such fiery eyes
> As we have seen him in the Capitol,
> Being cross'd in conference by some senators.

It might be made a picture of. Then Caesar (in the one speech he makes which is worthy of his intelligence), sketches Cassius so vividly that he is immortalised; and then Antony with one slight touch—full of flying power—

Yond Cassius has a lean and hungry look;
He thinks too much; such men are dangerous.

.   .   .   .   .   .

He is a great observer, and he looks
Quite through the deeds of men; he loves no plays,
As thou dost, Antony; he hears no music:
Seldom he smiles, and smiles in such a sort
As if he mock'd himself, and scorn'd his spirit
That could be moved to smile at anything.
Such men as he be never at heart's ease,
Whiles they behold a greater than themselves,
And therefore are they very dangerous.

Here and here alone Caesar speaks up to the level of his former self.
When he has passed by, Casca takes up the presentation, and we see, as
if we were on the spot, the scene when the crown is offered to Caesar,
and the mob, and the women, and Casca's own bitter envy. Then in
a single phrase Cicero is painted; the cultivated literary man who is
isolated from the common herd in dainty pride of culture.

CASSIUS: Did Cicero say anything?
CASCA: Ay, he spoke Greek.

Every blunt word of Casca lays bare his embittered and jealous heart,
and we can almost see the "quick metal" in his face. Even more vividly
is the heart of Brutus disclosed to us in this masterly dialogue. The
desperate thought which has been born in him—that Caesar must be
silenced—grows steadily while he listens to Cassius and questions Casca.
He is thinking of what Caesar has done, and of that alone. He questions,
questions, that he may be sure that Caesar is trying for the crown, that
he may set his mind at rest. Though he says little, it is enough to enable
us to follow his soul in doubt. Must I slay Caesar whom I love? Is there
no way out of it? I must have time to think. To-morrow, Cassius, come
to me, or I will come to you. His mind runs round the circumference of
his thought, but never quite enters the circle; hesitating, this way and
that dividing his dread, his impulse, and his duty. And so, in this slow
progress of his thought to its shaping, we leave him for a time. He leaves
Cassius alone, who comments on his character: "Noble, yet so simple
that he may be wrought into my conspiracy."

The night falls then, and the third Scene opens amid a great tempest, full of terror and portents. The meaning of it in the play is put afterwards on Calpurnia's lips:

The heavens themselves blaze forth the death of Princes.

We have seen how often Shakespeare used the common belief that Nature mixed herself up with those great human events which, striking at chief men, struck at humanity. Nay, more, he made Nature reflect the passions of men when they reached intensity. He writes as if he believed that a spiritual power in Nature was in touch with the deep things in man and in his history. We remember the storm which accompanies the murder of Duncan; the fury of the elements which reflects and heightens the agony of Lear. And here, to develop this thought of his, and at the same time to dramatise it, here presents at length what each of his characters thinks of the storm. And it affects them all in a different way. This suppression of his own idea, and this out-creation of it in other lives than his own, other thoughts than his own, is most masterly in this scene, and most effective on the stage.

Casca, the envious scoffer, who respects nothing, is like many of his tribe, smitten by the storm into superstitious terror. With his sword drawn, breathless and staring, thinking the world is ending, he meets Cicero; and the little sketch of Cicero is delightful. He is perfectly unmoved by the terror of the night; as quiet as if all the stars were shining in a peaceful sky—only astonished by the state of mind in which Casca presents himself. Hear how placid are his sentences—

Good even, Casca: brought you Caesar home?
Why are you breathless? and why stare you so?

And to Casca's relation of the awful sights—a lion met near the Capitol, a man with a burning hand, men all on fire walking the streets, the owl shrieking at noonday, and the skies dropping fire—he replies in a philosophic strain as if he were in his study; and then asks about the news of the day, as if he were at his club—

Indeed, it is a strange-disposed time:
But men may construe things after their fashion,

> Clean from the purpose of the things themselves.
> Comes Caesar to the Capitol to-morrow?

This is the educated, cultivated man to whom, absorbed in literary and political interests, the wild games of Nature (who to his mind pursues her natural course even in storm) are of no importance. Just so might Burke or Darwin have looked on the elemental war.

Neither does Cassius care a straw for the raging of the tempest, but not for Cicero's reason. The fury of hate in his heart is greater than the fury of the storm. The lightning and the elemental roar express his soul, and he walked in them with joy. He sees in the dreadful prodigies of the night the warning of Caesar's end—Heaven itself is speaking its wrath with Caesar. Then, as the tyrannic hate within him seeks fresh forms of expression, he says no longer that the storm is the message of divine wrath. It is itself the image of Caesar. It is he who is the dreadful night of Rome; it is he that thunders, lightens, opens graves, and roars like the lion, in the Capitol. He is our fear and destruction.

Finally the hate and envy of Cassius break out into that impassioned speech by which he bursts open the heart of Casca, and claims him as a brother in his envy—and in his conspiracy.

> And why should Caesar be a tyrant then?
> Poor man! I know he would not be a wolf
> But that he sees the Romans are but sheep:
> He were no lion, were not Romans hinds.
> Those that with haste will make a mighty fire
> Begin it with weak straws: what trash is Rome,
> What rubbish and what offal, when it serves
> For the base matter to illuminate
> So vile a thing as Caesar! But, O grief!
> Where hast thou led me? I perhaps speak this
> Before a willing bondman; then I know
> My answer must be made. But I am arm'd,
> And dangers are to me indifferent.

He ends by saying to Casca that "three parts of Brutus is ours already,"

and the man entire
Upon the next encounter yields him ours.

This phrase, while it marks the slowness in the growth of Brutus's resolution, which Shakespeare has so carefully wrought out, introduces us to the next scene in which Brutus at last makes up his mind. The storm still goes on—"the exhalations whizzing in the air" give light enough to read by—but the rain has ceased. Brutus is walking in his orchard, and the dawn is near at hand. He too has cared nothing for the storm. His soul is stormier, with its dreadful purpose, than are the heavens. Shakespeare lays bare this soul, restlessly ranging over motives, possibilities, casuistries, and settling finally into the resolve to slay for the general good the man he loves; not because Caesar has done anything as yet against liberty, but because he may—and, "lest he may, I will prevent him." What Caesar is, he says, if given greater power,

> Would run to these and these extremities:
> And therefore think him as a serpent's egg
> Which, hatch'd, would as his kind grow mischievous,
> And kill him in the shell.

'Tis a mean argument; and only a philosopher would use it and think it good. Once, during the soliloquy, the unphilosophic side of Brutus contradicts it—

> To speak truth of Caesar,
> I have not known when his affections sway'd
> More than his reason.

Then he gets back to his mere philosophy, changing and shifting.

Some say that in this soliloquy Brutus is unlike his previous character. But Shakespeare is representing a mind travelling over a host of arguments for and against the deed it considers. The disordered spirit of Brutus is tossed to and fro; even now he cannot come to certainty. It needs to settle him down into full resolve, that Rome should call on him for help. And the sealed papers flung in at his window, crying to him to "awake, and strike and redress, in the name of his great ancestor who drove out the Tarquin," finally secure his resolution. Then he looks back on the long struggle, and in his loneliness paints the tempest of thought through which he has passed—marvellous words they are—half of the philosopher, half of the man who has loved Caesar, and not one line of a man of the world.

> Since Cassius first did whet me against Caesar
> I have not slept.
> Between the acting of a dreadful thing
> And the first motion, all the interim is
> Like a phantasma or a hideous dream:
> The Genius and the mortal instruments
> Are then in council, and the state of man,
> Like to a little kingdom, suffers then
> The nature of an insurrection.

Now, when at last the mind of Brutus is free from doubt, the conspirators arrive. They are in the garden, the storm is dying away; and the presentation to the eye of the whole scene is rendered more vivid by the little dialogue (while Brutus and Cassius talk apart) of Casca and Cinna about the part of the heaven where the sun arises. They talk of "where the east is" while they wait to arrange how the foremost man of all the world is to die. This is Shakespeare's way, as it is the way of human life, of mingling the common with the uncommon, the great with the small, the deeds which shake the world with a brawl at an inn in Eastcheap.

Then Brutus, developing still more the high-mindedness of his character, will have no oath taken. No need for that if they are Romans who know they have an unselfish cause to maintain; every drop of whose blood is guilty if they break their promise. This is far too lofty a strain for the conspirators, whom other motives drive. They do not even answer him. Such words as

> The even virtue of our enterprise

must have struck cold on the passions of envious Casca and jealous Cassius. The loneliness of Brutus comes home to us.

Then emerges also his folly as a politician. It is the retired student, engaged only in ideas, who speaks when it is proposed to slay Antony as well as Caesar. Our course, he says, would be too bloody then. Would we could kill Caesar's spirit, and not Caesar. Mark Antony is nothing without Caesar.

This is too childish-foolish for this world. Brutus has no eye for men, or for affairs. He never even thinks of Octavius. He has not measured the latent power of Antony, nor does he measure him justly after the murder. He hands the whole of Rome over to him when he lets him speak over Caesar's body. His position as a politician is ridiculous; his position as a noble thinker is honourable. Caesar dead, Antony was not only Antony, but Caesar as well; and Caesar is nowhere more alive than when he sways the hearts of the Roman people in the speech of Antony. The only way the conspiracy could have succeeded was, once Caesar was slain, by the slaughter of those that loved Caesar. Napoleon understood that; so did Antony and Octavius. The tender-heartedness and the personal morality of Brutus were, in the circumstances, fatal to his cause. All this is the careful drawing of Shakespeare, who did not work (as I have often said) with the careless indifference which some think an attribute of genius.

Yet when we turn from the futile politician, and the philosopher ignorant of the world, to the man, with what charm does his tender-heartedness arrive! The conspirators depart; Brutus is left alone. He calls his attendant, Lucius. The boy is fast asleep. And Brutus, looking at him, loves his youth, and will not disturb him—

> Boy! Lucius! Fast asleep! It is no matter;
> Enjoy the honey-heavy dew of slumber:
> Thou hast no figures nor no fantasies,
> Which busy care draws in the brains of men;
> Therefore thou sleep'st so sound.

And this interlude of the tenderness which lay beneath the stoicism of Brutus is continued by the scene with Portia which instantly follows, and on which I have already commented.

The morning comes, and we are placed in Caesar's house. The storm has not quite passed away, and the doomed man enters, to be met by his wife who urges him to stay from the Capitol. There is that which is terrible in the insolent pride Caesar shows throughout this scene. There is that which is pitiable in the weakness with which he yields to his wife, and then, when his pride is appealed to, to the conspirators. This kind of pride is the very top of weakness. All the evil omens are in vain. His pompous and inflated speeches, intolerable when he is speaking in the third person, seem to challenge the gods, and to despise all men but himself. Shakespeare, like a Greek dramatist, meant them to contain his fate and the cause of it. They partly explain the hatred and envy of Cassius and the rest; and it is a fine piece of art which thus modifies our horror of his murder by our natural dislike to this tone of haughty defiance. And in the death scene this is continued. His insolence becomes so great that it seems to claim the dagger. He says he will spurn "like a cur" the man who would alter his will. "Hence!" he cries, as the conspirators press their suit upon him—"Hence! Wilt thou lift up Olympus?" Again Decius claims his friend's return from exile. Caesar answers,

> Doth not Brutus bootless kneel?

This motives the last blow, and brings us up to it without too great a shock.

Then follows the confusion of the conspirators, who do not know what to do; the dispersal of the people, and the conspirators left alone with their dead master. It is a wonderful scene; at first they do nothing but shout—

> Liberty! Freedom!—Tyranny is dead!
> Run hence, proclaim, cry it about the streets.

It is almost like the shout of Caliban—as foolish at least as his. Brutus bids the Senators not to be affrighted. Casca tells Brutus to speak to the people. "Where's Antony, where's Publius?" cry others. This is all these foolish persons think of doing after their momentous act. No prevision, nothing arranged, no measures for government,—and the whole world upturned!

Then they begin to talk, half-philosophic talk about life and death, and how their deed will be acted over on a future stage, as if they thought they were playing a tragedy, and had done nothing in reality. And Brutus, shaken to the centre of his stoicism, falls into melodrama quite outside his character; bids them bathe their arms in Caesar's blood, wash them up to the elbows, smear their swords, and, waving their red weapons in the marketplace, cry "Peace, freedom, and liberty."

At first all this seems, in the bloody circumstance, unnatural. But, in reality, nothing can be better done than Shakespeare has here done. The inner agitation of the conspirators shows itself in these absurdities. They begin to feel that they have shaken the world. They have let loose forces they cannot manage, and terror and confusion seize on their heart and brain. They dare not give voice to the overwhelming dread. And they take refuge in this surface-talk, in these inane boastings; even Brutus is shocked into melodrama. It is like Hamlet bursting into fantastic phrase after he has seen the ghost. It is almost a comfort when Antony—who is contending for his life, who knows what will follow on this deed, who sees the overthrow of Brutus and his own success, if only he can for a few hours secure his life from the conspirators' daggers—comes upon the scene. He is politic enough. He persuades Brutus that he will act with him. Cassius suspects him; but Brutus imputes his own single-eyed love of liberty to Antony, and consents, like an idiot, to Antony's speaking at Caesar's funeral. Antony is nobly managed. Were he only the hypocrite, we should despise him. Shakespeare does not leave it so. Even though his life is on the card, he cannot help breaking out into pity and praise when he sees his master dead, but he manages to pass this off as an offering to friendship, while he agrees in principle with what has been done. In him, and in Brutus, craft and simplicity stand face to face, and both men are true to the character Shakespeare has made for them. As a politician Antony is wise and Brutus a fool. As a man Brutus is noble and Antony ignoble—and yet not quite ignoble. His personal love and wrath for his friend, arising continually through his deceiving speeches, redeem him in our eyes. At last, he is left alone with the dead, and the long repressed rage bursts forth in that impassioned address to the pierced body of Caesar, wherein, in the last words, we see beforehand what is coming, when

> Caesar's spirit ranging for revenge,
> With Atè by his side come hot from hell,
> Shall in these confines with a monarch's voice
> Cry "Havoc," and let slip the dogs of war.

One catastrophe has been—the death of Caesar; but out of death Casear rises again, an avenging spirit. Another catastrophe, the death of Brutus, is at hand. It is the true catastrophe of the play—the overthrow of the Republican, the triumph of the Imperial, form of government. Caesar, *in* Antony, does this, and Caesar's true revenge is the victory of his idea.

The second scene closes the third Act. It is the scene of the speeches in the Forum. The speech of Brutus is entirely in character, doctrinaire, sententious; convinced, even to a touch of vanity, of his rightness; so convinced that he does not doubt the people being of his opinion (imputing his own thoughts to every man in the crowd); so convinced that he begs them, for his sake, to hear Antony. In every phrase Shakespeare writes down the folly of the man, his unimaginable unfitness to lead, to convince, or to understand a mob of citizens whom an imperialistic policy had debauched with gifts. Nevertheless, they cheer Brutus when he has done! Then Shakespeare, with one imaginative touch, makes it clear that they have completely misunderstood the action and the speech of Brutus.

ALL.	Live, Brutus! live, live!
1 CIT.	Bring him with triumph home unto his house.
2 CIT.	Give him a statue with his ancestors.
3 CIT.	*Let him be Caesar.*

Listen to that; the people wish to make him that which he hopes he has destroyed. He has slain Caesar that there may be no more Caesars. "Let him be Caesar," is the answer of the mob. Alone, alone, Brutus goes away, the fool of fancy, self-deceived.

Then Antony begins the speech that every schoolboy knows. It is charged with contempt of the mob. He plays on them as a musician on an instrument. The subtle changes of his speech, from praise of the conspirators—harmonising himself with the impression Brutus has made on the crowd—to praise of Caesar, dropping the first as he feels his listeners coming into sympathy with the second; his personal grief for Caesar breaking forth into tears that win him the sympathy of the people, and finally impassionate them into love of Caesar; his careful, reiterated appeal to their curiosity by his reserve with regard to Caesar's will till he has lashed them into insatiable eagerness; his final appeal to their hatred of ingratitude, the vice the people have always hated most; his exhibition of the dead body to their eyes: "Look, look and pity"—are one and all most masterly, and, as we read, it is finally the mighty intelligence of Shakespeare that impresses us more than even the mighty events of the history. The last appeal, with its fascinating touch of narrative—with its linking of each separate wound to the name of a conspirator—is full of a splendid knowledge of the way to excite a people:—

> If you have tears, prepare to shed them now.

Then comes that astonishing scene, in which Antony lashes the excitement of the mob into fury, in which we seem to see and hear the tumult growing, swelling, raging, till the Forum roars; till all Rome is so filled with madness of wrath that the mob slays Cinna the poet because he bears the name of Cinna the conspirator;—and Antony, left alone, while the mob rush forth to burn and slay, caps it all with triumphant cynicism—

> Now, let it work. Mischief, thou art afoot,
> Take thou what course thou wilt.

The rest, the fourth and fifth Acts of the play, are concerned with the fall of Brutus and the conspirators. The interest lessens slowly but steadily, till it dies away almost altogether in the fifth Act. It is only the interest of a death-bed; of the last and convulsive effort of Roman Republicanism, wounded to the death by the slaying of Caesar, to live again.

[. . .]

NOTE

1. There have been many men like Brutus whose aims were pure of self in the struggle of Ireland and in that of the working class, but there have been only too many who played the part of Cassius, Casca, and the rest.

"Letter from Birmingham Jail" (Martin Luther King, Jr.)

"The American Dream Unfulfilled: Martin Luther King, Jr. and the 'Letter from Birmingham Jail'"
by James A. Colaiaco, in *Phylon* (1984)

Introduction

In his essay on Martin Luther King, Jr.'s "Letter from Birmingham Jail," James Colaiaco provides "an exposition of [King's] philosophy of nonviolent direct action, especially civil disobedience. The idea of civil disobedience raised for King a fundamental philosophical issue: Are there any limits to the obedience which a citizen owes to the State? Put another way: Is a citizen under an absolute obligation to obey a law that he believes to be unjust?" With these questions, Colaiaco honors the fallen civil rights leader, whose acts brought about change and whose words so eloquently justified the nonviolent civil disobedience for which he is known.

Behold, here cometh the dreamer.
Let us slay him

Colaiaco, James A. "The American Dream Unfulfilled: Martin Luther King, Jr. and the 'Letter from Birmingham Jail.'" Phylon 45.1 (1984): 1–18.

> And we shall see what will become of his dreams.
>
> *Genesis* 37: 10–20

The spring of 1963 witnessed the publication of one of the most significant documents in the history of the American civil rights movement: Martin Luther King, Jr.'s "Letter From Birmingham Jail."[1] Few works of prose equal the letter in eloquence or moral force. It has been compared with Lincoln's Gettysburg Address, Emile Zola's letter in defense of Dreyfus, and John F. Kennedy's Inaugural Address. Among King's writings, only his "I Have A Dream" speech, delivered in the nation's capital on August 28, 1963, has received more acclaim.

Like many great political documents, the "Letter From Birmingham Jail" was composed during a time of crisis. Throughout April and May, 1963, national attention was focused on Birmingham, Alabama as King and his followers led a series of demonstrations that resulted in the overthrow of the city's segregation ordinances.[2] King's campaign of nonviolent direct action was a far-reaching success. The events in Birmingham proved to be a turning point in the battle for civil rights, after which the forces of segregation in the South began to crumble. Birmingham aroused the nation's conscience by exposing the evils of racism. While the demonstrators remained committed to nonviolence, millions of Americans were shocked by scenes on television and in the press of city police, led by commissioner Eugene "Bull" Conner, subjecting blacks to night sticks, high-pressure fire hoses, and fierce attack dogs. In the midst of the campaign, King was arrested for violating a state court injunction forbidding demonstrations. It was the thirteenth time that he had been jailed for defending civil rights. Placed in solitary confinement, King feared that the campaign would be defeated. But only briefly. Summoning up great courage, he secretly wrote his famous letter, a compelling statement of his philosophy of nonviolent direct action, and an eloquent presentation of his dream of justice and equality for black Americans.

Not only is the "Letter From Birmingham Jail" the best exposition of King's method and goals, but it also exerted great influence in winning broad support for the civil rights movement. As King asserted in an interview with Alex Haley in 1965: "The letter helped to focus greater international attention upon what was happening in Birmingham."[3] And it was this worldwide attention that furthered the civil rights cause. King continued: "And I am sure that without Birmingham, the march on Washington wouldn't have been called—which in my mind was one of the most creative steps the negro struggle has taken. . . . It was also the image of Birmingham which, to a great extent, helped to bring the Civil Rights Bill into being in 1963."[4] Because the letter is such a powerful expression of King's views, and because it articulates the aspirations of blacks in the 1960's better than any other document, it is fitting that today, more than twenty years later, we recall the circumstances of its composition, and analyze its contents.

The "Letter From Birmingham Jail" was written in response to "An Appeal for Law and Order and Common Sense," published by eight white Alabama clergymen in the *Birmingham News*, charging that the recent direct actions in the city had been "unwise and untimely."[5] Referring to "some of our Negro citizens, directed and led in part by outsiders," the clergymen urged blacks to withdraw their support from the demonstrations. As the leading "outsider," the statement was clearly directed at Martin Luther King, Jr.

When King saw the published statement, his first inclination may have been not to respond. He said that if he were to answer every criticism of his work and ideas, his secretaries would be overburdened by the correspondence, and he would have "no time for constructive work."[6] But because the criticism came from fellow clergymen—of the Protestant, Catholic and Jewish faiths—King realized that even sincere people of good will might misunderstand him and the civil rights movement. Moreover, with widespread attention aroused by the events in Birmingham, he saw the value in presenting his case to the entire nation. Sensing that the future of the American civil rights movement largely depended upon the success of the cause in Birmingham, King decided to respond immediately, in the form of an open letter. There could be no thought of waiting until after the turmoil of the day had subsided, when he could return to the comfortable confines of his study. The letter—a synthesis of ideas he had been developing for several years in speeches and articles—was begun in the margins of the newspaper in which the statement appeared, continued on scraps of paper, and concluded on a pad furnished by his attorneys. The completed letter, approximately 7000 words in length, was then smuggled out of jail. Polished for publication, the "Letter From Birmingham Jail" was first issued as a pamphlet in 1963. It soon appeared in several national periodicals, and it is estimated that nearly a million copies were circulated in churches throughout the land.

As King prepared to begin his letter, dated April 16, 1963, he was mindful of the slow and often frustrating progress of the American civil rights movement. In 1954, the United States Supreme Court issued its historic decision in *Brown v. Board of Education*. Yet, nine years later, the Southern states continued to defy the law forbidding segregation in the public schools. In 1955, King had been thrust suddenly into national prominence as the young Baptist pastor who organized a successful massive boycott of the segregated Montgomery, Alabama bus system. Two years later, in 1957, he was elected president of the Southern Christian Leadership Conference (SCLC), a newly founded organization dedicated to bringing justice and equality to black people. In 1960, thousands of students participated in sit-ins to protest segregated public facilities throughout the South. The following year, courageous freedom riders, mobilized by the Congress of Racial Equality (CORE), risked their lives to integrate bus stations in Mississippi and Alabama. In 1962, King and the SCLC suffered a temporary setback as poor planning contributed to the failure of the campaign to desegregate Albany, Georgia. The same year saw James Meredith become the first black student to enroll in the University of Mississippi. In 1963, as the nation prepared to celebrate the centenary of President Abraham Lincoln's Emancipation proclamation, King was sadly aware that black Americans were still deprived of fundamental human rights. As long as the Southern states continued to oppose the full integration of blacks into society, as long as blacks throughout the nation were denied justice and equality, the dream embodied in America's Declaration of Independence and the Constitution would remain unfulfilled.

The recent events in Birmingham also undoubtedly were fixed in King's mind as he contemplated how to respond to his critics. The direct-action campaign had been conceived in January 1963, when King pledged in a speech that he and his followers would not cease in their efforts until "Pharaoh lets God's people go."[7] That same month, George Wallace, having received the largest popular vote in Alabama gubernatorial history, made an inauguration vow of "segregation now, segregation tomorrow, segregation forever."[8] The Birmingham campaign (called "Project C"—the "C" stood for confrontation) was formally launched on April 3 with the issuance by King and his aides of the "Birmingham Manifesto," a review of the deplorable circum-stances that made the upcoming direct action necessary.[9] After a few days of sit-ins, on April 6, a group of demonstrators was taken away peacefully by police after they had marched on City Hall. Eugene "Bull" Conner then secured an injunction directing the demonstrators to discontinue their activities. For the first time, King would violate a court order. In consultation with his staff, he decided that he would be one of the first to set the example of civil disobedience.[10] On Good Friday, April 12, nearly a thousand blacks lined the streets as King and the Reverend Ralph Abernathy led a small group of protesters towards downtown Birmingham. After marching eight blocks, they were arrested and escorted to jail as a crowd of supporters sang "We Shall Overcome." In solitary confinement, King would now devote himself to composing his "Letter From Birmingham Jail."

From the outset, King realized that his letter had to address several important questions: As an Atlanta resident, what right did he have to organize a direct-action campaign in Birmingham? What does nonviolent civil disobedience entail? Does civil disobedience stem from a coherent philosophy? Is it moral for blacks to disobey laws? Does civil disobedience breed anarchy? Why should black Americans not continue to wait patiently for civil rights? Is King an extremist? If he could answer these questions effectively, King would defuse much of the criticism of himself and his methods, and increase support for the civil rights movement throughout the United States.

King begins his letter by meeting the charge that he is an intruder. He reminds his readers that he is president of the Southern Christian Leadership Conference, which has affiliates throughout the South. He informs them that several months earlier, the Alabama Christian Movement for Human Rights, an affiliate of the SCLC headed by the Reverend Fred Shuttlesworth, had invited him to Birmingham to participate in nonviolent efforts to secure equal rights for blacks. Thus King is in Birmingham by affiliation and by invitation.

Yet there is a more fundamental reason for King's presence in Birmingham in the spring of 1963. He feels a moral obligation to oppose the city's segregation practices. "More basically, I am in Birmingham because injustice is here."[11] Employing metaphors of particular significance to fellow clergymen, King compares himself with the Old and New Testament prophets who left their villages to carry the word of God to the world. He points to the example of St. Paul, who left Tarsus to carry the gospel of Jesus Christ to the Greco-Roman world. The comparison with St. Paul is even more apt than

King suggests. King's letter, written in a jail cell, calls to mind that Paul composed some of his great epistles to his disciples while he was imprisoned in Rome. King professes that he too must carry a gospel beyond his home town—the gospel of freedom. Convinced of "the interrelatedness of all communities and states," he proclaims: "I cannot sit idly by in Atlanta and not be concerned about what happens in Birmingham." King clinches his argument: "Injustice anywhere is a threat to justice everywhere."[12]

Having refuted the charge that he is an intruding agitator, King transcends the immediate criticisms of his recent activities and launches into the most important part of his letter: an exposition of his philosophy of nonviolent direct action, especially civil disobedience. The idea of civil disobedience raised for King a fundamental philosophical issue: Are there any limits to the obedience which a citizen owes to the State? Put another way: Is a citizen under an absolute obligation to obey a law that he believes to be unjust? Such questions have long concerned man, and continue to preoccupy us today in the 1980s. The justification for civil disobedience is usually either the doctrine of a higher law or some theory of natural or human rights. The ancient Greek dramatist Sophocles immortalized Antigone, a young heroine who is sentenced to death after defying a law of her king that conflicted with higher divine law. Since the ancient Greeks, several philosophers, from Aquinas to John Locke, have recognized the right of the individual to disobey laws that are contrary to the eternal law of God. The American Founding Fathers brought forth a new nation on the basis of the natural right of civil disobedience. The nineteenth-century Abolitionists defied the fugitive slave laws on the grounds that they opposed the law of God. Henry David Thoreau practiced civil disobedience and wrote a classic essay on the subject. Mahatma Gandhi achieved worldwide fame for his nonviolent resistance to unjust laws, first in South Africa, then in his native India. Since the Second World War, the question of civil disobedience has become increasingly important in the United States. The civil rights movement, resistance to the Vietnam War, and, most recently, a series of anti-nuclear protests have emphasized the right of individuals to disobey laws that conflict with moral principles. The most outstanding example in the Western world of the effectiveness of mass civil disobedience is the American civil rights movement under its greatest leader, Martin Luther King, Jr.

King realized the importance of setting forth clearly and cogently his philosophy of non-violent direct action and civil disobedience. His critics must be made aware that the recent protests were not spontaneous acts of frustration, but the product of careful planning and a coherent set of principles. He states that there are four basic steps to a nonviolent campaign: (1) the collection of facts, to determine whether injustices exist; (2) negotiation; (3) self-purification; and (4) direct action, including boycotts, sit-ins, marches, and civil disobedience. Since publicity focuses mostly on the final step, King saw that it was necessary to show that direct action is the last resort, undertaken only after sufficient fact-gathering and attempts at negotiation have occurred, and only after the protesters have been dedicated to nonviolence. As King asserts, the demonstrations in Birmingham began only after the first three steps had been taken.

The first step, the collection of facts, is obviously important. No nonviolent protest movement can gain the support of public opinion, or claim that it represents the cause of justice, unless it has gathered clear evidence of injustice. As King observes, the record of racial injustice in Birmingham was blatant and well-known. Birmingham was probably the most segregated city in the United States. Blacks had been treated unjustly in the courts, and their homes and churches frequently had been bombed with impunity. In September 1962, after a successful boycott of Birmingham's downtown stores, civil rights activists, led by the Reverend Fred Shuttlesworth, began negotiations with members of the economic community. After promises were made by the merchants that they would remove their offensive Jim Crow signs and cooperate in efforts to integrate the city's eating facilities, the civil rights leaders agreed to halt all demonstrations. But the blacks soon faced the grim reality that they had been the victims of false promises. The majority of the signs remained; the segregationist policies continued.[13]

King explains that negotiations proving fruitless, the blacks had no alternative but to begin a campaign of nonviolent direct action. But before protests could begin, a process of "self-purification" was necessary to prepare the demonstrators for the trials ahead. Purification was essential to the success of a nonviolent campaign. Unless protesters were purged of all feelings of bitterness towards their oppressors, unless they were prepared to love their enemies, unless they were willing to suffer both verbal and physical abuse without retaliating, their movement would degenerate into violence. As King reveals: "We repeatedly asked ourselves: 'Are you able to accept blows without retaliating?' 'Are you able to endure the ordeal of jail?'"[14] King was convinced that no matter how extreme the provocation, violence is immoral. Moreover, he maintained that the end never justifies the means. As he declared near the conclusion of his letter: "Over the past few years I have consistently preached that nonviolence demands that the means we use must be as pure as the ends we seek. I have tried to make clear that it is wrong to use immoral means to attain moral ends."[15] King believed that it is impossible to achieve a moral end by immoral means without harming the soul and making oneself unworthy of the end.

As King wrote about nonviolence, he no doubt recalled the numerous instances in which civil rights activists had maintained their courage and discipline and responded to their oppressors with love. The wave of student sit-ins that swept the South in 1960 demonstrated to the nation that racist oppression could be resisted nonviolently. One year later, freedom riders set a moral example when they willingly endured the suffering of savage beatings while attempting to integrate peacefully bus stations in Anniston, Birmingham, and Montgomery, Alabama. Inspired by examples such as these, prospective demonstrators for the Birmingham campaign in 1963 had to pass stringent tests before being permitted to join King's ranks. After being carefully selected, volunteers were prepared by attending nonviolent workshops in which they listened to sermons on nonviolence and participated in socio-dramas that simulated the challenges they would have to face. Moreover, volunteers had to sign a "commitment card," pledging adherence to the Ten Commandments of the nonviolent movement. The first required that volunteers "meditate daily on the teachings and life of Jesus;" the fifth, that they "walk and talk in the manner of love, for God is love;" the eighth, that they "refrain from the violence of fist, tongue, or heart."[16] Only after instilling such discipline could King be confident that his direct-action campaign would adhere to nonviolence.

King's philosophy of nonviolence was a synthesis of the teachings of Jesus Christ and Mahatma Gandhi. While Jesus provided the motivating ideal of love, Gandhi provided the method of mass nonviolent direct action. King first became interested in Gandhi when, as a young student at Crozer Theological Seminary, he travelled to

Philadelphia to attend a lecture on the Indian leader by Mordecai W. Johnson, then president of Howard University, who had recently returned from a trip to India. At this time, King was engaged in a quest for a method to eliminate social evil. He was deeply impressed by Gandhi's famous Salt March to the Sea, and by his nonviolent methods—boycotts, strikes, marches, and mass civil disobedience.[17] He was also struck by Gandhi's concept of *Satyagraha*, or Soul Force, as an instrument for overcoming evil. Although committed to the love ethic of Jesus, King was for a time unsure of how such love could be employed to solve social problems. He was aware that some people interpreted Christianity to mean passive nonresistance to evil. Yet if this were the correct view of Christ's teaching, a solution to the problem of racial injustice was hopeless. Moreover, King believed that to accept passively an unjust system is to cooperate with the evil of that system. His study of Gandhi convinced him that Christianity did not mean nonresistance to evil, but nonviolent resistance to evil. The Christian can resist evil vigorously, but with nonviolence and love rather than violence and hate. Nevertheless, not until the Montgomery bus boycott of 1955–56 did King perceive the applicability of Gandhi's method of mass nonviolent resistance to the American civil rights cause. Henceforth, he would embrace nonviolence not as a mere tactic, but as a philosophy of life. King's devotion to Gandhi was deepened by a trip to India with his wife Coretta in 1959 as the special guests of Prime Minister Nehru. King had an opportunity to study with some of Gandhi's disciples and to pay tribute to the late Indian leader. Arriving in New Delhi, he told a throng of reporters that he came not as a tourist, but as a pilgrim.

King was aware that the tactic of nonviolent direct action involves an inherent paradox. Although he believed that violence is immoral, his nonviolent methods were most successful when they provoked violence from oppressors. King and his followers always hoped to achieve their goals without becoming the victims of violence. But because the racist community was usually unyielding, civil rights activists found that when they used soul force, they were often met by physical force. Segregationists charged that the protesters should be blamed because they provoked the violence. Until the protesters began their activities, the segregationists lamented, peace reigned in the community. They contended that the protesters deserved to be beaten and arrested because their actions precipitated violence and destroyed law and order. But this argument rests on the dangerous assumption that the lack of conflict in a community is evidence of the presence of justice.

[...]

King understood that to say that one ought to obey just laws and disobey unjust laws merely begs the question of how one distinguishes between the two. For an answer, he is compelled to seek an authority that transcends the State. Since civil disobedients cannot look to the State to tell them whether its laws are just or not, King relies upon the rich Western tradition of natural law. The philosophy of natural law has a twenty-five hundred year history. It refers to moral principles, found innately in the human conscience, that originate in God and exist independently of the State. Since the State is sovereign, all its laws are "legal." Yet, throughout history, civil disobedients have recognized that civil law is not always just, and that human beings must be able to appeal to a higher law—divine or natural law—whenever a command of the State conflicts with their moral principles. Natural law is, therefore, King's guide. "A just law is a man-made code that squares with the moral law or the law of God. An unjust law is a code that is out of harmony with the moral law."[18] King finds support in one of the greatest Christian philosophers: "To put it in the terms of St. Thomas Aquinas: An unjust law is a human law that is not rooted in eternal law and natural law."[19] King reminds those who tend to regard civil law as sacrosanct that the early Christians disobeyed laws that were contrary to their conscience; moreover, the Boston Tea Party was "a massive act of civil disobedience." On the other hand, the actions of Adolf Hitler were perfectly "legal" though morally reprehensible.[20]

[...]

King was careful not to offend his fellow clergymen unduly. To stir their slumbering consciences was sufficient. Indeed, he hoped to stir the consciences of millions of professed Christians throughout the nation. He expresses heartfelt thanks to those who acted independently of organized religion and joined "the struggle for freedom." Maintaining a conciliatory tone, King also insists that although he wept over the laxity of the church, his disappointment stems from deep love: "Yes, I love the church. How could I do otherwise? I am in the rather unique position of being the son, the grandson and the great-grandson of preachers. Yes, I see the church as the body of Christ. But oh! How we have blemished and scarred that body through social neglect and through fear of being nonconformists."[21] The gospel of individual salvation must be supplemented by a social gospel. King reminds his readers that the early Christians were champions for the cause of humanity and justice. He warns that unless the church returns to its original sacrificial spirit, "it will lose its authenticity, forfeit the loyalty of millions, and be dismissed as an irrelevant social club with no meaning for the twentieth century."[22]

As King nears the conclusion of his letter, he injects a note of optimism into his message. Not only is the letter an exposition of his philosophy, but it is intended also to inspire his supporters to continue their efforts in the civil rights cause. He therefore expresses confidence that ultimately they will be victorious:

> I have no despair about the future. I have no fear about the outcome of our struggle in Birmingham, even if our motives are at present misunderstood. We will reach the goal of freedom in Birmingham and all over the nation, because the goal of America is freedom. Abused and scorned though we may be, our destiny is tied up with America's destiny. Before the pilgrims landed at Plymouth, we were here. Before the pen of Jefferson etched the majestic words of the Declaration of Independence across the pages of history, we were here. For more than two centuries our forefathers labored in this country without wages; they made cotton king; they built the homes of their masters while suffering gross injustice and shameful humiliation—and yet out of a bottomless vitality they continued to thrive and develop. If the inexpressible cruelties of slavery could not stop us, the opposition we now face will surely fail. We will win our freedom because the sacred heritage of our nation and the eternal will of God are embodied in our echoing demands.[23]

By connecting the victory of the civil rights cause to the destiny of America, King is appealing to the conscience of the nation by underscoring what Gunnar Myrdal described in 1944 as the "American Dilemma"—the conflict between our devotion to the American creed of democracy and our actual practice. Indeed, a nation that took pride in its heritage of freedom, and yet denied fundamental human rights to a race that had played so great a role in its history, was certainly confronted by a dilemma. A nation that took pride in itself as a haven for the homeless and the oppressed, and yet allowed so many of its citizens to languish in miserable poverty, has much for which to be ashamed. King no doubt was struck by the irony in the fact that while America was defending the cause of freedom throughout the world, she was denying it to twenty million citizens at home.

Before closing, King pays a final tribute to all those who have sacrificed for the cause of justice. Anticipating his "I Have A Dream" speech of a few months later, King—stressing again a major theme of his letter—links the success of the civil rights movement to the fulfillment of the American dream:

> One day the South will recognize its real heroes. They will be the James Merediths, with the noble sense of purpose that enables them to face jeering and hostile mobs, and with the agonizing loneliness that characterizes the life of the pioneer. They will be old, oppressed, battered Negro women, symbolized in a seventy-two-year-old woman in Montgomery, Alabama, who rose up with a sense of dignity and with her people decided not to ride segregated buses, and who responded with ungrammatical profundity to one who inquired about her weariness: "My feets is tired, but my soul is at rest." They will be the young high school and college students, the young ministers of the gospel and a host of their elders, courageously and nonviolently sitting in at lunch counters and willingly going to jail for conscience sake. One day the South will know that when these disinherited children of God sat down at lunch counters, they were in reality standing up for what is best in the American dream and for the most sacred values in our Judaeo-Christian heritage, thereby bringing our nation back to those great wells of democracy which were dug deep by the founding fathers in their formulation of the Constitution and Declaration of Independence.[24]

When Martin Luther King, Jr. put down his pen in April 1963, he had composed the manifesto of the American civil rights movement. The "Letter From Birmingham Jail" is the most eloquent and effective statement of King's philosophy, methods and goals. He had presented his dream of justice and equality for the black Americans. He had expounded his philosophy of nonviolent direct action. He had demonstrated that the decision of blacks to disobey unjust segregation laws is founded upon natural law. He had shown that civil disobedience does not create anarchy because the civil disobedients, in an effort to awaken the conscience of the community, are willing to accept the penalty of imprisonment for disobeying those laws that they believe are unjust. He had explained that blacks cannot and will not continue to wait for the granting of their fundamental human rights. He had answered the charge of extremism by showing that his actions were consistent with a great heritage of men who have been willing to sacrifice their lives for liberty and justice. In an appeal to the nation, King had proclaimed that the achievement of civil rights for blacks was necessary for the nation to fulfill the promise embodied in the American dream.

Martin Luther King, Jr.'s method of nonviolent direct action was ultimately victorious in Birmingham. But not without weeks of further struggle. On April 20, 1963, King and Ralph Abernathy were released on bond after eight days in jail. Tried and convicted of criminal contempt a few days later, they appealed and remained free on bond pending the final disposition of their case. Throughout the first week of May, the protests continued and were met by increasing police brutality. On May 2, the nation was stunned when almost a thousand children were arrested as they marched peacefully towards downtown Birmingham to the strains of "We Shall Overcome." The protesters stepped up their pace. Eventually, nearly three thousand were imprisoned as they proceeded to flood the city's business district. Finally, on May 7, a truce was called by Birmingham's business leaders. The direct action had crippled the city's economy and marshaled the public opinion of the nation behind the protesters. King's method had been vindicated; nonviolent direct action had led to negotiation. On May 10, an accord was reached that met essentially all of the blacks' demands. The city's eating facilities would be desegregated; and blacks would be hired by business and industry. Though the white establishment would later fail to fulfill its promises completely, the profound effect of the Birmingham demonstrations on the national conscience and on subsequent federal legislation cannot be denied. On the night following the accord, King flew home to Atlanta. He wanted to be with his family; he also planned to preach at his family's Ebenezer Baptist Church.

Yet King's visit home would be unexpectedly brief. On the night of his arrival in Atlanta, the accord was endangered as discontented whites bombed King's Birmingham headquarters and the home of his brother. Civil rights leaders feared that they had again been victims of false promises. To King's distress, many young blacks, no longer able to contain their frustration, resorted to rioting. Rushing back to Birmingham, his presence in the streets helped to curtail further violence. Tensions ultimately subsided after President John F. Kennedy publicly praised the justness of the cause of Birmingham's blacks, and declared that the federal government would guarantee the accord. The next few weeks saw more victories for King and the civil rights movement. On May 20, 1963, the United States Supreme Court finally ruled that Alabama's segregation laws were unconstitutional. Then, on June 11, President Kennedy announced to the nation that he was requesting Congress to enact a comprehensive Civil Rights Bill. In a nationally televised address, the President—in words echoing those of King—proclaimed: "Now the time has come for this nation to fulfill its promise. The events in Birmingham and elsewhere have so increased the cries for equality that no city or state or legislative body can prudently choose to ignore them."[25]

King died without his dream becoming a reality. When he was cut down by an assassin's bullet in Memphis on April 4, 1968, America had only begun to fulfill its promise. Since his death, blacks have taken important strides towards freedom and equality, but much remains to be done.

Martin Luther King, Jr. has left an enduring legacy. King's genius lay in his extraordinary vision. His was a vision of an America true to the sacred ideals of liberty, justice, and equality embodied in the Declaration of Independence and the Constitution. His was a vision of an America that fulfilled the promise of these ideals for all people, black and white alike. In the last years of his life, as King became involved in the campaign to combat poverty, he was a symbol for all the poor and downtrodden of the nation. As he ventured into the peace movement with public statements condemning the war in Vietnam, he became a leader in the cause of international justice and brotherhood. Yet King's greatest contribution was that he provided charismatic leadership to a civil rights movement that ranks in the annals of history as one of humanity's supreme accomplishments.

The night before he died, Martin Luther King, Jr. delivered a speech that concluded with the following prophetic words:

We've got some difficult days ahead. But it doesn't matter with me now. Because I've been to the mountain-top. And I don't mind. Like anybody, I would like to live a long life. Longevity has its place. But I'm not concerned about that now. I just want to do God's will. And He's allowed me to go to the mountain. And I've looked over. And I've seen the promised land. I may not get there with you. But I want you to know tonight, that we, as a people will get to the promised land. And I'm happy tonight. I'm not worried about anything. I'm not fearing any man. Mine eyes have seen the glory of the coming of the Lord.[26]

The dreamer is dead. It is for us, the living, to determine what will become of his dream.

NOTES

1. Quotations from the "Letter From Birmingham Jail" are taken from the book, *Why We Can't Wait* by Martin Luther King, Jr. Copyright? 1963, 1964 by Martin Luther King, Jr. Reprinted with permission of Harper and Row, Publishers, Inc.

2. For the narrative of the events in Birmingham, see the following: King, *Why We Can't Wait*; David L. Lewis, *King: A Biography* (2nd ed., Urbana, 1978); and Stephen B. Oates, *Let The Trumpet Sound: The Life of Martin Luther King, Jr.* (New York, 1982).

3. *The Playboy Interview*, edited by G. Barry Golson, (Wideview Books, 1981), pp. 118–19.

4. Ibid., pp. 118–19.

5. King, *Why We Can't Wait*, p. 77.

6. Ibid.

7. Oates, *Let The Trumpet Sound*, p. 213.

8. Ibid., p. 222.

9. Ibid., p. 216

10. King, *Why We Can't Wait*, p. 69.

11. Ibid., p. 78.

12. Ibid., pp. 78–79.

13. Ibid., pp. 45–47.

14. Ibid., p. 80.

15. Ibid., p. 98.

16. Ibid., p. 61.
17. For the influence of Gandhi on King, see King, *Stride Toward Freedom: The Montgomery Story* (New York, 1958), pp. 84–5; 96–8; 103; 217–18.
18. King, *Why We Can't Wait*, p. 85.
19. Ibid.
20. Ibid., p. 87.
21. Ibid., p. 95.
22. Ibid., p. 96.
23. Ibid., pp. 97–8.
24. Ibid., p. 99.
25. Lewis, op. cit., p. 209.
26. Flip Schulke, *Martin Luther King, Jr.: A Documentary . . . Montgomery To Memphis* (New York, 1976), Speeches and Sermons, "I've Been To The Mountaintop," p. 224.

THE SPEECHES OF MALCOLM X

"Rhetorical Resistance and the Conscience of the World: Civil Disobedience in the Speeches of Malcolm X"
by John Becker, independent scholar

A captivating orator and leader of the Black Nationalist movement, Malcolm X was one of the most famous and infamous figures in the struggle for civil rights in America during the 1960s. Speaking from the margins of the civil rights movement, either as the official spokesperson for Elijah Muhammad and his church, the Nation of Islam, or as the head of his own secular political organization, the Organization for Afro-American Unity, Malcolm stirred audiences with his controversial statements about race and political activism. Launching vitriolic critiques of the U.S. government and the civil rights movement led by Dr. Martin Luther King, Jr., Malcolm was uncompromising in his scathing judgment of institutions and ways of thinking that, in his opinion, held African Americans in bondage—psychologically, economically, and physically. Opposed to any sort of premature appeasement and wary of any course of action that would allow the oppressors of blacks to dictate how they should conduct their struggle for equal rights and political representation, Malcolm appealed to the angriest and most disenfranchised victims of racial injustice. His life, as recorded by Alex Haley in *The Autobiography of Malcolm X* (1965), was plagued by prejudice and marked by radical change. From street hustler to devout Muslim, from incarceration to international media fame, from staunch separatist to human rights advocate, Malcolm was a truly protean figure, capable of transforming himself according to the dictates of his conscience regardless of what had come before.

In many ways, his legacy of public addresses shares this protean quality. While many of Malcolm's statements reinforce his public image as an advocate of violent, revolutionary upheaval and racial separatism—an image that has been appropriated by militant groups like the Black Panthers and the predominantly socialist commentators and editors who have reprinted his speeches—many of his statements make this image problematic. The mainstream media's representations of Malcolm during his lifetime, starting with Mike Wallace's television special, *The Hate That Hate Produced* (1959), have undoubtedly helped disseminate a similarly simplistic and reductive portrait. But such caricatures do not reflect the variety of positions Malcolm held during the course of his political career, nor do they seriously consider the form of resistance Malcolm chose to employ. One of Malcolm's many commentators, Michael Eric Dyson, provides insight into this method as he recounts the formative influence of Malcolm X and Martin Luther King on his intellectual life:

> King's death and Malcolm's life forced me to grapple with the best remedy for resisting racism.
>
> As a result, I turned more frequently to a means of communication and combat that King and Malcolm had favored and that had been nurtured in me by my experience in the black church: rhetorical resistance. In African-American cultures, acts of rhetorical resistance are often more than mere words. They encompass a complex set of symbolic expressions and oral interactions with the "real" world. These expressions and interactions are usually supported by substantive black cultural traditions—from religious worship to social protest—that fuse speech and performance. (15–16)

Thus, for Dyson, Malcolm's rhetorical strategies not only prescribe specific courses of action, but also demonstrate the type of resistance Malcolm advocated. In his speeches, Malcolm often spoke about violent acts. Because of this, many have assumed Malcolm condoned violence. To further complicate the issue, his speeches advocate civil disobedience under specific conditions and also critique civil disobedi-ence and passive resistance as methods of political reform. In the end, Malcolm offers a "broader interpretation" of the civil rights movement and the means of resistance at its disposal ("The Ballot" 31).

At first glance, Malcolm X seems to oppose the strategies of civil disobedience used by Martin Luther King and his supporters. On many occasions, Malcolm specifically denigrated and belittled the "nonviolent direct action" of leaders like King, whom he describes in his "Message to the Grass Roots" as submissive and complicit "Uncle Toms":

> Just as the slavemaster [of the past] used Tom, the house Negro, to keep the field Negroes in check, the same old slavemaster today has Negroes who are nothing but modern Uncle Toms, twentieth-century Uncle Toms, to keep you and me in check, to keep us under control, keep us passive and peaceful and nonviolent. ("Message" 12)

Such inflammatory statements typify Malcolm, especially during his tenure as spokesman for the Nation of Islam, a religious organiza-tion that advocated racial separatism and demonized whites. For Malcolm, civil rights leaders like King were "not a part of the Negro revolution" because they were teaching oppressed blacks to refrain from defending themselves ("Message" 13). Such a strategy might ultimately have been the only way for a black minority of twenty-two million citizens to resist and change the unjust policies of a white majority. But Malcolm refuses to rule out more drastic measures. In this same speech, Malcolm cites Mao's revolution in China, the Mau Mau uprising in Kenya, as well as the Algerian struggle for indepen-dence as proof that revolution is necessarily violent (8–9). He then prescribes revolutionary action for oppressed blacks: "And you, sitting around here like a knot on the wall, saying, 'I'm going to love these folks no matter how much they hate me.' No, you need a revolution" (9). At other times, Malcolm seems to condone violence solely as a means self-defense, extolling the moral code of the Koran: "Our reli-gion teaches us to be intelligent. Be peaceful, be courteous, obey the law, respect everyone; but if someone puts his hand on you, send him to the cemetery" (12). These contradictions beg the question: What qualifies as revolutionary action?

Malcolm marshals acts of civil disobedience in the same speech to illustrate what he calls "the black revolution":

> [President Kennedy] said he was going to put out a civil-rights bill. And when he mentioned the civil-rights bill and the Southern crackers started talking about how they were going to boycott or filibuster it, then the Negroes started talking—about what? That they were going to march on Washington, march on the Senate, march on the White House, march on the Congress, and tie it up, bring it to a halt, not let the government proceed. They even said they were going out to the airport and lay down on the runway and not let any planes land. I'm telling you what they said. That was revolution. That was revolution. That was the black revolution. ("Message" 14)

These acts, applauded by Malcolm for their revolutionary character, differ in magnitude but not in kind from the nonviolent protests led by Martin Luther King, Jr. and other civil rights leaders. The distinction between the revolution he champions and the strategies of civil disobedience employed by King is difficult to discern. In his speech "The Black Revolution," delivered six months after "Message to the Grass Roots," Malcolm concludes that though the history of revolutions is animated by violence and bloodshed, America is in the unique position of being "the first country on this earth that can actually have a bloodless revolution" ("Black Revolution" 56). Such a revolution can only be accomplished, according to Malcolm, if " . . . the black man [is] given full use of the ballot in every one of the fifty states" (57). This "bloodless revolution" of the ballot "would wipe out the Southern segregationism that now controls America's foreign policy, as well as America's domestic policy" (57).

In another speech from this period, "At the Audubon," Malcolm prescribes a strategy for participation in the democratic process that might effectively empower African Americans. By not registering with any particular party, Malcolm claims that politicians will try to placate blacks and treat them as a politically relevant voting bloc:

> "Register" means being in a position to take political action any time, any place and in any manner that would be beneficial to you and me; being in a position to take advantage of our position. Then we'll be in a position to be respected and

recognized. But as soon as you get registered, and you want to be a Democrat or a Republican, you are aligning. And once you are aligning, you have no bargaining power—none whatsoever. . . . [By] being registered as independents, it means we can do whatever is necessary, wherever it's necessary, and whenever the time comes. ("Audubon" 133)

Such a strategy is but one example of what Malcolm, in his landmark speech "The Ballot or the Bullet," calls a "politically mature" understanding of how voting can be used to enact revolutionary change (30). This call for shrewd civic participation seems to preclude violent revolutionary action, though Malcolm always maintains that the failure of such strategies justifies using the "bullet."

Thus, Malcolm endorses at various times the full spectrum of responses available to oppressed blacks, from the concerted use of political power, to nonviolent protest and civil disobedience, and, finally, to acts of violence—both defensive and, as his consistent use of examples of armed uprising implies, revolutionary.

This stance, captured by Malcolm's oft-repeated phrase "by any means necessary," seems to exclude him from what the majority of political philosophers and legal commentators consider to be an advocate of legitimate civil disobedience. Scholars such as Hugo Adam Bedau, John Rawls, and many others claim that "justifiable" civil disobedience is nonviolent by definition (Bedau 51). Rawls's influential definition of civil disobedience is as follows: "a public, nonviolent, conscientious yet political act contrary to law usually done with the aim of bringing about a change in the law or policies of the government" (Rawls 104). But such a definition, as well as the theories Rawls extrapolates from it, "[presupposes] that the majority has a sense of justice." Rawls anticipates such an objection:

> [. . . One] might reply that moral sentiments are not a significant political force. What moves men are various interests, the desires for power, prestige, wealth, and the like. Although they are clever at producing moral arguments to support their claims, between one situation and another their opinions do not fit into a coherent conception of justice. . . . Unquestionably there is much truth in this contention, and in some societies it is more true than in others." (Rawls 117).

Rawls ends up answering this objection by limiting his discussion to civil disobedience in societies where the "sense of justice" prevails over these baser motivations. In an ideal, or, as Rawls phrases it, a "nearly-just" State, acts of civil disobedience are attempts at persuasion that allow the disenfranchised to force a confrontation between a society's policies and its "sense of justice." But Malcolm did not consider the United States one of these "nearly-just" societies:

> Don't change the white man's mind—you can't change his mind, and that whole thing about appealing to the moral conscience of America—America's conscience is bankrupt. She lost all conscience a long time ago. . . . If [Uncle Sam] had a conscience, he'd straighten this thing out with no more pressure being put upon him. ("Ballot" 40)

If such a society refuses to respond favorably to methods of persuasion, Malcolm argues that the only recourse of the oppressed is coercion:

> They don't know what morals are. They don't try and eliminate an evil because it's evil, or because it's illegal, or because it's immoral; they eliminate it only when it threatens their existence. ("Ballot" 40)

In fact, some have argued that civil disobedience always involves varying degrees of coercion. Nonviolent mass protest seems to draw some of its persuasive power from its potential to turn violent. Additionally, armed revolt might be imminent if the demands of such a protest are not met. The political philosopher John Morreall notes how even the most benign examples of civil disobedience involve coercion:

> When a group of students (presumably justifiably) takes over an administration building in attempts to get certain policies changed which were not changed through rational appeals to the administration, they are usually attempting to get as large an audience as possible to listen to the rationality of their proposals. But this is not all they are doing, for they could get just as large an audience through completely legal means. They are also trying to apply pressure upon the administration, they

are adding the force of coercion to the reasonableness of their demands. (Morreall 137)

Howard Zinn, in *Disobedience and Democracy*, similarly rejects the claim that legitimate civil disobedience must be exclusively nonviolent. Zinn's thoughts on the subject are insightful:

> I would define civil disobedience more broadly, as "the deliberate violation of law for a vital social purpose."... [This] would leave open the question of the *means* of disobedience, but with two thoughts in mind: 1. That one of the moral principles guiding the advocate of civil disobedience is his belief that a nonviolent world is one of his ends, and that nonviolence is more desirable than violence as a means; 2. That in the inevitable tension accompanying the transition from a violent world to a nonviolent one, the choice of means will almost never be pure, and will involve such complexities that the simple distinction between violence and nonviolence does not suffice as a guide. (Zinn 40)

Insisting on the underlying "pragmatism" of even the most principled application of civil disobedience, Zinn quotes from the writings of its most nonviolent practitioner, Mohandas Gandhi. These statements are reminiscent of Malcolm's pronouncements throughout his political career:

> Gandhi himself wrote at certain times (1919 and 1921) in *Young India*: "No rules can tell us how this disobedience may be done and by whom, when and where, nor can they tell us which laws foster untruth. It is only experience that can guide us...." And: "I do believe that where there is only a choice between cowardice and violence I would advise violence." (Zinn 42)

The first statement is very similar to Malcolm's assertion that the "rules" of protest established by the leadership of the civil rights movement, designed to appease a government unable or unwilling to protect the rights of blacks, should not be heeded. For Malcolm, "the black revolution," if circumscribed and contained by white America, would be ineffectual.

The second quote of Gandhi's that Zinn uses to further his argument against the exclusively nonviolent nature of civil disobedience is also reflected in Malcolm's rhetoric, which saw little substantive change resulting from the nonviolent resistance of King and others. Such a strategy fostered the Civil Rights Act in 1964, but racist discrimination and segregationist violence continued. Malcolm, like Gandhi, when confronted with an "either/or" choice between ineffectual pacifism and violent action, favored the latter. But, as Zinn notes, such comments betray a "pragmatic" attitude toward social change, one where " . . . circumstances and results determine tactics" (Zinn 42). This pragmatic stance, where results and context have precedence over abstract principles, lies at the heart of what Malcolm saw as lacking in the civil rights movement. Malcolm describes this stance in a letter he wrote while completing his pilgrimage to Mecca:

> You may be shocked by these words coming from me. But on this pilgrimage, what I have seen, and experienced, has forced me to re-arrange much of my thought-patterns previously held, and to toss aside some of my previous conclusions. This was not too difficult for me. Despite my firm convictions, I have been always a man who tries to face facts, and to accept the reality of life as new experience and new knowledge unfolds it. I have always kept an open mind, which is necessary to the flexibility that must go hand in hand with every form of intelligent search for truth. ("Letters" 60)

Certainly, the variety of positions Malcolm takes in his speeches reflects the intellectual adaptability and willingness to change he so eloquently professes above.

In his late speech, "Not Just an American Problem, But a World Problem," Malcolm assumes the posture of an educator, one who gives his audience the tools to make autonomous moral and political judgments. Such a stance seems less myopic, less concerned with advancing a particular agenda than with cultivating independent thought and an awareness of the world beyond America's borders. Malcolm saw racism in a global context; this context, he hoped, would be beneficial to the civil rights struggle and its participants.

So I have to give you the background, in order for you to understand some of the current problems that are developing here on this earth. And in no time can you understand the problems between Black and white people here in Rochester or Black and white people in Mississippi or Black and white people in California, unless you understand the basic problem that exists between Black and white people not confined to the local level, but confined to the international, global level on this earth today. When you look at it in that context, you'll understand it. But if you only try and look at it in the local context, you'll never understand it. You have to see the trend that is taking place on this earth. And my purpose for coming here tonight is to try and give you as up-to-date an understanding of it as is possible. ("Not Just an American" 147)

Separatism rhetoric in Malcolm's speeches declines after his break with Elijah Muhammad, and is replaced in this speech by the pursuit of true "brotherhood." Malcolm's frames the argument in terms that appeal to a higher moral conscience, a secular conscience based on a global awareness of injustice and the common plight of the oppressed:

[… We] realize that we have to fight against the evils of a society that has failed to produce brotherhood for every member of that society. This in no way means that we're antiwhite, antiblue, antigreen, or antiyellow. We're antiwrong. We're antidiscrimination. We're antisegregation. We're against anybody who wants to practice some form of segregation or discrimination against us because we don't happen to be a color that's acceptable to you. We believe in fighting that. ("Not Just an American" 149)

Malcolm X was intimately involved in many political spheres—Nation of Islam separatism, Black Nationalism, and civil rights activism—as both advocate and critic. At times he leveled rhetorical attacks at the nonviolent strategy of civil disobedience pursued by King and Gandhi before him. What was the substance of these critiques? That African Americans would never have a political voice and be free from racial oppression as long as blacks answered segregationist violence with professions of Christian brotherly love and nonviolent protest. Blaming the federal government for the injustices of the Jim Crow South and the ghettoized North, Malcolm argues that the only way to get Washington to change is to bring the plight of African Americans before the United Nations. The struggle for civil rights, as Malcolm shrewdly notes in his later speeches, necessarily confines the struggle of African Americans to the domestic sphere. By simply restating the grievance, christening it a struggle for "human rights," Malcolm and the civil rights movement leadership could legitimately bring the issue before a governing body with a "higher authority," a body that might substitute for the moral conscience of America that King and others were having such difficulty appealing to. This appeal was both disobedient and civil: disobedient to the federal government, which tried to stop Malcolm from making an appearance at the Organization for African Unity; but civil since such an appeal was within the framework of international law that the United States had agreed to, at least in theory.

Though Malcolm preaches the importance of self-defense, calling for black men to form rifle clubs to stem endemic racial violence, he explicitly justifies such action in terms of the second amendment of the Constitution and the pursuit of civil rights. For Malcolm, the leadership of the civil rights movement was too prone to influence by the white liberal establishment, too quick to appease the white world to make any meaningful difference before the "powder keg" of race relations in the United States exploded ("Black Revolution" 48). These concerns proved to be valid: After the deaths of Malcolm and King, riots broke out across the country as blacks despaired over the tragic loss of their most dedicated advocates and the continuing climate of racial oppression and disenfranchisement. This explosion of civil disorder validated much of what Malcolm had to say.

What happens if you appeal to the conscience of your nation, its inner sense of justice and need for consistency before the law, and your efforts fail? This is the question that plagued Malcolm, the question he spent his political career trying to answer. At times he embraced the rhetoric of revolution and separatism; at other times he called for acts of mass protest and civil disobedience. Ultimately, the conscience Malcolm appealed to is not just the conscience of a nation, but of the world.

WORKS CITED AND CONSULTED

Arendt, Hannah. "Civil Disobedience." *Crises of the Republic*. New York: Harcourt Brace Jovanovich, 1972. 49–102.

Bedau, Hugo Adam, ed. *Civil Disobedience in Focus*. London: Routledge, 1991.

Bedau, Hugo Adam. "Civil Disobedience and Personal Responsibility." Bedau 49–67.

Cone, James H. *Martin & Malcolm & America: A Dream or a Nightmare*. Maryknoll, NY: Orbis Books, 1991.

Dyson, Michael Eric. *Making Malcolm: The Myth and Meaning of Malcolm X*. New York: Oxford University Press, 1995.

Malcolm X, with Alex Haley. *The Autobiography of Malcolm X*. New York: Grove Press, 1965.

Malcolm X. "At the Audubon." New York, 13 December 1964. *Malcolm X Speaks* 88–104.

———. "The Ballot or the Bullet." Cleveland, 3 April 1964. *Malcolm X Speaks* 23–44.

———. "The Black Revolution." New York, 8 April 1964. *Malcolm X Speaks* 45–57.

———. *By Any Means Necessary*. 1970. Edited by George Breitman. New York: Pathfinder Press, 1992.

———. *February 1965: The Final Speeches*. Edited by Steve Clark. New York: Pathfinder Press, 1992.

———. "Letters from Abroad." Jedda, Saudi Arabia, 20 April 1964. *Malcolm X Speaks* 58–60.

———. *Malcolm X Speaks: Selected Speeches and Statements*. 1965. Edited by George Breitman. New York: Pathfinder Press, 1989.

———. "Message to the Grass Roots." Detroit, 10 November 1963. *Malcolm X Speaks* 3–17.

———. "Not Just an American Problem, But a World Problem." Rochester, 16 February 1965. *February 1965: The Final Speeches* 143–70.

———. *Speeches at Harvard*. Edited by and introduction by Archie Epps. New York: Paragon House, 1991.

Morreall, John. "The Justifiability of Violent Civil Disobedience." Bedau 130–43.

Rawls, John. "Definition and Justification of Civil Disobedience." Bedau 103–21.

Terrill, Robert E. *Malcolm X: Inventing Radical Judgment*. East Lansing, MI: Michigan State University Press, 2004.

Zinn, Howard. *Disobedience and Democracy*. New York: Vintage, 1968.

NATIVE SON
(RICHARD WRIGHT)

"Richard Wright and Albert Camus:
The Literature of Revolt"
by Steven J. Rubin, in
International Fiction Review (1981)

INTRODUCTION

Steven J. Rubin focuses on personal revolt in Richard Wright's *Native Son* and Albert Camus' *The Stranger*, justifying the acts of civil disobedience that the two novels' protagonists perform. Ultimately, he finds that: "Although the motivating forces behind their actions differ, both protagonists conform to a similar pattern: alienation, a sense of frustration with conventional order and values, an accidental murder, a realization of the meaning of that murder in terms of their role in society, a separation (physical and emotional) from their world, and a final coming to terms with their individual fates." Thus, he concludes that both Bigger Thomas, the central character in *Native Son*, and Meursault, the central character in *The Stranger*, find peace within themselves by realizing that their "actions, although self-destructive, [are] the only

---

Rubin, Steven J. "Richard Wright and Albert Camus: The Literature of Revolt." *International Fiction Review* 8.1 (Winter 1981): 12–6.

possible responses to the series of injustices and irrationalities within [their] existence."

⤮

The early fiction of Richard Wright, comprised of short stories written
in the thirties and culminating in *Native Son* (1940), is primarily an
expression of personal outrage and frustration. Although Wright's
literary heritage has been traced to the American Naturalists,[1] recent
readings of his works suggest that Wright was not as confined by
that tradition as has generally been believed.[2] Working within the
framework of social protest, Wright probed other more metaphysical
issues, which were later to become of even greater importance to him.
In dramatizing the plight of each of his heroes, from Big Boy in "Big
Boy Leaves Home," to Bigger Thomas in *Native Son*, Wright explored
the motivating forces behind their actions. As their personal dramas
unfolded, he developed such themes as the possibility of freedom,
man's isolation and alienation, the inherent irrationality of modern
American society, and the nature and form of personal rebellion
within that society.

Native Son is, as Edward Margolies in *The Art of Richard Wright*
points out, as much a psychological novel with clear existential implications, as it is sociological.[3] Bigger Thomas is not only a Black man struggling against an oppressive white society, but also Wright's archetypal
rebel, desperately seeking recognition and meaning within a world that
has offered him none. Alienated from the mainstream of society and
betrayed by his own environment, Bigger, like Wright's earlier heroes,
searches for an effective means of vanquishing his personal sense of
worthlessness. Ironically, like the protagonists of *Uncle Tom's Children*,
Bigger's revolt is simultaneously victorious and self-destructive.

The literature of revolt is born from the recognition on the part of
many modern writers that meaning and purpose are not an integral
part of the universe in which man finds himself. *Native Son*, written at
a time when Wright was preoccupied with social issues, also represents
an examination of the nature of personal rebellion, a theme which
dominated much of the thinking of such modern European writers as
André Malraux, Jean-Paul Sartre, and especially Albert Camus.

In its most universal form, rebellion, according to Camus, involves
a protest against the condition in which man finds himself [. . . .]

Finding the world to be unjust, the rebel protests against being a part of the universe and attempts to reorder his world according to his own version of justice. The act of revolting, even when it involves a level of injustice to match that which is prevalent in society, results in apocalyptical moments of freedom and power. The result, according to Camus, is not only a new respect for one's self, but also a new sense of order and unity in the universe. This acceptance of a self-imposed order is what ultimately moves both Camus's Meursault (*L'Etranger*), and Wright's Bigger Thomas toward a peaceful reconciliation with their fates.

In Wright's first volume of short stories, *Uncle Tom's Children* (1938), physical rebellion becomes the dominant theme and the means by which his characters achieve freedom and identity. Wright's early heroes seek fulfillment of their personality and a purpose to their otherwise meaningless existence through violent action. In similar fashion, Bigger Thomas, confused and alone, can find no conventional way to bridge the gap between his aspirations and the reality of his condition. In "How Bigger Was Born," Wright explained the need for rebellion: "In *Native Son* I tried to show that man, bereft of a culture and unanchored by property, can travel but one path if he reacts positively, but unthinkingly to the prizes and goals of civilization; and that path is emotionally blind rebellion."[4]

As the novel opens, Bigger is seen as a man conditioned by hatred and a sense of racial exclusion: "I just can't get used to it," Bigger said. "I swear to God I can't, I know I oughtn't think about it, but I can't help it. Everytime I think about it I feel like somebody's poking a red-hot iron down my throat. God-dammit, look! We live here and they live there. We black and they white. They got things and we ain't. They do things and we can't. It's just like living in jail. Half the time I feel like I'm on the outside of the world peeping in through a knot-hole in the fence."[5] Throughout Book I, "Fear," Bigger is portrayed as a man in conflict, not only with white society, but also with his surroundings, his family, his peers, and ultimately with himself. Bigger is not able to escape the sordidness of his condition through religion, as does his mother, or through alcohol, as does his mistress Bessie. For him there are no external evasions, and as his anxiety and frustration mount Bigger begins to feel a sense of impending disaster: "Bigger felt an urgent need to hide his growing and deepening feeling of hysteria;

he had to get rid of it or else he would succumb to it . . . his self-trust was gone. Confidence could only come again now through action so violent that it would make him forget" (*Native Son*, pp.30–1).

Bigger takes a job as a chauffeur for the Daltons, a wealthy white philanthropic family who support the NAACP but are nevertheless one of the city's biggest slum landlords. Through a strange series of circumstances Bigger, in a moment of fear and panic, kills their daughter Mary. The murder, although ostensibly a mistake, is an accident only in the narrowest sense, for Bigger has long dreamed of such an act. The full meaning of his crime does not become clear to him until after the murder, but he had long had a foreboding of such violence: "I feel like something awful's going to happen to me. . . . Naw, it ain't like something going to happen to me. It's . . . It's like I was going to do something I can't help" (*Native Son*, p. 24). Bigger fantasizes about destruction, of dropping bombs on the white world, and in one rare moment of insight even admits to the possibility of murder as an antidote to his extreme anguish and despair: "He knew that the moment he allowed what his life meant to enter fully into his consciousness, he would either kill himself or someone else" (*Native Son*, p. 14).

Bigger's killing of Mary becomes the one meaningful act of his life, giving him a new sense of freedom and identity and a capacity for action on a grand scale. Up to this time Bigger has cowered in fear before the white world. Now, as he plots his next move, the many options that are opened give him a new sense of power and possibility: "He lay again on the bed, his mind whirling with images born of a multitude of impulses. He could run away; he could remain; he could even go down and confess what he had done. The mere thought that these avenues of action were open to him made him feel free, that his life was his, that he held his future in his hands" (*Native Son*, p. 179).

Out of apparent fear of betrayal, Bigger brutally slays his mistress Bessie. These two acts place him irrevocably outside the social order of all men, both white and black. Unlike his killing of Mary, the murder of Bessie is neither accidental nor truly necessary for his protection. It is simply proof of his new ability to act. Although Bigger is afraid he will overwhelmed by a feeling of guilt, this second murder, like the first, gives him a sense of liberation and an even greater control over his destiny: "In all of his life these two murders were the most meaningful things that had ever happened to him. He was living, truly and deeply.... Never had he had the chance to live out the consequences of his actions; never had his will been so free as in this night and day of fear and murder and flight" (*Native Son*, p. 225).

Bigger is finally discovered to be the murderer and is captured after a search of the entire Black section of Chicago. Max, a white Communist Party lawyer, becomes his attorney and presents an impassioned plea, linking Bigger's deviant actions to his environment and the transgressions of a prejudiced society. Privately, however, Max, whose thinking does not go beyond sociological explanations, is somewhat bewildered as to Bigger's true motivation. Bigger tries to explain that his action has made him understand himself as a man: "What I killed for I *am*! ... What I killed for must've been good! ... When a man kills, it's for something.... I didn't know I was really alive in this world until I felt things hard enough to kill for 'em" (*Native Son*, pp. 391–2).

[...] In Camus' novel *L'Etranger*, 1942 (*The Stranger* 1946), Meursault's metaphysical rebellion originates because he finds himself adrift and isolated in a meaningless society. Bigger, like Meursault, is alone in a world which has lost all metaphysical and moral foundation. Without God and without absolutes, he lacks an *a priori* basis for moral and ethical choice. As Wright explained: "All Bigger Thomases, white and black, felt tense, afraid, nervous, hysterical, and restless.... These personalities were mainly consequent upon men and women living in a world whose fundamental assumptions could no longer be taken for granted; ... a world in which God no longer existed as a daily focal point in men's lives; a world in which men could no longer retain their faith in an ultimate hereafter."[6]

[...]

In the final pages of *Native Son*, Bigger Thomas, condemned to death, [attempts] to understand the relationship between man and the absurdity of his environment. Rejecting the solace of religion, he is determined to die alone, as he has lived. In talking with Max, however, he realizes that other men have lived and felt as he has. He is finally able to send a belated gesture of fraternity to Jan, whose help Bigger has rejected throughout. As Max is leaving his cell for the last time, Bigger calls out to him: "Tell ... Tell Mister ... Tell Jan hello."

As his death approaches, Bigger, like Meursault, is free of fear of life and death. He has finally made peace with himself by realizing that his actions, although self-destructive, were the only possible responses to the series of injustices and irrationalities within his existence. As his execution nears, Bigger has no remorse; instead he is seen with "a faint, wry bitter smile" (*Native Son*, p. 392).

[... There] is a basic difference in the pattern of revolt and its motivation between Wright's Bigger Thomas and Camus' Meursault. Meursault's actions are the result of his comprehending the chaotic nature of the universe. Bigger acts out of hatred, fear, and an innate longing to be free. Uneducated and inarticulate, he reacts unthinkingly to the underlying contradictions of an American society which proclaims the inherent worth of the individual and yet everywhere denies that worth to the Black man. Unlike Meursault, Bigger is not aware of the metaphysical implications of his protest. It is only after his action that he begins to experience a new knowledge of himself, his existence, and the nature of his surroundings. Directed immediately against the white majority, his rebellion eventually assumes a universal dimension and ultimately is, like that of Meursault and Ellison's invisible hero, a protest against the entire scheme of things.

Native Son is as much a study of an alienated and lonely individual struggling to understand his existence, as it is an examination of racial prejudice and its effects. Bigger is forced into an alien existence because of the irrational and unjust nature of the society in which he lives. For Bigger, the opposite poles of aspiration and satisfaction can only be briefly united through violence. Murder becomes, paradoxically, the one creative act of his life: "He had murdered and had created a new life for himself" (*Native Son*, p. 101). Like Cross Damon, Wright's Dostoevskian hero in *The Outsider* (1953), Bigger is able to kill without remorse, for good and evil have become meaningless to him. Killing has become part of Bigger's definition of himself; and although Wright does not attempt to justify or condone murder, he does strive to explain the necessity of Bigger's actions.

Although *The Outsider* has many obvious parallels to the work of Sartre, Camus, and the post–World War II European writers, there is little to indicate that Wright was influenced by the French existentialists during the writing of *Native Son*. His vision of an absurd world emanated more from firsthand experience in America than from literary sources. Wright clearly perceived the inconsistencies of the American system and tried to show, through Bigger Thomas, a man struggling within that system. Living in a society that had placed him next to obscurity, Bigger turns to violence as the only meaningful action open to him.

"What peculiar personality formation results," Wright later asked, "when millions of people are forced to live lives of outward submissiveness while trying to keep intact in their hearts a sense of worth of their own humanity."[7] The answer, in part, is given by Wright in *Native Son*. Written in 1940, the novel gives an early indication of Wright's existential vision and the themes that were to preoccupy his thinking in the years to come.

NOTES

1. Wright's literary relation to the American Naturalists was first articulated by Alfred Kazin, *On Native Grounds* (New York: Reynal and Hitchcock, 1942), p. 372; and later by Robert Bone, *The Negro Novel in America* (New Haven: Yale University Press), pp. 142–43.
2. Among the most interesting of Wright studies dealing with this issue are Richard E. Baldwin, "The Creative Vision of *Native Son*," *Massachusetts Review* 14 (Spring 1973), 378–90; and John R. May, *Toward a New Earth* (Notre Dame: Notre Dame University Press, 1972), pp. 164–72.
3. Edward Margolies, *The Art of Richard Wright* (Carbondale: Southern Illinois University Press, 1969), p. 106.
4. Richard Wright, "How Bigger Was Born," *Saturday Review*, 1 June 1940, p. 4.
5. Richard Wright, *Native Son* (New York: Harper and Row, 1940), pp. 22–23. All further references to this work appear in the text.
6. Richard Wright, "How Bigger Was Born," pp. 17–18.
7. Richard Wright, Introduction, *Black Metropolis*. Edited by Horace R. Clayton and St. Claire Drake (New York: Harcourt and Brace, 1945).

THE PRINCE
(NICCOLÒ MACHIAVELLI)

"Civil Disobedience in *The Prince*"
by Raymond Angelo Belliotti,
State University of New York at Fredonia

An act of civil disobedience is an intentional, public violation of an ordinance that is clearly the law of the nation in which it takes place. Acts of civil disobedience flow from reasons of moral conscience and they usually are aimed at a change in the law or a related policy.

Acts of civil disobedience must be distinguished from commonplace lawlessness or inadvertent violations. Gunmen who rob banks and rapists who assault victims are not civilly disobedient. They are merely criminals. They are not motivated by higher social purposes; they do not hope to alter the laws prohibiting theft and rape; their actions are neither public demonstrations nor designed to rally mass support for their cause. Likewise, those who violate the law because of neglect, indifference, or ignorance are not civilly disobedient. Motorists who pass through a stop sign because they are paying insufficient attention to their task, hikers who mistakenly drop lit cigarettes in a forest, and foreigners who violate a law because they are unaware of the prohibition are not civilly disobedient.

Civil disobedience has a unique purpose: to inspire a social outcry to change existing law or policy by publicly demonstrating the alleged immorality of existing arrangements. Acts of civil disobedience aspire to win converts to their cause by stirring the moral sensibilities of the public. Classic cases of civil disobedience abound. In the nineteenth century, Henry David Thoreau refused to pay taxes in order to protest the Mexican-American War and the institution of slavery. In 1955, Rosa Parks refused to comply with the legal requirement that African Americans could occupy only the rear seats of public buses. During the first half of the twentieth century Mahatma Gandhi orchestrated numerous acts of civil resistance in leading India's struggle for independence from the British Empire. In the 1980s Nelson Mandela and Archbishop Desmond Tutu organized civilly disobedient acts as a way of protesting apartheid in South Africa. In all these cases, the participants were legally punished for their actions.

Acts of civil disobedience violate the law. Accordingly, the moral appropriateness of civilly disobedient action is problematic. The critical question surrounding civil disobedience is clear: When, if ever, may individual citizens justifiably substitute their understanding of right and wrong for the judgment of the state? After all, if citizens systematically refuse to comply with laws simply because they disagree with the appropriateness of those laws, public order would dissolve. Scores of laws are controversial, yet the state demands general compliance in order to nurture the common good and secure stability. A nation where civil disobedience is rampant is unlikely to remain unified. Still, certain organized acts of civil disobedience have earned widespread approval for inspiring healthy change that would not otherwise have been forthcoming. Where might we draw the line between justified civil disobedience and self-indulgent lawlessness?

At least five questions provide a framework for understanding justified civil disobedience. The first is the question of means: Will the civilly disobedient acts be nonviolent or will they involve violence? Usually, advocates of civil disobedience require nonviolence for both moral and strategic reasons. When people break the law nonviolently they implicitly affirm their general consent to the legal system and the social order. When they break the law violently they call into question their own motives. Moreover, nonviolent resistance is more likely to inspire others to rally to the cause. By displaying their own rectitude, civilly disobedient activists underscore their moral message and maximize their chances of winning public support for their cause.

The second question is the scope of the intended change in existing arrangements: Do the activists aim at reform or do they target an overthrow of the basic structures of government? Aiming at reform—the change of a certain law or a few policies—is less threatening to the general order and more likely to attract supporters than calling for revolution. At least, this is the case in a reasonably just state.

The third question is one of political context: Will the civilly disobedient acts occur in a democracy or republic that is reasonably just, or in a totalitarian state that is fundamentally unjust? If the activists operate in a democracy or republic, their message is more likely to be heard, their cause is more likely to gather support, and the governmental response is likely to be less harsh than in a totalitarian state. In a totalitarian state, one of the critical aspects of successful disobedience—public awareness of the event—is likely to be frustrated. Authoritarians rarely permit widespread publicity for dissenters.

The fourth question is one of past benefits: Has the state granted and have the activists accepted substantial benefits from the state in the past? Where the protestors have benefited greatly from the state in the past, their present opposition may be judged as ingratitude. This was an argument advanced by Socrates in Plato's dialogue *The Crito* (Plato 51d-54e). Where protestors have been systematically oppressed—Mandela and Tutu under apartheid, Parks under segregation laws, Gandhi under imperial rule—their case for justified civil disobedience is stronger.

The fifth question is one of future compliance: Should the protestors accept punishment as the lawful consequence of their disobedience, or should they refuse to accept punishment? The usual answer is that accepting punishment is morally and strategically wise. By accepting punishment for their lawlessness, the protestors affirm their general commitment to the rule of law and allegiance to their nation. Moreover, they are more likely to win public support for their cause by taking full responsibility for their actions and accepting punishment. The radical answer is that the protestors have no strong moral reason to accept punishment and doing so contradicts their central purpose: If they are convinced their actions are morally justified, why should they accept punishment for doing what is morally right? If they accept punishment, are they not compromising their moral message?

When is civil disobedience justified? The answer to this question is a matter of ongoing debate, but the following summarizes one plausible position. The first step is to address the issue of citizens substituting their own judgments for those of the state. In a reasonably just state, such as a democracy or republic, protestors are not substituting their sense of right and wrong for the judgment of the state. Instead, they are holding the state accountable for straying from its own standards. The state holds itself out—in public records, founding documents, and constitutional aspirations—as subscribing to certain fundamental values and basic political commitments. Where the state's laws transgress those stated values and commitments, the state has failed its own purposes. Citizens who hold the state accountable, through acts of civil disobedience intended to highlight the discrepancy, are merely demanding that the state live up to its expressed goals.

The second step is to restrict the justified range of civil disobedience. Protestors should organize civilly disobedient acts only against offensive laws and policies that cause serious injustice. Such laws and policies transgress the fundamental values and political commitments that define the state. They cause serious injury to a significant number of citizens.

The third step requires civil disobedience to be aimed at reform and to be conducted nonviolently. Lawless acts aimed at revolution are less civil disobedience and more civil insurrection. Although revolutionary activity is often justified, it goes far beyond civil disobedience. Remaining nonviolent, as noted above, underscores the moral message and maximizes prospects of earning public sympathy for the cause.

The fourth step insists that protestors accept punishment for their civilly disobedient actions. To be justified, civilly disobedient acts must fulfill both moral and strategic requirements. Punishment is the standard legal response to violating the law, and nonviolent protestors further their cause, both morally and strategically, by complying.

The fifth step recognizes that civil disobedience is, for practical purposes, a last resort. Other methods of affecting change should be tried prior to launching civilly disobedient deeds. The civilly disobedient acts must also have a reasonable expectation of achieving their results. Having the moral high ground is not enough to enact change. The strategic or prudential dimension—Are prospects for success reasonable? What ways of acting will maximize those prospects? How can public support best be won?—remains crucial.

Finally, the amount of harm caused by the civilly disobedient acts must be outweighed by the amount of good caused by the expected changes in the disagreeable laws or policies. That the activists must minimize the amount of harm they cause by their deeds should go without saying.

Two notions inform the advice Niccolò Machiavelli offers political rulers in *The Prince*, written around 1513. *Virtù* has been, more or less accurately, translated as efficiency, skill, strength, excellence, discipline, manliness, ability, virtue, effectiveness, will power, vigor, and a host of related attributes. For Machiavelli, *virtù* connotes an excellence relevant to a person's function. Human beings inhabit a world of scarce resources and keen competition that rests uncomfortably with our bottomless ambitions and passions. Worse, we are susceptible to the whims of *Fortuna*, which often conspire against our best-devised strategies. Only people embodying *virtù* are able to cope with *Fortuna*, confront adversity with renewed purpose, imagine and pursue grand deeds, and maintain their resolve and passion in a relentlessly competitive world.

Specifically, Machiavelli refers to military *virtù*, political *virtù*, civic *virtù*, moral *virtù*, and artistic *virtù*. The qualities of excellence defining each type will differ. The greatest men—those able to found, preserve, reform, and expand healthy political units—must exude military and political *virtù*. Such leaders must effectively size up the prevailing situation; reflect on the available choices, priorities, and probable consequences; and act decisively and successfully. Citizens in a healthy political unit must exhibit civic and moral *virtù* if the unit is to continue to flourish.

In *The Prince*, Machiavelli sometimes writes as if *Fortuna* is a personified, natural force that consciously and whimsically plays with the circumstances of human beings. At other times, he writes as if *Fortuna* is only the set of circumstances within which human beings must operate and choose alternatives (Ch. 25). Wise human beings can take proactive and reactive measures to soften *Fortuna*'s fury. The message to individual rulers is even crisper. Do not depend on past favorable *Fortuna*. Your fortunes will change. No person will enjoy positive *Fortuna* forever. Sometimes caution wins the day. Sometimes boldness succeeds. The character of the times determines proper action. For Machiavelli, the highest ends of governments are expansion and glory; the highest end for human beings is enduring glory, a form of immortality.

A host of slogans capture the gist of Machiavelli's advice to princes. He tells princes to "free yourself from the imperatives of conventional morality." Because of the unbridgeable gap between how people live and how they ought to live, princes who insist on acting on moral ideals will destroy themselves. Princes who refuse to cast aside conventional morality at critical times will fail because so many people act immorally. Princes must learn how to be not good, understand when to use that knowledge and when not to use it, in accord with necessity (Ch. 15, 18). In general, a prince should follow conventional morality where he can, but recognize that necessity often requires violating morality to advance the purposes of the state and prince (Ch. 15, 18, 19).

People are mystified by appearances. They judge the actions of everyone, especially those of princes, by their results. If a prince succeeds in founding, preserving, reforming, or expanding the power of the state—and thereby enhancing the well-being of its citizens—his methods will be evaluated favorably (Ch. 18). Machiavelli is not championing the evaluative notion that "good ends justify any means." Instead, he is describing the way the majority of people will be blinded by results when judging the ways those ends were attained. He suggests that if their self-interest were promoted by the results, people would brush away the wrongness of the means.

A prince's default position is following the scruples of conventional morality. But *necessità*—the basic human inclination toward self-interest; the scarcity of natural resources; the actual behavior of the vast majority of people; the competitive nature of international affairs; and the whims of *Fortuna*—will often require violating the demands of conventional morality as the only way to attain political ends: founding, preserving, reforming, or expanding the state. A healthy state is required if the prince is to achieve glory and the people are to enjoy security and order, and develop civic *virtù*.

For a prince to merely hold his subjects in fear is not enough. According to Machiavelli he must "cultivate the loyalty of the masses." A prince must transform what citizens first take as external rule into an internally accepted regime. The cornerstones of the program include showing the people how their self-interest is tightly bound with the well-being of the prince; recruiting a strong army and instituting sound laws; neutralizing the ambition of the nobles; implementing disciplined education; cultivating appropriate habits and customs; enlarging the prince's reputation; and demonstrating that the system works through grand military triumphs and a clear system of internal rewards and punishments.

According to Machiavelli, people are strongly inclined toward evil; they are turned to the good only by necessity; they judge mainly by appearances; they evaluate actions only by results; they seek merely to avoid being oppressed; they will desert the prince if he is defeated or captured; and, thus, they lack grand spirits. Still, their well-being and collective loyalty is pivotal to the prince's successful reign and to his reward of enduring glory.

A successful prince must also "establish strong armies and sound laws." He should recruit, train, and lead his own troops. A prince's reputation for strength must be based on his actual military capabilities. The prince's troops can include his subjects or citizens or dependents. To lose with his own men is preferable to winning with soldiers belonging to someone else or those who are hired guns (Ch. 13). As always, the prince should be self-sustaining and rely as little as possible upon outsiders (Ch. 10). Only if strong arms and sound laws are in place can a state cultivate civic *virtù* and begin to compete effectively in international affairs.

If natural resources are scarce, the ambition of glory-seekers is expansive, and world affairs consist of a series of competitions, then the prince must draw a tight circle around his area of concern—his state and citizens—and advance their interests to the detriment of those outside that circle. For Machiavelli, this is the nature of the world and of human beings. Care for the well-being of citizens or the common good does not extend beyond the state's borders. A prince should "operate within the world as it is." Glory is conferred in response to grand political and military achievements. These triumphs involve winners and losers. One sure way of losing is to operate from principles and values which lack currency in the world as it is and as it functions.

Like a proficient poker player, the prince tries to conceal the real strength of his holdings. Sometimes he wants to give the impression his position is stronger than it is in order to forestall internal opposition or external attack. At other times, he may feign vulnerability in order to invite aggression which he can easily quell. The deception in all cases is designed to amplify his overall standing. But no one, poker player or politician, can succeed through bluffs only. A firm basis of strength, not merely its illusion, is required. For princes, a strong military, a well-ordered polity, and avoiding the hatred of the people are prerequisites for continued success.

The ends of the state are the personal glory of the prince and the enhanced well-being of the citizens (Ch. 26). Machiavelli is clear in

The Prince that these ends require territorial expansion (Ch. 3, 7). The prince must "understand the critical ends of the state." The state must expand because, in Machiavelli's uncompromising worldview, the only other choice is enslavement. True, the prince burns with ambition and aspires to enduring glory. That glory can be attained only by invigorating the state and enlarging the common good.

The prince's deepest aspiration springs, true enough, from self-interest. But he comes to understand that what is in his self-interest cannot be gained selfishly. If selfishness is ignoring the interests of others when one should not, then the prince must shun it in order to satisfy his self-interest in enduring glory. From the standpoint of the people, the glory of the prince is a means to the common good. None of this assumes that the prince has purely selfless motives or even that his heart aches for the plight of his people. Accordingly, the well-being of citizens is part of the *definition* of personal glory, rather than merely a means of attaining it.

The prince must remember that "it is better to be feared than to be loved, but avoid being hated." For the prince, being both feared and loved by the people is the best situation. But accomplishing both at once is uncommon. If the prince cannot join these two emotions in his people, it is better to be feared than to be loved. This is the case because of Machiavelli's conception of human nature: People are generally ungrateful, cowardly, selfish, deceptive, greedy, and inconstant. As long as the prince serves their interests, they pledge loyalty and offer extravagant promises. Love is an emotion that binds people through obligation. People, who are basically wicked and self-interested, will shun that duty when convenient. Fear has a greater hold because it includes dread of punishment. Fear, then, is completely reliable and predictable (Ch. 17, 18).

At all costs, a prince must avoid being hated (Ch. 17, 19). The people will hate a prince only if the ruler confiscates their property or their women. When the prince has to kill, he should be able to articulate persuasive reasons and to make a clear case. Above all, he must not seize the property of citizens: "Men forget more quickly the death of a father than the loss of a father's estate" (Ch. 17).

The prince should take the lion and the fox as role models. The lion frightens wolves and the fox recognizes traps. Rulers who act only as lions do not fully understand the requirements of their office. The lion, as a metaphor for military might, can be tricked and neutralized by clever adversaries. The fox, as a metaphor for cunning and deception, cannot always defend itself from forceful enemies. The qualities of both beasts are needed by a successful prince (Ch. 18, 19).

Machiavelli disdains half-hearted measures, the kind we are tempted to apply when we are unsure of our position and options. The prince must be decisive and avoid neutrality. A prince gains respect by unreservedly allying himself with one party in a conflict and being equally opposed to the other party in the conflict. If a prince remains neutral, the victor in the dispute will injure him and the defeated party will revel in that injury. The prince will be conquered by the former and receive no aid from the latter (Ch. 21).

The theory and practice of civil disobedience postdate the writing of *The Prince* by over three centuries. Machiavelli, however, understands keenly the danger that social unrest poses for the prince and his nation-state. A divided country—one where civil disobedience and other social revolts are widely practiced—undermines the prince's efforts in international affairs and minimizes his prospects for rallying internal support for his policies. Thus, he advises the ruler to quell potential civil disobedience of every sort by fashioning the state and his own conduct appropriately. The prince is a monarch holding absolute power. According to Machiavelli, he will win the allegiance of the masses as long as he is militarily and politically effective, refrains from trifling with the women and property of his subjects, advances the material interests of the nation, and thereby avoids being hated. Such a monarch earns loyalty from his subjects by getting them to identify their collective self-interest with his interests. Under such circumstances, groups of citizens are highly unlikely to mount a public protest over this or that law. Given the absolute power of the prince, if a demonstration of this sort were initiated the likelihood that it would gain widespread public airing is miniscule. Accordingly, Machiavelli designs the political context of *The Prince* in order to frustrate the central purposes, methods, and prospects for successful civil disobedience.

If a prince is politically and militarily ineffective, if he is hated, or otherwise loses the allegiance of his subjects, the most likely result is civil insurrection or revolution. Citizens may well rise up, take up arms, and attack an incompetent or cruel monarch. Elsewhere Machiavelli celebrates Lucius Junius Brutus (ca. 545 BC–ca. 509 BC), who led the people of early Rome in a revolution that drove an unscrupulous monarch, Tarquin the Proud, out of Rome and installed a republic (*The Discourses* Book 1, Ch. 16; Book 3, Ch. 3). Machiavelli judged that deposed princes of this stripe received precisely what they earned by their ineptitude.

Accordingly, the political context of *The Prince* is an inhospitable setting for civil disobedience. The government is a monarchy, not a democracy or republic; public demonstrations would be quickly extinguished and would not receive widespread discussion; and citizens would be unlikely to target specific laws for reform. For Machiavelli, the central purposes of the nation—the personal glory of the prince and the enhanced well-being of the citizens—deserve nothing less.

WORKS CITED AND CONSULTED

Bedau, Hugo. *Civil Disobedience in Focus*. New York: Routledge, 1991.

Belliotti, Raymond Angelo. *Niccolò Machiavelli: The Laughing Lion and the Strutting Fox*. Lanham: Lexington Books, 2008.

Fortas, Abe. *Concerning Dissent and Civil Disobedience*. New York: Signet Broadside, 1968.

Machiavelli, Niccolò. *The Prince*. *Machiavelli: Selected Political Writings*. Edited and translated by David Wootton. Indianapolis: Hackett Publishing Company, 1994. 5–80.

———. *The Discourses*. *Machiavelli: Selected Political Writings*. Edited and translated by David Wootton. Indianapolis: Hackett Publishing Company, 1994. 81–217.

Plato, *The Crito*. *Plato: Collected Dialogues*. Translated by Hugh Tredennick. Edited by Edith Hamilton and Huntington Cairns. Princeton: Princeton University Press, 1973.

Price, Russell. "The Senses of *Virtù* in Machiavelli." *European Studies Review* 3 (1973): 315–45.

Zinn, Howard. *Disobedience and Democracy*. Cambridge, MA: South End Press, 2002.

THE SCARLET LETTER
(NATHANIEL HAWTHORNE)

"Civil Disobedience and *Realpolitik* in Nathaniel Hawthorne's *The Scarlet Letter*"
by Robert C. Evans,
Auburn University at Montgomery

In the rich and thought-provoking article "The Scarlet Letter of the Law: Hawthorne and Criminal Justice," Laura Hanft Korobkin raises many points relevant to any consideration of civil disobedience in Hawthorne's greatest novel. Korobkin not only discusses *The Scarlet Letter* in relation to the actual methods and procedures of the justice system in Puritan New England, but she also relates the book to political controversies that were raging when the novel was first written, published, and read. In particular, she shows how Hawthorne's text may have resonated for readers concerned with the problems created by the Fugitive Slave Law of 1850, which "placed all citizens"—even those living in the North—"under affirmative legal obligations not only to permit but also to assist in the capture and return of fugitive slaves" (428). Korobkin suggests that *The Scarlet Letter* raises two questions that would have seemed highly relevant to Hawthorne's contemporaries as they wrestled with their own and others' reactions to the Fugitive Slave Law:

> First, what obligations do individuals have to obey laws regulating private behavior, laws that directly conflict with the individuals' deeply held principles, and which they have had

243

no hand in making? And second, must submission to such a
law be viewed as integrity-destroying cowardice, or can it be
understood as courageous and even beneficial to the individual?
These questions sounded with particular resonance in 1850,
when the legitimacy of public law and criminal process was a
matter of intense national debate. (428)

No summary of Korobkin's subtle article can do justice to her
painstaking and thorough discussion; suffice it to say that she suggests
that Hester Prynne may have struck many of Hawthorne's first readers
as a model illustrating the virtues of outward obedience to civil laws.
By accepting the punishment Puritan authorities inflict on her, and by
continuing to live as an obedient member of the community, Hester
helps preserve that community even while she inwardly dissents from
some of its values. Rather than openly rebelling and thus provoking
discord and division, she is willing to remain in the community, live
a useful and public-spirited life, set an inspiring example, and look
forward to a day when the community will peacefully evolve, in ways
that correspond more with her own ideals. Korobkin admits that to
some of Hawthorne's contemporaries, "Hester's outward submission to
the strictures of Puritan law might well appear a shameful knuckling
under, the kind of failure of will that buys safety at the price of personal
integrity. Yet Hawthorne" (Korobkin continues) ultimately "convinces
us that Hester's behavioral acquiescence is both truly heroic and intellectually liberating. With Hester as a model, the novel suggests, readers
may find the courage not to rebel but to forego rebellion" (429).

Hester, from Korobkin's perspective, thus emerges as a more
compliant, more conservative, less radical, and less revolutionary
character than she is sometimes perceived to be. Hester may
think radical thoughts, but she fails to act in radical ways. Indeed,
Hawthorne even "implies that it is precisely because she need not
think about practical action that her mental explorations can be so
far-reaching" (434).

Hester's philosophical and historical conclusions can be radical,
even revolutionary, precisely because they are not muddied by
the messy and corrupting process of attempting change in the
real world. It is significant too that outward obedience is all that
the Puritan rule of law requires; its justice system punishes only

acts, not thoughts. Because community stability depends on each member's self-restraint, Hester's conformity to behavioral expectations helps hold the community together even when her thoughts may be at their bitterest. (435)

Certainly much evidence within the novel supports Korobkin's interpretation of Hester's character and behavior. This is especially true of her conduct in Chapter III of the book, in which she refuses to name her partner in sin but never protests the fundamental justice of her sentence. To lodge any such public protest, of course, might only have led to even harsher punishment, and so Hester mainly (and wisely) keeps her silence. Her only speech consists, ironically, of a refusal to speak (Hawthorne 49–50), and she even seems willing not only to suffer her own punishment but also to shoulder the punishment that should apply to the unknown father of her child: "would that I might endure his agony, as well as mine" (49). She is forthright in refusing to confess her lover's name ("Never!' . . . I will not speak!" (49–50)), but she never objects to the punishment imposed on her or to the laws that dictate that punishment.

By refusing to speak, Hester engages in a kind of passive resistance and civil disobedience (especially since her refusal is enacted in front of the entire community), but she stops short of engaging in any kind of active protest or any exceptionally provocative defiance of authority. She never challenges her judges, and she never rebukes the people of the town. Indeed, her disobedience is "civil" in nearly every sense of the word: It is polite; it is dignified; it is free from open anger or obvious rancor; and it seems to concede the right of the civil authorities to ordain the punishment they have chosen to impose. Her silence wins the (obviously self-interested) admiration of her secret lover, Arthur Dimmesdale ("Wondrous strength and generosity of a woman's heart! She will not speak!" [50]), although Hawthorne leaves it unclear whether Dimmesdale expresses his admiration loudly enough for anyone else to hear.

Hester's behavior in Chapter III thus seems to exhibit precisely the kind of "behavioral acquiescence" emphasized by Korobkin (429). Hester's only action is a refusal to act; her only words amount to a determination to stay silent. She stands on the scaffold for more than four hours, enduring the stares and scorn of the outraged community and the open condemnation (in an hour-long sermon) of the censuring clergy. When the authorities briefly urge her to act in a way she considers a violation of her personal conscience, she refuses, and those authorities are (somewhat surprisingly) willing to accept her refusal. She is punished only for the sin of adultery; no further or greater punishment is exacted as a result of her conduct on the scaffold. Hester thus manages to disobey in a way that fails to provoke any heightened outrage or any vindictive response. She makes her point quickly but firmly, and "the elder clergyman," recognizing "the impracticable state of the poor culprit's mind," soon launches into his already-prepared sermon (Hawthorne 50). It is as if the clergyman had anticipated Hester's defiance, is essentially untroubled by it (he almost seems to feel a kind of pity for her), and so moves on to the next stage of the preordained ritual. No one suggests that Hester should be physically threatened, whipped for disobedience, or tortured into confessing her lover's name. Hester has thus managed to defy authority in a way that fails to outrage the authorities assembled; she has managed to assert her independence from the community in a way that fails to provoke communal vengeance. She has engaged, in other words, in a successful act of civil disobedience: She has managed to show—before the whole assembled population—that it is possible, even for a relatively powerless woman, to stand her ground without pushing her defiance too far.

Far more disturbing, however—and also far more difficult to explain in the terms Korobkin has suggested—is Hester's behavior in a later episode of the novel. In Chapter VIII of *The Scarlet Letter* (titled "The Elf-Child and the Minister"), Hester and her infant daughter, Pearl, are present at the home of Governor Bellingham, where Hester has come to deliver a pair of embroidered gloves the governor has ordered. In the first half of the chapter, Hawthorne goes out of his way to emphasize the governor's wealth, pride, and love of material comforts (Hawthorne 73–74). In a nice bit of subtle irony, the narrator notes that despite this sort of materialism, men such as Bellingham were nevertheless always "prepared to sacrifice goods and life at the behest of duty" (73), although such phrasing leaves intriguingly unclear exactly *whose* life and goods they were willing to sacrifice. Similar irony attaches to a description of Arthur Dimmesdale, who also happens to be present (along with a prominent clergyman named Mr. Wilson, as well as Roger Chillingworth) at the governor's home during Hester's visit. The narrator notes that Dimmesdale's "health had severely suffered, of late, by his too unreserved self-sacrifice to the labors and duties of the pastoral relation," although the phrase "self-sacrifice" only helps remind us how little, in fact, he has actually sacrificed in the several years since Hester first stood upon the public scaffold and willingly bore sole blame for their mutual sin.

In any case, the governor, upon seeing Pearl, informs Hester that he and other men of authority have recently been discussing whether the infant should be removed from "the guidance" of Hester, whom he smugly calls "one who hath stumbled and fallen" (Hawthorne 75), as if he himself were free from sin. Hester at first answers "calmly, although growing more pale," but the more she speaks, the more significantly pointed her words become. Touching her scarlet letter, she says that "this badge hath taught me, it daily teaches me,—it is teaching me *at this moment*, [italics added]—lessons whereof my child may be the wiser and better, albeit they can profit nothing to myself" (75). Hesters phrasing is not only eloquent and rhetorically effective, but it is also (by the time she reaches the crucial phrase "at this moment") fairly sharp and even somewhat sarcastic. The words "at this moment" imply that Hester is presently enduring a lesson in patience, endurance, self-control, and humility—the kind of humility utterly lacking, it goes without saying, in the governor himself. Nevertheless, the governor persists, insisting that Pearl be examined (by Mr. Wilson) to determine "whether she hath had such Christian nurture as befits a child of her age" (75). Although the narrator notes that Pearl is indeed well versed in the tenets of the Christian religion, the girl refuses to cooperate with Wilsons questioning, a fact that only further frustrates the governor. With unintended irony, he exclaims (within a few feet of Dimmesdale, and certainly well within Dimmesdales hearing), "Here is a child of three years old, and she cannot tell who made her!" (76). Dimmesdale, of course, who has had a significant role in making the child, remains characteristically silent.

Perhaps partly for this reason, Hester becomes increasingly outspoken and rebellious. When the governor indicates that Pearl may be taken from her custody, Hester grabs the girl and draws her "forcibly into her arms, confronting the old Puritan magistrate with almost a fierce expression" (76). The narrator notes, in language that has remarkably explicit political overtones, that Hester "felt that she possessed indefeasible rights against the world, and was ready to defend them to the death" (76). At first, though, Hester does not openly state her rebellious feelings. Instead, she begins by appealing to a higher authority: "'God gave me the child!' cried she." Nevertheless, in the next sentence she becomes more openly confrontational: "He gave her, in requital of all things else, which *ye* had taken from me" (76; italics added). Hester's "ye" may refer to Bellingham in particular, to the assembled men in general, or to Puritan society more broadly, but in any of these senses it is far more defiant in tone than anything she has said before. She doesn't mention any sense of guilt for her own sin, and, rather than describing Pearl as a kind of punishment from God, she speaks (at least at first) of the child as a form of "requital" for everything else that had been "taken from" the mother.

Hester presents herself, in other words, as a victim—a view she had not earlier expressed in public. She next calls Pearl her "happiness," but then, perhaps realizing that this assertion will prove rhetorically ineffective, she immediately adds that Pearl is also her "torture, none the less!" (Hawthorne 76). The same kind of careful balance is repeated in the next two sentences: "Pearl keeps me here in life! Pearl punishes me too!" (76). She even claims that Pearl, in effect, is a living embodiment of "the scarlet letter, only capable of being loved, and so endowed with a million-fold power of retribution for my sin" (76). Only now, indeed, does Hester explicitly mention her own "sin" and thus seem to grant the justice of the judgment that has been imposed upon her. No sooner does she do so, however, than she openly expresses her most defiant statement yet: "Ye shall not take her! I will die first!" (76). One way to read that final sentence is as a threat to commit suicide; another way to read it is as a promise of her willingness to die in the process of violently opposing any attempt to take her child. In any case, her words are shockingly frank and are far more openly rebellious than anything she said (or did not say) earlier on the scaffold. The fact that she speaks as a loving mother, of course, wins her some sympathy, even from at least one of the Puritans himself. Mr. Wilson—described with nice equivocation as the "not unkind old minister"—tries to calm her by addressing her as a "poor woman" and by assuring her that "the child shall be well cared for" (76).

Hester, however, refuses to be placated. "'God gave her into my keeping,'" she repeats, "raising her voice almost to a shriek. 'I will not give her up!'" (76). And now, in a truly remarkable turn of events, Hester moves from brazenly outspoken civil disobedience to something different altogether: She now begins to engage in what might be called a form of hard-hitting, hard-ball *realpolitik*, demonstrating a kind of desperate cunning and skill that make her far more dangerous, uncontrolled, and unpredictable than perhaps at any other point in the novel. Turning to Dimmesdale, whom she has thus far ignored, she suddenly demands (in wonderfully effective and heavily accented monosyllables), "Speak thou for me!" (76). She then explicitly reminds him (in words that ironically echo words addressed by Mr. Wilson to Dimmesdale in the first scaffold scene [48–49]), "Thou wast my pastor, and hadst charge of my soul, and knowest me better than these men can" (76). In this sentence, as indeed throughout her address to Dimmesdale, Hester's words are double-edged. He did indeed have charge of her soul, but, as they both know, he also had access to her body. He has indeed "known" her in a different way than the other men present. He has "known" her sexually, but he also knows her strength of character, and so her statement to him is both a bit of implied flattery and also a subtle threat. When Hester once again states that she "will not lose the child," her words are once more double-edged: She will not lose Pearl, but she now seems willing to lose Dimmesdale and destroy his career by revealing him as Pearl's father. She once more demands, "Speak for me!" (76), but implied in these words is also a demand that he speak for Pearl, and also that he speak now if he hopes to save his own reputation. Here and throughout her speech, Hester's words are richly ambiguous. They are full of desperation, but they are also brimming with implied threats.

Hester speaks publicly, and all the assembled men hear her, but only Dimmesdale (and perhaps also Chillingworth) is in a position to catch the many ironies embedded in her language and to appreciate the fuller and deeper implications of the threats she is making. Thus, when Hester tells Dimmesdale that "thou hast sympathies which these men lack" (Hawthorne 76), she simultaneously appeals to his compassion, plays on his vanity, alludes to his sterling public reputation, reminds him of his past and present love for her and the girl, and implicitly threatens to reveal the precise nature of those "sympathies" if he should fail to comply with her demands. Likewise, when Hester tells Dimmesdale that "thou knowest what is in my heart, and what are a mother's rights, and how much the stronger they are, when that mother has but her child and the scarlet letter" (76), the complicated connotations of her words are exceptionally rich and pointed. Dimmesdale does indeed know what is in her heart, because he has had fuller access to her than any other man present except (possibly) Chillingworth. Dimmesdale must also realize that Hester now feels that her "rights" as a "mother" are far stronger than are his as a father or as a secret lover, and that she will not hesitate to expose him if he fails to assist her. It is, after all, largely thanks to Dimmesdale—and to his silence and weakness over the years—that Hester has only "her child and the scarlet letter" (76). Up to now, she has been unusually patient, loving, forgiving, and self-sacrificing in her dealings with Dimmesdale, but the whole secret burden of this speech is that those days may be about to end abruptly unless he helps her. Without ever threatening him explicitly (i.e., in ways that the governor or Mr. Wilson can comprehend), she nevertheless draws a very firm line in the sand—a line Dimmesdale can see even if it is invisible to the two men in authority.

Hester knows that her feelings of utter powerlessness have now, paradoxically, put her in a position of extreme power over Dimmesdale, and thus there is a tone not only of desperation but also of supreme confidence when she tells him, "Look to it! I will not lose the child! Look to it!" (77). The narrator instantly comments that "this wild and singular appeal . . . indicated that Hester Prynne's situation had provoked her to little less than madness" (77), but with the exception of the governor and Wilson, every other witness to the scene—including Hester, Dimmesdale, Chillingworth, the narrator, and Hawthorne's readers—knows that if Hester is crazy, she is crazy like a fox. She knows precisely what she is doing, and so (significantly) does Dimmesdale. Hester is playing a complicated game of chess with her secret lover, and he has just been checkmated. She presents herself as a victim (and genuinely feels herself to be one), but she is far from conceding defeat. No wonder Dimmesdale looks "pale" and "nervous"! No wonder he places his hand over his heart and seems to be "thrown into agitation" (77). In one sense, of course, he is genuinely agitated spiritually; his conscience is (and has long been) troubled. Significantly, however, Dimmesdale does not really make a positive step to act on Hester's behalf until he is threatened—until his secret (which is already known to God) is about to be revealed to men. Only then does Dimmesdale step forward. "There is truth in what she says," he solemnly announces, but he knows (and we and Chillingworth know) how much more truth there is in her words than the governor and Wilson are capable of realizing. "God gave her the child," Dimmesdale continues (thereby continuing once more to deflect his own responsibility). "This child of its father's guilt and its mother's shame hath come from the hand of God" (he proclaims) "to work in many ways upon her heart, who pleads so earnestly, and with such bitterness of spirit, the right to keep her" (77).

As these words should make obvious, Dimmesdale's phrasing is in many ways as double-edged and as full of hidden meanings as Hester's has already been. Thus, by referring to a "father's guilt," he not only lets Hester know that he does feel guilty; he also lets her know that she has been successful in arousing—and playing on— that guilt in the present episode. Similarly, by referring to Hester's "bitterness of spirit," he not only alludes to her general anger; he also signals that he understands why she may feel bitter at him in particular. The presence of Pearl does indeed "work in many ways upon [Hester's] heart," but the child's presence (combined with the mother's hidden threats) have also worked on Dimmesdale's. Thus, when Dimmesdale describes the effect Pearl has on Hester, he also implicitly describes the effect that both Pearl *and* Hester have upon himself: Every sight of them is, for him, "a retribution . . . ; a torture, to be felt at many an unthought of moment; a pang, a sting, an ever-recurring agony, in the midst of a troubled joy!" (77). Hester, indeed, has just proven how subtly she can manipulate Dimmesdale (when she feels she needs to) in order to achieve her own ends. She has just demonstrated how, by appealing to his conscience but also by implicitly threatening to expose him, she can make him speak and act as she desires.

Dimmesdale's arguments win the day, which is another way of saying that Hester (not to put too fine a point on it) blackmails Dimmesdale into winning a victory for her. Yes, she appeals to his conscience, but she also appeals (more pertinently) to his sense of self-interest and to his desire for self-protection. It is a stunning example of power politics within the pages of *The Scarlet Letter*, and it goes far beyond a simple example (as in the first scaffold scene) of civil disobedience. Roger Chillingworth, for one, cannot help but admire Hester's skill. After hearing Dimmesdale's plea, Chillingworth smilingly responds: "You speak, my friend, with a strange earnestness" (78). Chillingworth and Hester, of course, both know why Dimmesdale speaks so earnestly, even if Dimmesdale is as yet unaware of Chillingworth's real identity and of Chillingworth's precise knowledge. Chillingworth, though, knows exactly what has just happened, and perhaps, as a kind of Satanic figure, he even admires the spark of rebellion that has just flamed up in Hester.

Hester, too, seems to realize how important a victory she has just won. Later, as she is leaving the governor's home, she exchanges words with the governor's sister, Mistress Hibbins ("the same who, a few years later, was executed as a witch" [78–79]). Mistress Hibbins expresses her regret that Hester will not accompany her into the forest to meet "the Black Man" (i.e., Satan) (79).

> "Make my excuse to him, so please you!" answered Hester, with a triumphant smile. "I must tarry at home, and keep watch over my little Pearl. Had they taken her from me, I would willingly have gone with thee into the forest, and signed my name in the Black Man's book, too, and that with my own blood!" (79)

Possibly, of course, Hester is merely being sarcastic in responding to a woman she probably distrusts and who (she may feel) has just tried to insult her. In another sense, however, her threat does not seem merely sardonic or empty. Hester has just proven her willingness not only to defy the deputies of God but also, indeed, to manipulate and blackmail one of them. She has just proven her willingness—and her ability—to play hardball. No longer merely civilly disobedient, Hester has shown herself to be a potential and dangerous rebel. Feeling threatened in her "indefeasible rights" as a mother (76), she first appeals to her Heavenly Father but then ends by claiming (perhaps only jokingly) that if she had lost her child, she would have been willing to become a follower of Satan. Fortunately, thanks to the success of her subtle exercise in *realpolitik*, no one (especially not Dimmesdale) is forced to witness just how far Hester might really have been willing to go if she had been pushed beyond her limits of endurance.

WORKS CITED

Hawthorne, Nathaniel. *The Scarlet Letter*. Person, 3–166.

Korobkin, Laura Hanft. "The Scarlet Letter of the Law: Hawthorne and Criminal Justice." Person, 426–51.

Person, Leland, ed. *The Scarlet Letter and Other Writings*, by Nathaniel Hawthorne. New York: Norton, 2005.

THE TRIAL
(FRANZ KAFKA)

"Franz Kafka's *The Trial* and Civil Disobedience"
by Michael D. Sollars, Texas Southern University

The theme of civil disobedience—a protagonist struggling against a powerful, even menacing social body or tradition—has many notable antecedents in the long history of literature. Most historical examples of civil disobedience in literature present a predatory social body that is identifiable and definite, and capable of being faced and possibly defeated. The civil disobedience in more modern literature, on the other hand, often catapults the reader into a disorienting and indecipherable new world. Franz Kafka's novel *The Trial* (1925) is one of modernism's most poignant portrayals of the lone individual's defiance against a powerful, pervasive, yet indeterminate social consciousness.

Published posthumously in 1925, only one year after the author's death at the age of forty-one from tuberculosis, *The Trial* presents a blurred reality of the absurd and existentialism. This situation of a character thrust into a disorienting and frightening landscape—one sharply marked by the absurd—is so prevalent in Kafka's novels (other examples include *The Metamorphosis* (1915) and *The Castle* [1926]), that "Kafkaesque" is the literary term coined to describe such plots. And it is in *The Trial* that Kafka most poignantly reveals the individual's challenge against an encroaching and sinister social body.

Kafka's story of his protagonist Joseph K.'s plight against the Courts begins very much like Gregor Samsa's nightmare story in *The Metamorphosis*. In this, Kafka's earlier work, the young Gregor awakens one morning in his familiar bedroom to find himself transformed into a giant beetle. He spends the rest of his short life as the outsider, alienated from his family and society. Joseph K., beginning his thirtieth year, wakes one morning to find his familiar, stable world suddenly transformed into one that he finds confusing and threatening. What was once familiar becomes strange. K. is not greeted by the smiling face of his landlady who daily serves his breakfast. Instead he faces two coarse Court warders who have intruded into his lodgings to arrest him for reasons that are never disclosed. The reader, like Kafka, is equally off balance because K. is never taken away to be jailed by the two court officials; for the most part, his arrest only amounts to a quasi-official notice that he has fallen under the watchful eye and jurisdiction of the Law and the Courts, two social edifices against which K. must now spend all of his time and energy battling. K. never actually learns of any charges, general or specific, against him.

The initial catalyst—his arrest—begins Joseph K.'s defiance of the Law and the Courts, although his resistance ultimately proves to be insubstantial and ineffective. His first reaction to the arresting warders is disbelief, as he thinks that his co-workers are playing a game on him, for it is his birthday. He then turns his indignation toward the two clown-like thugs, insulting their lack of intelligence by assuming his own intellectual superiority over them. But Joseph K. has only now awakened to this strange world, and as such he fails to consider his own ignorance of the Courts. His hubris compels him to believe that he will quickly outsmart these policemen. But what K. believes to be his intellectual mastery pales in the face of the straightforward logic voiced by one of the crude warders named Fritz, who says to his colleague: "See, Willem, he admits that he does not know the Law and yet he claims he's innocent" (6–7). Nina Pelikan Straus points out in her article "Grand Theory on Trial: Kafka, Derrida and the Will to Power" that language in *The Trial* "inflicts an emotional and intellectual trauma upon Joseph K.—call it a nihilistic apprehension of the world and the self—from which he does not recover" (380).

As Joseph K. begins to accept the gravity of his situation, he then turns defiant toward the "wretched hirelings," his arresters. He says, "Plain stupidity is the only thing that can give them such assurance. A few words with a man on my own level of intelligence would make everything far clearer than hours of talk with these two" (7). But K.'s defiance at this point only seems to make it more clear to him that he has indeed become ensnared in the trap of the Courts. This he soon learns from the Inspector, an official over the two warders, who has set up a makeshift interrogation office in one of lodging rooms next to K.'s small sleeping room. K. denies to the Inspector that he has committed any offense. He then seeks to take the offense in his predicament: " . . . the real question is, who accuses me? What authority. . . . Are you officers of the law? . . . I demand a clear answer to these questions, and I feel sure that after an explanation we shall be able to part from each other on the best of terms" (11). K.'s expectation is twofold: He wants to confront the real authority lurking behind these front men, and he naively thinks that mere human discourse between intelligent beings will bring a mutually agreeable outcome to the situation.

Joseph K. has awakened to find not himself transformed, but the reality around him totally redefined. Only the day before he had remained comfortable in his existence, ignorant of the Court's unseen forces secretly marshalling against him. Now K. quickly learns that everyone around him—his landlady, the bank manager, and even strangers—are very familiar with his case. In K.'s world of the absurd, traditional meanings no longer suffice to answer the new reality before him, an enigmatic Court and Law that he must confront. K. possesses an idea of the Law and justice and his idea—the abstract principle—does not coincide with his new reality. The world that Joseph K. believes exists in the novel's opening pages is not the world he has actually awakened to find: "What authority could they represent? K. lived in a country with a legal constitution, there was universal peace, all the laws were in force; who dared seize him in his own dwelling?"(4). Kafka's words are shockingly prescient, as the indiscriminate arrests and executions of untold numbers by Germany during World War II would soon commence. Kafka did not live to see his sisters and others once close to him put to death in concentration camps.

Once K. is defeated in his attempts to bring quick remedy to his arrest through simple logical negotiations, his only recourse is defiance against the Law, Courts, and the Court's representatives. Kafka presents K. as an individual who becomes more and more isolated from society. Arnold Heidsieck writes, "When at first Joseph K. discovers the court offices in the attic they appear as something in limbo beyond the everyday world, something shadowy, homeless, not really existing" (16).

K. is not alone as an accused by the Law and Courts, as Kafka describes the the throng of defendants who inhabit the Courts. One

defendant that K. meets is an old man who has been coming to the
Court about his case for many years. K. asks the old man what he is
waiting for at the Court. The defendant offers no answer, as though
he does not know. Kafka suggests that the defendant has visited the
Courts for longer than he can recall. As John P. McGowan notes in
"*The Trial*: Terminable/Interminable," " . . . the individual is merely
one element in a network . . . Once pulled into this system, the individual has no choice but to play his role, to act out the part assigned to
him, thus insuring the maintenance of the equilibrium in the whole"
(3). The futility of one's action, and yet the futility of inaction, epitomizes the absurd condition for K.'s defiance against the Courts. K. is
cautioned time and again that he must attend to his case with all his
time and energies, warnings that K. refuses to follow. His intention is
not to become one of the many who have succumbed to a plaintive
and penitential existence.

Joseph K. finds himself alone, essentially trapped and lost, and
what aid and advice he receives is of questionable merit. For instance,
K. is befriended by the Manufacturer, a client at the bank where K.
works as the Chief Clerk. The money borrower shares his knowledge
about the Courts with K., warning him not to leave a stone unturned
in his defense. He also encourages K. to seek assistance from Titorelli,
a Court portrait painter.

K. finds the Court painter Titorelli in the artist's poor lodgings.
The shabbily dressed Titorelli, living in a small room owned by the
Courts, has inherited his post as a painter of judges from his father,
an earlier Court painter. K. learns that the Courts rely only on tradition and memory, what was done before, in every manner, even to the
point of keeping no written records. The judges even demand that they
be painted like the judges of old, and thus no portrait looks like the
subject. Surprisingly, it is the artist rather than the lawyer Huld who
offers K. the most information about the Courts. Titorelli explains that
there are three possible outcomes to K.'s case. There are three forms of
acquittal possible, and that it is up to K. to choose his outcome: definite acquittal, ostensible acquittal, or indefinite postponement.

Titorelli explains that once a judge grants an acquittal for K. to
please Titorelli and the judge's other friends, then K. will be a free
man. K., incredulous, says: "So then I am free." Titorelli qualifies
this outcome, though, by explaining that K. will only be "ostensibly
free, or more exactly, provisionally free" (158). He goes on to explain

that the low-level judges he knows lack the authority to grant a final acquittal, and that power belongs only to the highest Court, which is inaccessible. But then Titorelli clarifies even further that even once an acquittal has been given, the defendant can expect that one day in the future the courts will again take up his case for prosecution. This continues ad infinitum, with no complete release or expulsion. Titorelli's explanations give K. a headache and dash his hopes.

K. is encouraged to seek an advocate for his defense, one who knows the Courts well, and on the surface this seems a logical course of action. His uncle, Albert K., who visits K. from his countryside home, introduces K. to the elderly and bedridden Dr. Huld, a well-respected lawyer and a friend of many powerful judges. His influence has him attached to the Court in the Palace of Justice. K. seems only marginally interested Huld's words, even ignoring his grave warnings. K. then finds it surprising to see the Chief Clerk of the Court in Huld's bedchamber so late at night. As the men begin to discuss K.'s case, K., rather than develop strength for his case with the Chief Clerk, suddenly leaves the room and goes off to make love to Leni, Huld's young maid and nurse whom he has only met minutes before.

To turn his case over to Huld, K. would be following the dominant and prevalent attitude and recourse. But K. soon judges that Huld, who feels that K. will benefit from long delays in his case, is not an effective advocate. Huld tells K. very little about his case and the progress being made. K. never learns of the actual charges against him from Huld. This is certainly one of Kafka's points of irony, in that Huld is a powerful and influential advocate, but yet his abilities are limited. K. later goes to see Huld in order to dismiss him as his attorney, deciding instead to take the matters in his own hands in order to push for a speedier resolution of his case.

Kafka's Courts in *The Trial* are symbolic of the absurd concerning guilt, justice, and punishment. Any specific crimes K. has committed and charges against K. remain obscured. The reader also quickly realizes that it matters not whether a defendant is guilty or innocent, as the Courts are said to be resistant to all forms of proof and innocence. These are presented as ambiguous and menacing edifices to which everyone is tied and subject. These offices of inquiry are housed in the attics of most houses, in essence, blanketing the social body. These spaces are dark, stuffy, and filled with foul air. They are packed with defendants and those who work for the Courts. K. finds the Court to be a labyrinthian network of corrupt, power-driven officials (45). This is the social body, to which all fall subject, that K. intends to defy.

K.'s only encounter with the Courts is the Court of Inquiry, as he never is able to confront the actual final Court of Judgment. These Courts are never described and may or may not exist, and therefore any possible final judgment by this entity remains problematic. Titorelli the Painter, one familiar with the Courts, remarks to K. that he knows of no one who has been given unconditional acquittal—absolution and freedom by the Courts.

The Court of Inquiry finally summons Joseph K. to appear before it on a Sunday morning. K., who is uncertain as to the time and location of his case, becomes lost en route but eventually arrives in the offices of the Court by accident. It may also be that all K.'s choices and routes lead to the Court. This Court, like all Courts, is housed in the attic space of an old, dilapidated, and crowded building. Subterranean passageways lead from one Court to another. Kafka describes it as looking like a large, dark, and stuffy political meeting hall with one group seated on one side and another group on the other side. K. is admonished by the Examining Magistrate for being more than an hour late. To this K. retorts: "Whether I am late or not, I am here now" (39). K. hears loud applause from one side of the room, and this fills him with bravado. He now feels certain that he can win over the crowd, just as he earlier believed that he could outwit the Investigator. K. then attempts to seize control of the Court deliberations. He challenges the Court's authority by asserting that the proceedings can only be termed a "trial" if he, K., so asserts and allows it to be.

Then K. attempts a more demonstrative rebuke of the Examining Magistrate of the Court when the judge identifies K. as a house painter. K. recoils at this reference, asserting and clarifying at the same time that he is the chief clerk in a large bank. He snatches an old book or ledger from the hands of the official, bellowing: "Herr Examining Magistrate, I really don't fear this ledger of yours though it is a closed book to me . . ." (41). K.'s defiance takes on not a private but public defiance: " . . . what has happened to me . . . is representative of a misguided policy which is being directed against many other people as well. It is for these that I take up my stand here, not for myself" (41). But questions remain regarding K.'s outburst. Is he sincere in his declaration to fight for humanity, or is K. merely grandstanding, seizing the moment to embarrass the Examining Magistrate and thereby gain himself popularity in the Court?

As K. soon learns, he has not taken the proceedings seriously enough. Even his hope of release from the Court due to his mistaken identity fails. Kafka's portrayal of the Court's confusion concerning K.'s identity further underlines the corruptness of the proceedings. Actual identity matters little. Of course, the confusion over K.'s identity suggests to the reader the possibility that K. is innocent, at least in this particular instance. The momentum rushes to K.'s side and then we recognize that, despite his courage or bravado, he will no doubt fall to the machinations of the Court. Ultimately, K. discovers that the vast majority of the old men in the Court are Court officials, not onlookers or other defendants. Only one group is made up of defendants. Although his bravado is dimmed, his courage or resilience seems undiminished: "You scoundrels, I'll spare you future interrogations" (48).

Who is Joseph K.? His identity seems intentionally left obscure by Kafka. The author does not complete K.'s surname, only calling him K., and this, of course, begs the question as to K.'s full signification. We can only speculate that the K is intended for the author's own surname. The letter K also gives the protagonist an everyman identity. The reader is offered only a modicum of background information concerning K. He is a thirty-year-old man and works as a chief clerk at a large banking institution. He takes his work seriously. He rooms in a boarding house owned by Frau Grubach. He has an uncle named Albert K. He enjoys the presence of women. At one point the Chief Magistrate identifies K. as a house painter. In a discourse based on logic, this signification would indicate that the court has the wrong defendant in front of it. In Kafka's world of the absurd, the correct or incorrect identity of the accused makes no difference. This point reinforces the everyman motif. K. is also seen during the first half of the novel as self-absorbed. He prides himself on his superior intellect and looks down on the Court workers and officials. His attitude changes later in the novel when K. attempts to help the two warders (the same two who had earlier arrived to arrest him) keep from being whipped. This is one of the rare occasions when K. is not solipsistic.

But is K. guilty and, if so, of what? Throughout the novel K. denies any guilt to criminal action. And this is why he remains puzzled by the Court's determination to snare him. K.'s puzzlement as to his guilt propels his defiance of the Courts. The protagonist's rebellion remains directed and intent until later in the novel. K. is defeated. Perhaps he succumbs, refuses to fight on. Kafka is not clear on this point. Perhaps Kafka is suggesting some metaphysical guilt, a Christian guilt that surrounds humankind's Fall in the Garden of Eden. Kafka offers only fragmented, often disjointed, descriptions and images, mere suggestions, in *The Trial*. As a modernist work the form of the absurd, *The Trial* does not perform the traditional duty of explaining motives and actions or showing causal relations between events. Joseph K. never becomes acutely reflective about his life. He asserts his innocence, but makes no attempt to explore his past for the reader. Only toward the end of the novel, after K. is to be led off to his death, does he uncharacteristically contemplate his life:

> I always wanted to snatch at the world with twenty hands, and not for a very laudable motive, either. That was wrong, and am I to show now that not even a year's trial has taught me anything? ... Are people to say of me after I am gone that at the beginning of my case I wanted to finish it, and at the end of it I wanted to begin it again? I don't want that to be said. (225–26)

In the end, K.'s defiance gains him a certain dignity, apart from the barbaric forces set against him.

The final scene in the novel reveals that K. chooses to end his life with individual dignity. On K.'s thirty-first birthday, one year from the start of the novel, two men dressed in black suits and hats escort K. from his lodgings. He goes with them willingly. At this point he seems to have accepted his fate or sentence. His earlier struggles have ended. Kafka writes, " ... the important thing was that he suddenly realized the futility of resistance. There would be nothing heroic in it were he to resist ..." (225). In the face of overwhelming odds, he struggles to understand that "the only thing for me to go on doing is to keep my intelligence calm and analytical to the end" (225). He proceeds with his two executioners across dark, empty streets. At times K., rather than being led by the two men, leads them. At one moment, the three are confronted by a policeman, but K. leads his group away safely. Then K. takes up running, again leading the other two, until they come to a desolate stone quarry, a site emblematic of religious sacrifice. There K. is murdered "like a dog." Straus adds that "Joseph K.'s arrest and death served as a warning against the arbitrariness of certain dicta as practiced by imperial regimes, such as the Hapsburg and the Nazi . . . readers might discover that empires need no nation states to exert their traumatic powers and can be built in universities" (383).

To further understand the unique dilemma Joseph K. faces in his resistance to the social body, other literary antecedents may prove helpful. Reaching back first to Sophocles' tragedy *Antigone*, the young heroine Antigone is seen facing her own challenge in her defiance of the overreaching power of the State. Antigone's world and her reasons for her decision to defy King Creon are based on reason and logical considerations that connect her moral act with what she sees as divine purpose. She acts against the king because she recognizes that the law of the gods must take precedence over the law of man. More than two millennia later, the American Romantic writer Henry David Thoreau defied the government's position on slavery and war by not paying his poll taxes, and he was briefly jailed. As in Antigone's situation, Thoreau faced a definitive and exact foe: a government whose acts are unacceptable to the conscious-thinking individual. Both Antigone and Thoreau encountered a world in which reality's landscape can be surveyed in cause-and-effect terms and meaning. Antigone knows that her defiance of the State will result in her death, and she freely chooses this death. Joseph K., on the other hand, finds no "other" world apart from the individual self that can be understood or confronted directly. He cannot learn of the charges against him, how the Court functions, how and in what way he must answer the Court. The charges against Antigone are clearly stated. This "other" hidden world or set of laws remains inaccessible and threatening to Joseph K. He faces the world of the absurd, unlike Antigone and Thoreau, who react to a comprehensible, albeit detrimental, reality.

In the mid-twentieth century, the French writer and philosopher Albert Camus wrote what has become the defining statement of human life characterized as the absurd and existential—"The Myth of Sisyphus." In this essay, Camus recreates in modern language the tragic story of Sisyphus from Greek mythology. Sisyphus is punished by the gods for his defiance, and must push a huge boulder up the long slope of a mountain. Once he nears the summit, the boulder tumbles back down to the foot of the mountain where Sisyphus must again take up his eternal work, his punishment. Sisyphus's existence can be seen as absurd: Clearly he is the hamster turning his wheel, all the time hoping he can escape his cage. Sisyphus's punishment is capricious, his meaningless toil has no end, and there exists no reason or balance between human acts, applied justice, and resulting punishment.

It is in Camus' world of Sisyphus that Joseph K. certainly finds himself trapped. The unsuspecting young man is plunged into the machinations of the Law, which for Sisyphus is the capricious Greek gods. For K. the motives, decisions, and actions of the Law are never declared directly or revealed by revelation. Joseph K. can only conjecture why he has been caught up in the Law's labyrinth. Straus summarizes this dilemma in "Grand Theory on Trial: Kafka, Derrida and the Will to Power," explaining that: "*The Trial* is not about the impossibility of justice, but about what it is like for humans when justice morphs into an endless series of interpretations of the law controlled by a powerful but inaccessible interpreter" (382).

WORKS CITED

Carter, Steven. "Kafka's *The Trial*." *Explicator* 61.1 (Fall 2002).

Heidsieck, Arnold. "Logic and Ontology in Kafka's Fiction." *The German Review* 61.1 (Winter 1986): 11–17.

Kafka, Franz. *The Trial*. New York: Knopf, 1964.

Kittler, Wolf. "Burian Without Resurrection on Kafka's Legend 'Before the Law.'" *MLN* 121.3 (2006): 647–647.

McGowan, John P. "*The Trial*: Terminable/Interminable." *Twentieth Century Literature*. 26.1 (Spring 1980): 14.

Straus, Nina Pelikan. "Grand Theory on Trial: Kafka, Derrida and the Will to Power." *Philosophy and Literature*. 31.2 (2007): 378–393.

Yalom, Marilyn K. "Albert Camus and the Myth of *The Trial*." *Modern Language Quarterly*. 25.4 (Dec. 1964): 434.

✐ *Acknowledgments* ✐

Beauchamp, Gorman. "Of Man's Last Disobedience: Zamiatin's *We* and Orwell's *1984.*" *Comparative Literature Studies* 10.4 (Dec 1973) 285–301. Copyright by The Board of Trustees of the University of Illinois. Reprinted by permission

Brooke, Stopford A. "Julius Caesar." *Ten More Plays of Shakespeare*. London: Constable and Co., 1913. 58–90.

Colaiaco, James A. "The American Dream Unfulfilled: Martin Luther King, Jr. and the 'Letter from Birmingham Jail.'" Phylon 45.1 (1984): 1–18. Reprinted by permission. This article was published in a slightly revised form in *Martin Luther King, Jr.: Apostle of Militant Nonviolence* (Palgrave Macmillan, 1983).

Croiset, Alfred and Croiset, Maurice. "Aristophanes and His Contemporaries." *Abridged History of Greek Literature*. New York: MacMillan, 1904. 248–55.

Ehrenberg, Victor. *Sophocles and Pericles*. Oxford: Oxford Blackwell, 1954. 28–37, 54–61.

Kazin, Alfred. "Writing in the Dark." *Henry David Thoreau: Studies and Commentaries*. Edited by Walter Harding et al. Rutherford, NJ: Fairleigh Dickinson UP, 1972. 34–52. Copyright Associate University Presses, Inc. Reprinted by permission.

Oliver, Egbert S. "A Second Look at 'Bartleby.'" *College English* 6.8 (May 1945): 431–439.

Reid, Margaret A. "Langston Hughes: Rhetoric and Protest." *The Langston Hughes Review* 3.1 (1984 Spring): 13–20. Copyright The Langston Hughes Society. Reprinted by permission.

Rubin, Steven J. "Richard Wright and Albert Camus: The Literature of Revolt." *International Fiction Review* 8.1 (Winter 1981): 12–26. Reprinted by permission

Index